VOLUME II—PARTS 52 & 53

FEDERAL ACQUISITION REGULATION

ISSUED MARCH 2005 BY THE:

**GENERAL SERVICES ADMINISTRATION
DEPARTMENT OF DEFENSE
NATIONAL AERONAUTICS AND SPACE ADMINISTRATION**

(This edition includes the consolidation of all Federal Acquisition Circulars through 2001-27)

TITLE 48—FEDERAL ACQUISITION REGULATIONS SYSTEM

Chapter 1

FEDERAL ACQUISITION REGULATION

Volume I

FOREWORD

This March 2005 edition is a complete reissue of the Federal Acquisition Regulation (FAR). It includes all Federal Acquisition Circulars through 2001-27.

The FAR is the primary regulation for use by all Federal Executive agencies in their acquisition of supplies and services with appropriated funds. It became effective on April 1, 1984, and is issued within applicable laws under the joint authorities of the Administrator of General Services, the Secretary of Defense, and the Administrator for the National Aeronautics and Space Administration, under the broad policy guidelines of the Administrator, Office of Federal Procurement Policy, Office of Management and Budget.

The FAR precludes agency acquisition regulations that unnecessarily repeat, paraphrase, or otherwise restate the FAR, limits agency acquisition regulations to those necessary to implement FAR policies and procedures within an agency, and provides for coordination, simplicity, and uniformity in the Federal acquisition process. It also provides for agency and public participation in developing the FAR and agency acquisition regulation.

FEDERAL ACQUISITION REGULATION

General Structure and Subparts

SUBCHAPTER A—GENERAL

PART 1—FEDERAL ACQUISITION REGULATIONS SYSTEM
1.1	Purpose, Authority, Issuance
1.2	Administration
1.3	Agency Acquisition Regulations
1.4	Deviations from the FAR
1.5	Agency and Public Participation
1.6	Career Development, Contracting Authority, and Responsibilities
1.7	Determinations and Findings

PART 2—DEFINITIONS OF WORDS AND TERMS
2.1	Definitions
2.2	Definitions Clause

PART 3—IMPROPER BUSINESS PRACTICES AND PERSONAL CONFLICTS OF INTEREST
3.1	Safeguards
3.2	Contractor Gratuities to Government Personnel
3.3	Reports of Suspected Antitrust Violations
3.4	Contingent Fees
3.5	Other Improper Business Practices
3.6	Contracts with Government Employees or Organizations Owned or Controlled by Them
3.7	Voiding and Rescinding Contracts
3.8	Limitations on the Payment of Funds to Influence Federal Transactions
3.9	Whistleblower Protections for Contractor Employees
3.10	Contractor Code of Business Ethics and Conduct
3.11	Preventing Personal Conflicts of Interest for Contractor Employees Performing Acquisition Functions

PART 4—ADMINISTRATIVE MATTERS
4.1	Contract Execution
4.2	Contract Distribution
4.3	Paper Documents
4.4	Safeguarding Classified Information Within Industry
4.5	Electronic Commerce in Contracting
4.6	Contract Reporting
4.7	Contractor Records Retention
4.8	Government Contract Files
4.9	Taxpayer Identification Number Information
4.10	Contract Line Items
4.11	System for Award Management
4.12	Representations and Certifications
4.13	Personal Identity Verification
4.14	Reporting Executive Compensation and First-Tier Subcontract Awards
4.15	[Reserved]
4.16	Unique Procurement Instrument Identifiers
4.17	Service Contracts Inventory

SUBCHAPTER B—COMPETITION AND ACQUISITION PLANNING

PART 5—PUBLICIZING CONTRACT ACTIONS

5.1	Dissemination of Information
5.2	Synopses of Proposed Contract Actions
5.3	Synopses of Contract Awards
5.4	Release of Information
5.5	Paid Advertisements
5.6	Publicizing Multi-Agency Use Contracts
5.7	Publicizing Requirements Under the American Recovery and Reinvestment Act of 2009

PART 6—COMPETITION REQUIREMENTS

6.1	Full and Open Competition
6.2	Full and Open Competition After Exclusion of Sources
6.3	Other Than Full and Open Competition
6.4	Sealed Bidding and Competitive Proposals
6.5	Advocates for Competition

PART 7—ACQUISITION PLANNING

7.1	Acquisition Plans
7.2	Planning for the Purchase of Supplies in Economic Quantities
7.3	Contractor Versus Government Performance
7.4	Equipment Lease or Purchase
7.5	Inherently Governmental Functions

PART 8—REQUIRED SOURCES OF SUPPLIES AND SERVICES

8.1	Excess Personal Property
8.2	[Reserved]
8.3	[Reserved]
8.4	Federal Supply Schedules
8.5	Acquisition of Helium
8.6	Acquisition from Federal Prison Industries, Inc.
8.7	Acquisition from Nonprofit Agencies Employing People Who Are Blind or Severely Disabled
8.8	Acquisition of Printing and Related Supplies
8.9	[Reserved]
8.10	[Reserved]
8.11	Leasing of Motor Vehicles

PART 9—CONTRACTOR QUALIFICATIONS

9.1	Responsible Prospective Contractors
9.2	Qualifications Requirements
9.3	First Article Testing and Approval
9.4	Debarment, Suspension, and Ineligibility
9.5	Organizational and Consultant Conflicts of Interest
9.6	Contractor Team Arrangements
9.7	Defense Production Pools and Research and Development Pools

PART 10—MARKET RESEARCH

PART 11—DESCRIBING AGENCY NEEDS
11.1	Selecting and Developing Requirements Documents
11.2	Using and Maintaining Requirements Documents
11.3	Acceptable Material
11.4	Delivery or Performance Schedules
11.5	Liquidated Damages
11.6	Priorities and Allocations
11.7	Variation in Quantity
11.8	Testing

PART 12—ACQUISITION OF COMMERCIAL ITEMS
12.1	Acquisition of Commercial Items—General
12.2	Special Requirements for the Acquisition of Commercial Items
12.3	Solicitation Provisions and Contract Clauses for the Acquisition of Commercial Items
12.4	Unique Requirements Regarding Terms and Conditions for Commercial Items
12.5	Applicability of Certain Laws to the Acquisition of Commercial Items and Commercially Available Off-The-Shelf Items
12.6	Streamlined Procedures for Evaluation and Solicitation for Commercial Items

SUBCHAPTER C—CONTRACTING METHODS AND CONTRACT TYPES

PART 13—SIMPLIFIED ACQUISITION PROCEDURES
13.1	Procedures
13.2	Actions At or Below the Micro-Purchase Threshold
13.3	Simplified Acquisition Methods
13.4	Fast Payment Procedure
13.5	Test Program for Certain Commercial Items

PART 14—SEALED BIDDING
14.1	Use of Sealed Bidding
14.2	Solicitation of Bids
14.3	Submission of Bids
14.4	Opening of Bids and Award of Contract
14.5	Two-Step Sealed Bidding

PART 15—CONTRACTING BY NEGOTIATION
15.1	Source Selection Processes and Techniques
15.2	Solicitation and Receipt of Proposals and Information
15.3	Source Selection
15.4	Contract Pricing
15.5	Preaward, Award, and Postaward Notifications, Protests, and Mistakes
15.6	Unsolicited Proposals

PART 16—TYPES OF CONTRACTS

16.1	Selecting Contract Types
16.2	Fixed-Price Contracts
16.3	Cost-Reimbursement Contracts
16.4	Incentive Contracts
16.5	Indefinite-Delivery Contracts
16.6	Time-and-Materials, Labor-Hour, and Letter Contracts
16.7	Agreements

PART 17—SPECIAL CONTRACTING METHODS

17.1	Multi-year Contracting
17.2	Options
17.3	[Reserved]
17.4	Leader Company Contracting
17.5	Interagency Acquisitions
17.6	Management and Operating Contracts
17.7	Interagency Acquisitions: Acquisitions by Nondefense Agencies on Behalf of the Department of Defense

PART 18—EMERGENCY ACQUISITIONS

18.1	Available Acquisition Flexibilities
18.2	Emergency Acquisition Flexibilities

SUBCHAPTER D—SOCIOECONOMIC PROGRAMS

PART 19—SMALL BUSINESS PROGRAMS

19.1	Size Standards
19.2	Policies
19.3	Determination of Small Business Status for Small Business Programs
19.4	Cooperation with the Small Business Administration
19.5	Set-Asides for Small Business
19.6	Certificates of Competency and Determinations of Responsibility
19.7	The Small Business Subcontracting Program
19.8	Contracting with the Small Business Administration (The 8(a) Program)
19.9	[Reserved]
19.10	[Reserved]
19.11	Price Evaluation Adjustment for Small Disadvantaged Business Concerns
19.12	Small Disadvantaged Business Participation Program
19.13	Historically Underutilized Business Zone (HUBZone) Program
19.14	Service-Disabled Veteran-Owned Small Business Procurement Program
19.15	Women-Owned Small Business (WOSB) Program

PART 20—RESERVED

PART 21—RESERVED

PART 22—APPLICATION OF LABOR LAWS TO GOVERNMENT ACQUISITIONS

22.1	Basic Labor Policies
22.2	Convict Labor
22.3	Contract Work Hours and Safety Standards Act
22.4	Labor Standards for Contracts Involving Construction
22.5	Use of Project Labor Agreements for Federal Construction Projects
22.6	Contracts For Materials, Supplies, Articles, and Equipment Exceeding $15,000
22.7	[Reserved]
22.8	Equal Employment Opportunity
22.9	Nondiscrimination Because of Age
22.10	Service Contract Labor Standards
22.11	Professional Employee Compensation
22.12	Nondisplacement of Qualified Workers Under Service Contracts
22.13	Equal Opportunity for Veterans
22.14	Employment of Workers with Disabilities
22.15	Prohibition of Acquisition of Products Produced by Forced or Indentured Child Labor
22.16	Notification of Employee Rights Under the National Labor Relations Act
22.17	Combating Trafficking in Persons
22.18	Employment Eligibility Verification

PART 23—ENVIRONMENT, ENERGY AND WATER EFFICIENCY, RENEWABLE ENERGY TECHNOLOGIES, OCCUPATIONAL SAFETY, AND DRUG-FREE WORKPLACE

23.1	Sustainable Acquisition Policy
23.2	Energy and Water Efficiency and Renewable Energy
23.3	Hazardous Material Identification and Material Safety Data
23.4	Use of Recovered Materials and Biobased Products
23.5	Drug-Free Workplace
23.6	Notice of Radioactive Material
23.7	Contracting for Environmentally Preferable Products and Services
23.8	Ozone-Depleting Substances
23.9	Contractor Compliance with Environmental Management Systems
23.10	Federal Compliance with Right-to-Know Laws and Pollution Prevention Requirements
23.11	Encouraging Contractor Policies to Ban Text Messaging While Driving

PART 24—PROTECTION OF PRIVACY AND FREEDOM OF INFORMATION

24.1	Protection of Individual Privacy
24.2	Freedom of Information Act

PART 25—FOREIGN ACQUISITION

25.1	Buy American—Supplies
25.2	Buy American—Construction Materials
25.3	Contracts Performed Outside the United States
25.4	Trade Agreements
25.5	Evaluating Foreign Offers—Supply Contracts
25.6	American Recovery and Reinvestment Act—Buy American statute—Construction Materials
25.7	Prohibited Sources
25.8	Other International Agreements and Coordination
25.9	Customs and Duties
25.10	Additional Foreign Acquisition Regulations
25.11	Solicitation Provisions and Contract Clauses

PART 26—OTHER SOCIOECONOMIC PROGRAMS

26.1	Indian Incentive Program
26.2	Disaster or Emergency Assistance Activities
26.3	Historically Black Colleges and Universities and Minority Institutions
26.4	Food Donations to Nonprofit Organizations

SUBCHAPTER E—GENERAL CONTRACTING REQUIREMENTS

PART 27—PATENTS, DATA, AND COPYRIGHTS

27.1	General
27.2	Patents and Copyrights
27.3	Patent Rights under Government Contracts
27.4	Rights in Data and Copyrights
27.5	Foreign License and Technical Assistance Agreements

PART 28—BONDS AND INSURANCE

28.1	Bonds and Other Financial Protections
28.2	Sureties and Other Security for Bonds
28.3	Insurance

PART 29—TAXES

29.1	General
29.2	Federal Excise Taxes
29.3	State and Local Taxes
29.4	Contract Clauses

PART 30—COST ACCOUNTING STANDARDS ADMINISTRATION

30.1	General
30.2	CAS Program Requirements
30.3	CAS Rules and Regulations [Reserved]
30.4	Cost Accounting Standards [Reserved]
30.5	Cost Accounting Standards for Educational Institutions [Reserved]
30.6	CAS Administration

PART 31—CONTRACT COST PRINCIPLES AND PROCEDURES

31.1	Applicability
31.2	Contracts with Commercial Organizations
31.3	Contracts with Educational Institutions
31.4	[Reserved]
31.5	[Reserved]
31.6	Contracts with State, Local, and Federally Recognized Indian Tribal Governments
31.7	Contracts with Nonprofit Organizations

PART 32—CONTRACT FINANCING

32.1	Non-Commercial Item Purchase Financing
32.2	Commercial Item Purchase Financing
32.3	Loan Guarantees for Defense Production
32.4	Advance Payments for Non-Commercial Items
32.5	Progress Payments Based on Costs
32.6	Contract Debts
32.7	Contract Funding
32.8	Assignment of Claims
32.9	Prompt Payment
32.10	Performance-Based Payments
32.11	Electronic Funds Transfer

PART 33—PROTESTS, DISPUTES, AND APPEALS

33.1	Protests
33.2	Disputes and Appeals

SUBCHAPTER F—SPECIAL CATEGORIES OF CONTRACTING

PART 34—MAJOR SYSTEM ACQUISITION

34.0	General
34.1	Testing, Qualification and Use of Industrial Resources Developed Under Title III, Defense Production Act
34.2	Earned Value Management System

PART 35—RESEARCH AND DEVELOPMENT CONTRACTING

PART 36—CONSTRUCTION AND ARCHITECT-ENGINEER CONTRACTS

36.1	General
36.2	Special Aspects of Contracting for Construction
36.3	Two-Phase Design-Build Selection Procedures
36.4	[Reserved]
36.5	Contract Clauses
36.6	Architect-Engineer Services
36.7	Standard and Optional Forms for Contracting for Construction, Architect-Engineer Services, and Dismantling, Demolition, or Removal of Improvements

PART 37—SERVICE CONTRACTING

37.1	Service Contracts—General
37.2	Advisory and Assistance Services
37.3	Dismantling, Demolition, or Removal of Improvements
37.4	Nonpersonal Health Care Services
37.5	Management Oversight of Service Contracts
37.6	Performance-Based Acquisition

PART 38—FEDERAL SUPPLY SCHEDULE CONTRACTING
38.1	Federal Supply Schedule Program
38.2	Establishing and Administering Federal Supply Schedules

PART 39—ACQUISITION OF INFORMATION TECHNOLOGY
39.1	General
39.2	Electronic and Information Technology

PART 40—RESERVED

PART 41—ACQUISITION OF UTILITY SERVICES
41.1	General
41.2	Acquiring Utility Services
41.3	Requests for Assistance
41.4	Administration
41.5	Solicitation Provision and Contract Clauses
41.6	Forms
41.7	Formats

SUBCHAPTER G—CONTRACT MANAGEMENT

PART 42—CONTRACT ADMINISTRATION AND AUDIT SERVICES
42.1	Contract Audit Services
42.2	Contract Administration Services
42.3	Contract Administration Office Functions
42.4	Correspondence and Visits
42.5	Postaward Orientation
42.6	Corporate Administrative Contracting Officer
42.7	Indirect Cost Rates
42.8	Disallowance of Costs
42.9	Bankruptcy
42.10	[Reserved]
42.11	Production Surveillance and Reporting
42.12	Novation and Change-of-Name Agreements
42.13	Suspension of Work, Stop-Work Orders, and Government Delay of Work
42.14	[Reserved]
42.15	Contractor Performance Information
42.16	Small Business Contract Administration
42.17	Forward Pricing Rate Agreements

PART 43—CONTRACT MODIFICATIONS
43.1	General
43.2	Change Orders
43.3	Forms

PART 44—SUBCONTRACTING POLICIES AND PROCEDURES
44.1	General
44.2	Consent to Subcontracts
44.3	Contractors' Purchasing Systems Reviews
44.4	Subcontracts for Commercial Items and Commercial Components

FEDERAL ACQUISITION REGULATION — STRUCTURE

PART 45—GOVERNMENT PROPERTY
45.1	General
45.2	Solicitation and Evaluation Procedures
45.3	Authorizing the Use and Rental of Government Property
45.4	Title to Government Property
45.5	Support Government Property Administration
45.6	Reporting, Reutilization, and Disposal

PART 46—QUALITY ASSURANCE
46.1	General
46.2	Contract Quality Requirements
46.3	Contract Clauses
46.4	Government Contract Quality Assurance
46.5	Acceptance
46.6	Material Inspection and Receiving Reports
46.7	Warranties
46.8	Contractor Liability for Loss of or Damage to Property of the Government

PART 47—TRANSPORTATION
47.1	General
47.2	Contracts for Transportation or for Transportation-Related Services
47.3	Transportation in Supply Contracts
47.4	Air Transportation by U.S.-Flag Carriers
47.5	Ocean Transportation by U.S.-Flag Vessels

PART 48—VALUE ENGINEERING
48.1	Policies and Procedures
48.2	Contract Clauses

PART 49—TERMINATION OF CONTRACTS
49.1	General Principles
49.2	Additional Principles for Fixed-Price Contracts Terminated for Convenience
49.3	Additional Principles for Cost-Reimbursement Contracts Terminated for Convenience
49.4	Termination for Default
49.5	Contract Termination Clauses
49.6	Contract Termination Forms and Formats

PART 50—EXTRAORDINARY CONTRACTUAL ACTIONS AND THE SAFETY ACT
50.1	Extraordinary Contractual Actions
50.2	Support Anti-terrorism by Fostering Effective Technologies Act of 2002

PART 51—USE OF GOVERNMENT SOURCES BY CONTRACTORS
51.1	Contractor Use of Government Supply Sources
51.2	Contractor Use of Interagency Fleet Management System (IFMS) Vehicles

SUBCHAPTER H—CLAUSES AND FORMS

PART 52—SOLICITATION PROVISIONS AND CONTRACT CLAUSES
52.1	Instructions for Using Provisions and Clauses
52.2	Text of Provisions and Clauses
52.3	Provision and Clause Matrix

PART 53—FORMS
53.1 General
53.2 Prescription of Forms
53.3 Illustration of Forms

APPENDIX

INDEX PAGES 1-144 [REMOVED]

VOLUME II—PARTS 52 & 53

FEDERAL ACQUISITION REGULATION

ISSUED MARCH 2005 BY THE:

GENERAL SERVICES ADMINISTRATION
DEPARTMENT OF DEFENSE
NATIONAL AERONAUTICS AND SPACE ADMINISTRATION

(This edition includes the consolidation of all Federal Acquisition Circulars through 2001-27)

TITLE 48—FEDERAL ACQUISITION REGULATIONS SYSTEM

Chapter 1

FEDERAL ACQUISITION REGULATION

Volume II

FOREWORD

This March 2005 edition is a complete reissue of the Federal Acquisition Regulation (FAR). It includes all Federal Acquisition Circulars through 2001-27. The effective date of the overall FAR remains April 1, 1984.

The FAR is the primary regulation for use by all Federal Executive agencies in their acquisition of supplies and services with appropriated funds. It became effective on April 1, 1984, and is issued within applicable laws under the joint authorities of the Administrator of General Services, the Secretary of Defense, and the Administrator for the National Aeronautics and Space Administration, under the broad policy guidelines of the Administrator, Office of Federal Procurement Policy, Office of Management and Budget.

The FAR precludes agency acquisition regulations that unnecessarily repeat, paraphrase, or otherwise restate the FAR, limits agency acquisition regulations to those necessary to implement FAR policies and procedures within an agency, and provides for coordination, simplicity, and uniformity in the Federal acquisition process. It also provides for agency and public participation in developing the FAR and agency acquisition regulations.

FEDERAL ACQUISITION REGULATION

SUBCHAPTER H—CLAUSES AND FORMS

PART 53—FORMS

Sec.
53.000 Scope of part.
53.001 Definitions.

Subpart 53.1—General

53.100 Scope of subpart.
53.101 Requirements for use of forms.
53.102 Current editions.
53.103 Exceptions.
53.104 Overprinting.
53.105 Computer generation.
53.106 Special construction and printing.
53.107 Obtaining forms.
53.108 Recommendations concerning forms.
53.109 Forms prescribed by other regulations.
53.110 Continuation sheets.
53.111 Contract clause.

Subpart 53.2—Prescription of Forms

53.200 Scope of subpart.
53.201 Federal acquisition system.
53.201-1 Contracting authority and responsibilities (SF 1402).
53.202 [Reserved]
53.203 [Reserved]
53.204 Administrative matters.
53.204-1 Safeguarding classified information within industry (DD Form 254, DD Form 441).
53.204-2 [Reserved]
53.205 Publicizing contract actions.
53.205-1 Paid advertisements.
53.206 [Reserved]
53.207 [Reserved]
53.208 [Reserved]
53.209 Contractor qualifications.
53.209-1 Responsible prospective contractors.
53.210 [Reserved]
53.211 [Reserved]
53.212 Acquisition of commercial items.
53.213 Simplified acquisition procedures (SF's 18, 30, 44, 1165, 1449, and OF's 336, 347, and 348).
53.214 Sealed bidding.
53.215 Contracting by negotiation.
53.215-1 Solicitation and receipt of proposals.
53.216 Types of contracts.
53.216-1 Delivery orders and orders under basic ordering agreements (OF 347).
53.217 [Reserved]
53.218 [Reserved]
53.219 Small business programs.
53.220 [Reserved]
53.221 [Reserved]
53.222 Application of labor laws to Government acquisitions (SF's 308, 1093, 1413, 1444, 1445, 1446, WH-347).
53.223 [Reserved]
53.224 [Reserved]
53.225 [Reserved]
53.226 [Reserved]
53.227 [Reserved]
53.228 Bonds and insurance.
53.229 Taxes (SF's 1094, 1094-A).
53.230 [Reserved]
53.231 [Reserved]
53.232 Contract financing (SF 1443).
53.233 [Reserved]
53.234 [Reserved]
53.235 Research and development contracting (SF 298).
53.236 Construction and architect-engineer contracts.
53.236-1 Construction.
53.236-2 Architect-engineer services (SF's 252 and 330).
53.237 [Reserved]
53.238 [Reserved]
53.239 [Reserved]
53.240 [Reserved]
53.241 [Reserved]
53.242 Contract administration.
53.242-1 Novation and change-of-name agreements (SF 30).
53.243 Contract modifications (SF 30).
53.244 [Reserved]
53.245 Government property.
53.246 [Reserved]
53.247 Transportation (U.S. Commercial Bill of Lading).
53.248 [Reserved]
53.249 Termination of contracts.
53.250 [Reserved]
53.251 Contractor use of Government supply sources (OF 347).

Subpart 53.3—Illustration of Forms

53.300 Scope of subpart.
53.301 Standard forms.
53.302 Optional forms.
53.303 Agency forms.
    53.301-18 SF 18, Request for Quotation.
    53.301-24 SF 24, Bid Bond.
    53.301-25 SF 25, Performance Bond.
    53.301-25-A SF 25-A, Payment Bond.
    53.301-25-B SF 25-B, Continuation Sheet (For SF's 24, 25, and 25-A).
    53.301-26 SF 26, Award/Contract.
    53.301-28 SF 28, Affidavit of Individual Surety.
    53.301-30 SF 30, Amendment of Solicitation/ Modification of Contract.

53.301-33	SF 33, Solicitation, Offer and Award.	53.301-1402	SF 1402, Certificate of Appointment.
53.301-34	SF 34, Annual Bid Bond.	53.301-1403	SF 1403, Preaward Survey of Prospective Contractor (General).
53.301-35	SF 35, Annual Performance Bond.		
53.301-44	SF 44, Purchase Order—Invoice—Voucher.	53.301-1404	SF 1404, Preaward Survey of Prospective Contractor—Technical.
53.301-120	SF 120, Report of Excess Personal Property.	53.301-1405	SF 1405, Preaward Survey of Prospective Contractor—Production.
53.301-120-A	SF 120-A, Continuation Sheet (Report of Excess Personal Property).	53.301-1406	SF 1406, Preaward Survey of Prospective Contractor—Quality Assurance.
53.301-126	SF 126, Report of Personal Property for Sale.		
		53.301-1407	SF 1407, Preaward Survey of Prospective Contractor—Financial Capability.
53.301-126-A	SF 126-A, Report of Personal Property for Sale (Continuation Sheet).		
		53.301-1408	SF 1408, Preaward Survey of Prospective Contractor—Accounting System.
53.301-252	SF 252, Architect-Engineer Contract.		
53.301-273	SF 273, Reinsurance Agreement For A Bonds Performance Bond.	53.301-1409	SF 1409, Abstract of Offers.
		53.301-1410	SF 1410, Abstract of Offers—Continuation.
53.301-274	SF 274, Reinsurance Agreement For A Bonds Statute Payment Bond.		
		53.301-1413	SF 1413, Statement and Acknowledgment.
53.301-275	SF 275, Reinsurance Agreement in Favor of the United States.		
		53.301-1414	SF 1414, Consent of Surety.
53.301-294	SF 294, Subcontracting Report for Individual Contracts.	53.301-1415	SF 1415, Consent of Surety and Increase of Penalty.
53.301-298	SF 298, Report Documentation Page.		
53.301-308	SF 308, Request for Wage Determination and Response to Request.	53.301-1416	SF 1416, Payment Bond for Other Than Construction Contracts.
		53.301-1418	SF 1418, Performance Bond for Other Than Construction Contracts.
53.301-330	Architect-Engineer Qualifications.		
53.301-1034	SF 1034, Public Voucher for Purchases and Services Other Than Personal.	53.301-1420	SF 1420, Performance Evaluation—Construction Contracts.
		53.301-1421	SF 1421, Performance Evaluation (Architect-Engineer).
53.301-1034A	SF 1034A, Public Voucher for Purchases and Services Other Than Personal—Memorandum Copy.		
		53.301-1423	SF 1423, Inventory Verification Survey.
53.301-1035	SF 1035, Public Voucher for Purchases and Services Other Than Personal, Continuation Sheet.	53.301-1424	SF 1424, Inventory Disposal Report.
		53.301-1427	SF 1427, Inventory Schedule A—Continuation Sheet (Metals in Mill Product Form).
53.301-1035A	SF 1035A, Public Voucher for Purchases and Services Other Than Personal— Memorandum, Continuation Sheet.		
		53.301-1428	SF 1428, Inventory Schedule.
		53.301-1429	SF 1429, Inventory Schedule—Continuation Sheet.
53.301-1093	SF 1093, Schedule of Withholdings Under the Construction Wage Rate Requirements Statute (40 U.S.C. Chapter 31, Subchapter IV, section 3144) and/or the Contract Work Hours and Safety Standards Statute (40 U.S.C. Chapter 37, section 3703).	53.301-1435	SF 1435, Settlement Proposal (Inventory Basis).
		53.301-1436	SF 1436, Settlement Proposal (Total Cost Basis).
		53.301-1437	SF 1437, Settlement Proposal for Cost-Reimbursement Type Contracts.
		53.301-1438	SF 1438, Settlement Proposal (Short Form).
53.301-1094	SF 1094, U.S. Tax Exemption Form.		
53.301-1094A	SF 1094A, Tax Exemption Forms Accountability Record.	53.301-1439	SF 1439, Schedule of Accounting Information.
53.301-1165	SF 1165, Receipt for Cash—Subvoucher.	53.301-1440	SF 1440, Application for Partial Payment.

53.301-1442	SF 1442, Solicitation, Offer, and Award (Construction, Alteration, or Repair).	SF 35	Annual Performance Bond
		SF 273	Reinsurance Agreement for a Miller Act Performance Bond
53.301-1443	SF 1443, Contractor's Request for Progress Payment.	SF 274	Reinsurance Agreement for a Miller Act Payment Bond
53.301-1444	SF 1444, Request for Authorization of Additional Classification and Rate.	SF 275	Reinsurance Agreement in Favor of the United States
53.301-1445	SF 1445, Labor Standards Interview.	SF 294	Subcontracting Report for Individual Contracts
53.301-1446	SF 1446, Labor Standards Investigation Summary Sheet.	SF 295	Summary Subcontract Report
53.301-1447	SF 1447, Solicitation/Contract.	SF 308	Request for Wage Determination and Response to Request
53.301-1449	SF 1449, Solicitation/Contract/Order for Commercial Items.	SF 330	Architect-Engineer Qualifications
53.302-17	Optional Form 17, Offer Label.	SF 1403	Preaward Survey of Prospective Contractor (General)
53.302-90	Optional Form 90, Release of Lien on Real Property.	SF 1404	Preaward Survey of Prospective Contractor—Technical
53.302-91	Optional Form 91, Release of Personal Property from Escrow.	SF 1405	Preaward Survey of Prospective Contractor—Production
53.302-307	Optional Form 307, Contract Award.	SF 1406	Preaward Survey of Prospective Contractor—Quality Assurance
53.302-308	Optional Form 308, Solicitation and Offer—Negotiated Acquisition.	SF 1407	Preaward Survey of Prospective Contractor—Financial Capability
53.302-309	Optional Form 309, Amendment of Solicitation.	SF 1408	Preaward Survey of Prospective Contractor—Accounting System
53.302-312	[Reserved]	SF 1409	Abstract of Offers
53.302-336	Optional Form 336, Continuation Sheet.	SF 1410	Abstract of Offers—Continuation.
		SF 1414	Consent of Surety
53.302-347	Optional Form 347, Order for Supplies or Services.	SF 1415	Consent of Surety and Increase of Penalty
53.302-348	Optional Form 348, Order for Supplies or Services Schedule—Continuation.	SF 1416	Payment Bond for Other Than Construction Contracts
53.302-1419	Optional Form 1419, Abstract of Offers—Construction.	SF 1418	Performance Bond for Other Than Construction Contracts
53.302-1419A	Optional Form 1419A, Abstract of Offers—Construction, Continuation Sheet.	SF 1423	Inventory Verification Survey
		SF 1424	Inventory Disposal Report
53.303-DD-254	Department of Defense DD Form 254, Contract Security Classification Specification.	SF 1427	Inventory Schedule A—Continuation Sheet (Metals in Mill Product Form)
		SF 1428	Inventory Schedule
53.303-DD-441	Department of Defense DD Form 441, Security Agreement.	SF 1429	Inventory Schedule—Continuation Sheet
53.303-WH-347	Department of Labor Form WH-347, Payroll (For Contractor's Optional Use).	SF 1435	Settlement Proposal (Inventory Basis)
		SF 1436	Settlement Proposal (Total Cost Basis)
Forms Authorized for Local Reproduction		SF 1437	Settlement Proposal for Cost-Reimbursement Type Contracts
SF 18	Request for Quotation	SF 1438	Settlement Proposal (Short Form)
SF 24	Bid Bond	SF 1439	Schedule of Accounting Information
SF 25	Performance Bond		
SF 25A	Payment Bond	SF 1440	Application for Partial Payment
SF 25B	SF 25-B, Continuation Sheet (For SF's 24, 25, and 25-A)	SF 1445	Labor Standards Interview
		SF 1446	Labor Standards Investigation Summary Sheet
SF 28	Affidavit of Individual Surety		
SF 33	Solicitation, Offer and Award	SF 1449	Solicitation/Contract/Order for Commercial Items
SF 34	Annual Bid Bond		

OF 90	Release of Lien on Real Property	OF 309	Amendment of Solicitation
OF 91	Release of Personal Property from Escrow	OF 312	Small Disadvantaged Business Participation Report
OF 307	Contract Award	OF 347	Order for Supplies or Services
OF 308	Solicitation and Offer—Negotiated Acquisition		

Subpart 53.1—General

53.000 Scope of part.
This part—

(a) Prescribes standard forms (SF's) and references optional forms (OF's) and agency-prescribed forms for use in acquisition;

(b) Contains requirements and information generally applicable to the forms; and

(c) Illustrates the forms.

53.001 Definitions.
"Exception," as used in this part, means an approved departure from the established design, content, printing specifications, or conditions for use of any standard form.

Subpart 53.1—General

53.100 Scope of subpart.
This subpart contains requirements and information generally applicable to the forms prescribed in this regulation.

53.101 Requirements for use of forms.
The requirements for use of the forms prescribed or referenced in this part are contained in Parts 1 through 52, where the subject matter applicable to each form is addressed. The specific location of each requirement is identified in Subpart 53.2.

53.102 Current editions.
The form prescriptions in Subpart 53.2 and the illustrations in Subpart 53.3 contain current edition dates. Contracting officers shall use the current editions unless otherwise authorized under this regulation.

53.103 Exceptions.
Agencies shall not—

(a) Alter a standard form prescribed by this regulation; or

(b) Use for the same purpose any form other than the standard form prescribed by this regulation without receiving in advance an exception to the form.

53.104 Overprinting.
Standard and optional forms (obtained as required by 53.107) may be overprinted with names, addresses, and other uniform entries that are consistent with the purpose of the form and that do not alter the form in any way. Exception approval for overprinting is not needed.

53.105 Computer generation.
(a) The forms prescribed by this part may be computer generated without exception approval (see 53.103), provided—

(1) There is no change to the name, content, or sequence of the data elements, and the form carries the Standard or Optional Form number and edition date (see 53.111); or

(2) The form is in an electronic format covered by the American National Standards Institute (ANSI) X12 Standards published by the Accredited Standards Committee X12 on Electronic Data Interchange or a format that can be translated into one of those standards.

(b) The standards listed in paragraph (a)(2) of this section may also be used for submission of data set forth in other parts for which specific forms have not been prescribed.

53.106 Special construction and printing.
Contracting offices may request exceptions (see 53.103) to standard forms for special construction and printing. Examples of common exceptions are as follows:

STANDARD FORMS	SPECIAL CONSTRUCTION AND PRINTING
(a) SF 18—	(1) With vertical lines omitted (for listing of supplies and services, unit, etc.);
	(2) As reproducible masters; and/or
	(3) In carbon interleaved pads or sets.
(b) SF's 26, 30, 33, 1447—	As die-cut stencils or reproducible masters.
(c) SF 44—	(1) With serial numbers and contracting office name and address; and/or
	(2) On special weight of paper and with the type of construction, number of sets per book, 2and number of parts per set as specified by the contracting officer. (Executive agencies may supplement the administrative instructions on the inside front cover of the book.)
(d) SF 1442—	(1) As die-cut stencils or reproducible masters; and/or
	(2) With additional wording as required by the executive agency. (However, the sequence and wording of the items appearing on the prescribed form should not be altered.

53.107 Obtaining forms.
(a) Executive agencies shall obtain standard and optional forms from the General Services Administration (GSA) by using GSA Supply Catalog—Office Products (see 41 CFR 101-26.302). Standard forms adapted for computer preparation (see 53.105) or with special construction and printing (see 53.106) that are not available from GSA may be ordered directly from the Government Printing Office (GPO).

(b) Contractors and other parties may obtain standard and optional forms from the Superintendent of Documents, GPO, Washington, DC 20402. Standard and optional forms not available from the Superintendent of Documents may be obtained from the prescribing agency.

(c) Agency forms may be obtained from the prescribing agency.

53.108 Recommendations concerning forms.

Users of this regulation may recommend new forms or the revision, elimination, or consolidation of the forms prescribed or referenced in this regulation. Recommendations from within an executive agency shall be submitted to the cognizant council in accordance with agency procedures. Recommendations from other than executive agencies should be submitted directly to the FAR Secretariat.

53.109 Forms prescribed by other regulations.

Certain forms referred to in Subpart 53.2 are prescribed in other regulations and are specified by the FAR for use in acquisition. For each of these forms, the prescribing agency is identified by means of a parenthetical notation after the form number. For example, SF 1165, which is prescribed by the Government Accountability Office (GAO), is identified as SF 1165 (GAO).

53.110 Continuation sheets.

Except as may be otherwise indicated in the FAR, all standard forms prescribed by the FAR may be continued on (a) plain paper of similar specification, or (b) specially constructed continuation sheets (*e.g.,* OF 336). Continuation sheets shall be annotated in the upper right-hand corner with the reference number of the document being continued and the serial page number.

53.111 Contract clause.

Contracting officers shall insert the clause at 52.253-1, Computer Generated Forms, in solicitations and contracts that require the contractor to submit data on Standard or Optional Forms prescribed by this regulation; and, unless prohibited by agency regulations, forms prescribed by agency supplements.

Subpart 53.2—Prescription of Forms

53.200 Scope of subpart.

This subpart prescribes standard forms and references optional forms and agency-prescribed forms for use in acquisition. Consistent with the approach used in Subpart 52.2, this subpart is arranged by subject matter, in the same order as, and keyed to, the parts of the FAR in which the form usage requirements are addressed. For example, forms addressed in FAR Part 14, Sealed Bidding, are treated in this subpart in section 53.214, Sealed Bidding; forms addressed in FAR Part 43, Contract Modifications, are treated in this subpart in section 53.243, Contract modifications. The following example illustrates how the subjects are keyed to the parts in which they are addressed:

53.243 Contract Modifications (SF 30).

▶ SECTION (KEYED TO FAR PART CONTAINING SUBJECT MATTER: USAGE REQUIREMENTS FOR SF 30 ARE ADDRESSED IN PART 43, CONTRACT MODIFICATIONS)

▶ PART AND SUBPART (INVARIABLE)

53.201 Federal acquisition system.

53.201-1 Contracting authority and responsibilities (SF 1402).

SF 1402 (10/83), Certificate of Appointment. SF 1402 is prescribed for use in appointing contracting officers, as specified in 1.603-3.

53.202 [Reserved]

53.203 [Reserved]

53.204 Administrative matters.

53.204-1 Safeguarding classified information within industry (DD Form 254, DD Form 441).

The following forms, which are prescribed by the Department of Defense, shall be used by agencies covered by the Defense Industrial Security Program if contractor access to classified information is required, as specified in and the clause at 52.204-2:

(a) *DD Form 254* (Department of Defense (DoD)), *Contract Security Classification Specification.* (See 4.403(c)(1).)

(b) *DD Form 441* (DoD), *Security Agreement.* (See paragraph (b) of the clause at 52.204-2.)

53.204-2 [Reserved]

53.205 Publicizing contract actions.

53.205-1 Paid advertisements.

SF 1449, prescribed in 53.212, shall be used to place orders for paid advertisements as specified in 5.503.

53.206 [Reserved]

53.207 [Reserved]

53.208 [Reserved]

53.209 Contractor qualifications.

53.209-1 Responsible prospective contractors.

The following forms are prescribed for use in conducting preaward surveys of prospective contractors, as specified in 9.106-1, 9.106-2, and 9.106-4:

(a) *SF 1403* (Rev. 9/88), *Preaward Survey of Prospective Contractor (General).* SF 1403 is authorized for local reproduction.

(b) *SF 1404* (Rev. 9/88), *Preaward Survey of Prospective Contractor—Technical.* SF 1404 is authorized for local reproduction.

(c) *SF 1405* (Rev. 9/88), *Preaward Survey of Prospective Contractor—Production.* SF 1405 is authorized for local reproduction.

(d) *SF 1406* (Rev. 11/97), *Preaward Survey of Prospective Contractor—Quality Assurance.* SF 1406 is authorized for local reproduction.

(e) *SF 1407* (Rev. 9/88), *Preaward Survey of Prospective Contractor—Financial Capability.* SF 1407 is authorized for local reproduction.

(f) *SF 1408* (Rev. 9/88), *Preaward Survey of Prospective Contractor—Accounting System.* SF 1408 is authorized for local reproduction.

53.210 [Reserved]

53.211 [Reserved]

53.212 Acquisition of commercial items.

SF 1449 (Rev. 2/2012), *Solicitation/Contract/Order for Commercial Items.* SF 1449 is prescribed for use in solicitations and contracts for commercial items. Agencies may prescribe additional detailed instructions for use of the form.

53.213 Simplified acquisition procedures (SF's 18, 30, 44, 1165, 1449, and OF's 336, 347, and 348).

The following forms are prescribed as stated in this section for use in simplified acquisition procedures, orders under

53.214

existing contracts or agreements, and orders from required sources of supplies and services:

(a) *SF 18* (Rev. 6/95), *Request for Quotations*, or *SF 1449* (Rev. 2/2012), *Solicitation/Contract/Order for Commercial Items*. SF 18 is prescribed for use in obtaining price, cost, delivery, and related information from suppliers as specified in 13.307(b). SF 1449, as prescribed in 53.212, or other agency forms/automated formats, may also be used to obtain price, cost, delivery, and related information from suppliers as specified in 13.307(b).

(b) *SF 30* (Rev. 10/83), *Amendment of Solicitation/Modification of Contract*. SF 30, prescribed in 53.243, may be used for modifying purchase orders, as specified in 13.307(c)(3).

(c) *SF 44* (Rev. 10/83), *Purchase Order Invoice Voucher*. SF 44 is prescribed for use in simplified acquisition procedures, as specified in 13.306.

(d) *SF 1165* (6/83 Ed.), *Receipt for Cash-Subvoucher*. SF 1165 (GAO) may be used for imprest fund purchases, as specified in 13.307(e).

(e) *OF 336* (4/86 Ed.), *Continuation Sheet*. OF 336, prescribed in 53.214(h), may be used as a continuation sheet in solicitations, as specified in 13.307(c)(1).

(f) *SF 1449* (Rev. 2/2012) *Solicitation/Contract/Order for Commercial Items* prescribed in 53.212, *OF 347* (Rev. 2/2012), *Order for Supplies or Services*, and *OF 348* (Rev. 4/06), *Order for Supplies or Services—Schedule Continuation*. SF 1449, OF's 347 and 348 (or approved agency forms/automated formats) may be used as follows:

(1) To accomplish acquisitions under simplified acquisition procedures, as specified in 13.307.

(2) To establish blanket purchase agreements (BPA's), as specified in 13.303-2, and to make purchases under BPA's, as specified in 13.303-5.

(3) To issue orders under basic ordering agreements, as specified in 16.703(d)(2)(i).

(4) As otherwise specified in this chapter (*e.g.*, see 5.503(a)(2), 8.406-1, 36.701(b), and 51.102(e)(3)(ii)).

53.214 Sealed bidding.

The following forms are prescribed for use in contracting by sealed bidding (except for construction and architect-engineer services):

(a) *SF 26* (Rev. 3/2013), *Award/Contract*. SF 26 is prescribed for use in awarding sealed bid contracts for supplies or services in which bids were obtained on SF 33, Solicitation, Offer and Award, as specified in 14.408-1(d)(1). Block 18 may only be used for sealed-bid procurements.

(b) *SF 30, Amendment of Solicitation/Modification of Contract*. SF 30, prescribed in 53.243, shall be used in amending invitations for bids, as specified in 14.208(a).

(c) *SF 33* (Rev. 9/97), *Solicitation, Offer and Award*. SF 33 is prescribed for use in soliciting bids for supplies or services and for awarding the contracts that result from the bids, as specified in 14.201-2(a)(1), unless award is accomplished by SF 26.

(d) *SF 1447* (Rev. 2/2012), *Solicitation/Contract*. SF 1447 is prescribed for use in soliciting supplies or services and for awarding contracts that result from the bids. It shall be used when the simplified contract format is used (see 14.201-9) and may be used in place of the SF 26 or SF 33 with other solicitations and awards. Agencies may prescribe additional detailed instructions for use of the form.

(e) [Reserved]

(f) *SF 1409* (Rev. 9/88), *Abstract of Offers*, and *SF 1410* (9/88), *Abstract of Offers—Continuation*. SF 1409 and SF 1410 are prescribed for use in recording bids, as specified in 14.403(a).

(g) *OF 17* (Rev. 12/93), *Offer Label*. OF 17 may be furnished with each invitation for bids to facilitate identification and handling of bids, as specified in 14.202-3(b).

(h) *OF 336* (Rev. 3/86), *Continuation Sheet*. OF 336 may be used as a continuation sheet in solicitations, as specified in 14.201-2(b).

53.215 Contracting by negotiation.

53.215-1 Solicitation and receipt of proposals.

The following forms are prescribed, as stated in the following paragraphs, for use in contracting by negotiation (except for construction, architect-engineer services, or acquisitions made using simplified acquisition procedures):

(a) *SF 26* (Rev. 3/2013), *Award/Contract*. SF 26, prescribed in 53.214(a), may be used in entering into negotiated contracts in which the signature of both parties on a single document is appropriate, as specified in 15.509. Block 18 may not be used for negotiated procurements.

(b) *SF 30* (Rev. 10/83), *Amendment of Solicitation/Modification of Contract*. SF 30, prescribed in 53.243, may be used for amending requests for proposals and for amending requests for information, as specified in 15.210(b).

(c) *SF 33* (Rev. 9/97), *Solicitation, Offer and Award*. SF 33, prescribed in 53.214(c), may be used in connection with the solicitation and award of negotiated contracts. Award of such contracts may be made by either OF 307, SF 33, or SF 26, as specified in 53.214(c) and 15.509.

(d) *OF 17* (Rev. 12/93), *Offer Label*. OF 17 may be furnished with each request for proposals to facilitate identification and handling of proposals, as specified in 15.210(c).

(e) *OF 307* (Rev. 9/97), *Contract Award*. OF 307 may be used to award negotiated contracts as specified in 15.509.

(f) *OF 308* (Rev. 9/97), *Solicitation and Offer-Negotiated Acquisition*. OF 308 may be used to support solicitation of negotiated contracts as specified in 15.210(a). Award of such contracts may be made by OF 307, as specified in 15.509.

SUBPART 53.2—PRESCRIPTION OF FORMS 53.228

(g) *OF 309* (Rev. 9/97), Amendment of Solicitation. OF 309 may be used to amend solicitations of negotiated contracts, as specified in 15.210(b).

53.216 Types of contracts.

53.216-1 Delivery orders and orders under basic ordering agreements (OF 347).

OF 347, Order for Supplies or Services. OF 347, prescribed in 53.213(f) (or an approved agency form), may be used to place orders under indefinite delivery contracts and basic ordering agreements, as specified in 16.703(d)(2)(i).

53.217 [Reserved]

53.218 [Reserved]

53.219 Small business programs.

The following standard form is prescribed for use in reporting small business (including Alaska Native Corporations and Indian tribes), veteran-owned small business, service-disabled veteran-owned small business, HUBZone small business, small disadvantaged business (including Alaska Native Corporations and Indian tribes) and women-owned small business subcontracting data, as specified in Part 19: SF 294, (Rev. 10/2014) Subcontracting Report for Individual Contracts. SF 294 is authorized for local reproduction.

53.220 [Reserved]

53.221 [Reserved]

53.222 Application of labor laws to Government acquisitions (SF's 308, 1093, 1413, 1444, 1445, 1446, WH-347).

The following forms are prescribed as stated below, for use in connection with the application of labor laws:

(a) [Reserved]

(b) [Reserved]

(c) *SF 308* (DOL) (Rev. 2/2013), Request for Wage Determination and Response to Request. (See 22.404-3(a) and (b).)

(d) *SF 1093* (Rev. 2/2013), Schedule of Withholdings Under the Construction Wage Rate Requirements Statute (40 U.S.C. Chapter 31, Subchapter IV, section 3144) and/or the Contract Work Hours and Safety Standards Statute (40 U.S.C. Chapter 37, section 3703). (See 22.406-9(c)(1).)

(e) *SF 1413* (Rev. 4/2013), Statement and Acknowledgment. SF 1413 is prescribed for use in obtaining contractor acknowledgment of inclusion of required clauses in subcontracts, as specified in 22.406-5.

(f) Form *SF 1444* (Rev. 4/2013), Request for Authorization of Additional Classification and Rate. (See 22.406-3(a) and 22.1019.)

(g) *SF 1445* (Rev. 12/96), Labor Standards Interview. (See 22.406-7(b).)

(h) *SF 1446* (Rev. 4/2013.), Labor Standards Investigation Summary Sheet. (See 22.406-8(d).)

(i) Form *WH-347* (DOL), Payroll (For Contractor's Optional Use). (See 22.406-6(a).)

53.223 [Reserved]

53.224 [Reserved]

53.225 [Reserved]

53.226 [Reserved]

53.227 [Reserved]

53.228 Bonds and insurance.

The following standard forms are prescribed for use for bond and insurance requirements, as specified in Part 28:

(a) *SF 24* (Rev. 10/98) Bid Bond. (See 28.106-1.) SF 24 is authorized for local reproduction.

(b) *SF 25* (Rev. 3/2013) Performance Bond. (See 28.106-1(b).) SF 25 is authorized for local reproduction.

(c) *SF 25A* (Rev. 3/2013) Payment Bond. (See 28.106-1(c).) SF 25A is authorized for local reproduction.

(d) *SF 25B* (Rev. 10/83), Continuation Sheet (For Standard Forms 24, 25, and 25A). (See 28.106-1(c).)

(e) *SF 28* (Rev. 6/03) Affidavit of Individual Surety. (See 28.106-1(e) and 28.203(b).) SF 28 is authorized for local reproduction.

(f) *SF 34* (Rev. 1/90), Annual Bid Bond. (See 28.106-1(f).) SF 34 is authorized for local reproduction.

(g) *SF 35* (Rev. 1/90), Annual Performance Bond. (See 28.106-1.) SF 35 is authorized for local reproduction.

(h) *SF 273* (Rev. 4/2013) Reinsurance Agreement for a Bond statute Performance Bond. (See 28.106-1(h) and 28.202-1(a)(4).) SF 273 is authorized for local reproduction.

(i) *SF 274* (Rev. 4/2013) Reinsurance Agreement for a Bond statute Payment Bond. (See 28.106-1(i) and 28.202-1(a)(4).) SF 274 is authorized for local reproduction.

(j) *SF 275* (Rev. 10/98) Reinsurance Agreement in Favor of the United States. (See 28.106-1(j) and 28.202-1(a)(4).) SF 275 is authorized for local reproduction.

(k) *SF 1414* (Rev. 10/93), Consent of Surety. SF 1414 is authorized for local reproduction.

(l) *SF 1415 (Rev. 7/93), Consent of Surety and Increase of Penalty.* (See 28.106-1(l).) SF 1415 is authorized for local reproduction.

(m) *SF 1416 (Rev. 10/98) Payment Bond for Other than Construction Contracts.* (See 28.106-1(m).) SF 1416 is authorized for local reproduction.

(n) *SF 1418 (Rev. 2/99) Performance Bond For Other Than Construction Contracts.* (See 28.106-1(n).) SF 1418 is authorized for local reproduction.

(o) *OF 90 (Rev. 1/90), Release of Lien on Real Property.* (See 28.106-1(o) and 28.203-5(a).) OF 90 is authorized for local reproduction.

(p) *OF 91 (1/90 Ed.), Release of Personal Property from Escrow.* (See 28.106-1(p) and 28.203-5(a).) OF 91 is authorized for local reproduction.

53.229 Taxes (SF's 1094, 1094-A).

SF 1094 (Rev. 12/96), U.S. Tax Exemption Form, and SF 1094A (Rev. 12/96), Tax Exemption Forms Accountability Record. SF's 1094 and 1094A are prescribed for use in establishing exemption from State or local taxes, as specified in 29.302(b).

53.230 [Reserved]

53.231 [Reserved]

53.232 Contract financing (SF 1443).

SF 1443 (7/09), Contractor's Request for Progress Payment. SF 1443 is prescribed for use in obtaining contractors' requests for progress payments.

53.233 [Reserved]

53.234 [Reserved]

53.235 Research and development contracting (SF 298).

SF 298 (2/89), Report Documentation Page. SF 298 is prescribed for use in submitting scientific and technical reports to contracting officers and to technical information libraries, as specified in 35.010.

53.236 Construction and architect-engineer contracts.

53.236-1 Construction.

The following forms are prescribed, as stated below, for use in contracting for construction, alteration, or repair, or dismantling, demolition, or removal of improvements.

(a) [Reserved]

(b) [Reserved]

(c) [Reserved]

(d) *SF 1442 (4/85 Ed.), Solicitation, Offer and Award (Construction, Alteration, or Repair).* SF 1442 is prescribed for use in soliciting offers and awarding contracts expected to exceed the simplified acquisition threshold for—

(1) Construction, alteration, or repair; or

(2) Dismantling, demolition, or removal of improvements (and may be used for contracts within the simplified acquisition threshold), as specified in 36.701(a).

(e) *OF 347 (Rev. 2/2012), Order for Supplies or Services.* OF 347, prescribed in 53.213(f) (or an approved agency form), may be used for contracts under the simplified acquisition threshold for—

(1) Construction, alteration, or repair; or

(2) Dismantling, demolition, or removal of improvements, as specified in 36.701(b).

(f) *OF 1419 (11/88 Ed.), Abstract of Offers—Construction, and OF 1419A (11/88 Ed.), Abstract of Offers—Construction, Continuation Sheet.* OF's 1419 and 1419A are prescribed for use in recording bids (and may be used for recording proposal information), as specified in 36.701(c).

53.236-2 Architect-engineer services (SF's 252 and 330).

The following forms are prescribed for use in contracting for architect-engineer and related services:

(a) *SF 252 (Rev. 10/83), Architect-Engineer Contract.* SF 252 is prescribed for use in awarding fixed-price contracts for architect-engineer services, as specified in 36.702(a). Pending issuance of a new edition of the form, Block 8, Negotiation Authority, is deleted.

(b) *SF 330 (Rev. 3/2013), Architect-Engineer Qualifications.* SF 330 is prescribed for use in obtaining information from architect-engineer firms regarding their professional qualifications, as specified in 36.702(b)(1) and (b)(2).

53.237 [Reserved]

53.238 [Reserved]

53.239 [Reserved]

53.240 [Reserved]

53.241 [Reserved]

53.242 Contract administration.

53.242-1 Novation and change-of-name agreements (SF 30).

SF 30, Amendment of Solicitation/Modification of Contract. SF 30, prescribed in 53.243, shall be used in connection with novation and change of name agreements, as specified in 42.1203(h).

53.243 Contract modifications (SF 30).

SF 30 (Rev. 10/83), Amendment of Solicitation/ Modification of Contract. SF 30 is prescribed for use in amending invitation for bids, as specified in 14.208; modifying purchase and delivery orders, as specified in 13.302-3; and modifying contracts, as specified in 42.1203(h), 43.301, 49.602-5, and elsewhere in this regulation. The form may also be used to amend solicitations for negotiated contracts, as specified in 15.210(b). Pending the publication of a new edition of the form, Instruction (b), Item 3 (effective date), is revised in paragraphs (3) and (5) as follows:

(b) Item 3 (effective date).

* * * * *

(3) For a modification issued as a confirming notice of termination for the convenience of the Government, the effective date of the confirming notice shall be the same as the effective date of the initial notice.

* * * * *

(5) For a modification confirming the termination contracting officer's previous letter determination of the amount due in settlement of a contract termination for convenience, the effective date shall be the same as the effective date of the previous letter determination.

53.244 [Reserved]

53.245 Government property.

The following forms are prescribed, as specified in this section, for use in reporting, reutilization, and disposal of Government property and in accounting for this property:

(a) *SF 120 (GSA), Report of Excess Personal Property,* and *SF 120A (GSA), Continuation Sheet (Report of Excess Personal Property).* (See 45.602-3 and 41 CFR 102-36.215.)

(b) *SF 126 (GSA), Report of Personal Property for Sale,* and *SF 126A (GSA), Report of Personal Property for Sale (Continuation Sheet).* (See FPMR 101-45.303 (41 CFR 101-45.303.))

(c) *SF 1423 (Rev. 5/04), Inventory Verification Survey.* (See 45.602-1(b)(1) .)

(d) *SF 1424 (Rev. 5/2004), Inventory Disposal Report (See 45.605).* SF 1424 is authorized for local reproduction.

(e) *SF 1428 (Rev. 6/2007), Inventory Disposal Schedule,* and *SF 1429 (Rev. 5/2004), Inventory Disposal Schedule—Continuation Sheet.* (See 45.602-1, 49.303-2, 52.245-1, and 53.249(b).) SF's 1428 and 1429 are authorized for local reproduction.

53.246 [Reserved]

53.247 Transportation (U.S. Commercial Bill of Lading).

The commercial bill of lading is the preferred document for the transportation of property, as specified in 47.101.

53.248 [Reserved]

53.249 Termination of contracts.

(a) The following forms are prescribed for use in connection with the termination of contracts, as specified in Subpart 49.6:

(1) *SF 1034 (GAO), Public Voucher for Purchases and Services Other than Personal.* (See 49.302(a).)

(2) *SF 1435 (Rev. 9/97), Settlement Proposal (Inventory Basis).* (See 49.602-1(a).) Standard Form 1435 is authorized for local reproduction.

(3) *SF 1436 (Rev. 5/2004), Settlement Proposal (Total Cost Basis).* (See 49.602-1(b).) Standard Form 1436 is authorized for local reproduction.

(4) *SF 1437 (Rev. 9/97), Settlement Proposal for Cost-Reimbursement Type Contracts.* (See 49.602-1(c) and 49.302.) Standard Form 1437 is authorized for local reproduction.

(5) *SF 1438 (Rev. 5/2004), Settlement Proposal (Short Form).* (See 49.602-1(d).) Standard Form 1438 is authorized for local reproduction.

(6) *SF 1439 (Rev. 7/89), Schedule of Accounting Information.* (See 49.602-3.) Standard Form 1439 is authorized for local reproduction.

(7) *SF 1440 (Rev. 7/89), Application for Partial Payment.* (See 49.602-4.) Standard Form 1440 is authorized for local reproduction.

(b) *SF 1428 (Rev. 6/2007), Inventory Disposal Schedule,* and *Standard Form 1429 (Rev. 5/2004), Inventory Disposal Schedule—Continuation Sheet*, shall be used to support termination settlement proposals listed in paragraph (a) of this section, as specified in 49.602-2.

53.250 [Reserved]

53.251 Contractor use of Government supply sources (OF 347).

OF 347, Order for Supplies or Services. OF 347, prescribed in 53.213(f), may be used by contractors when requisitioning from the VA, as specified in 51.102(e)(3)(ii).

Subpart 53.3—Illustration of Forms

53.300 Scope of subpart.

This subpart contains illustrations of forms used in acquisitions.

53.301 Standard forms.

This section illustrates the standard forms that are specified by the FAR for use in acquisitions. The forms are illustrated in numerical order. The subsection numbers correspond with the standard form numbers (*e.g.,* Standard Form 18 appears as 53.301-18).

53.302 Optional forms.

This section illustrates the optional forms that are specified by the FAR for use in acquisitions. The numbering system is as indicated in 53.301.

53.303 Agency forms.

This section illustrates agency forms that are specified by the FAR for use in acquisitions. The forms are arranged numerically by agency. The numbering system is as indicated in 53.301.

* * * * * *

This page intentionally left blank.

Standard Form 18

REQUEST FOR QUOTATION (THIS IS NOT AN ORDER)	THIS RFQ ☐ IS ☐ IS NOT A SMALL BUSINESS SET-ASIDE	PAGE OF PAGES

1. REQUEST NO.	2. DATE ISSUED	3. REQUISITION/PURCHASE REQUEST NO.	4. CERT. FOR NAT. DEF. UNDER BDSA REG. 2 AND/OR DMS REG. 1 ▶	RATING

5a. ISSUED BY	6. DELIVER BY (Date)

5b. FOR INFORMATION CALL (NO COLLECT CALLS)		7. DELIVERY	
NAME	TELEPHONE NUMBER	☐ FOB DESTINATION	☐ OTHER (See Schedule)
	AREA CODE	NUMBER	9. DESTINATION
			a. NAME OF CONSIGNEE

8. TO:

a. NAME	b. COMPANY	b. STREET ADDRESS
c. STREET ADDRESS		c. CITY
d. CITY	e. STATE	f. ZIP CODE	d. STATE	e. ZIP CODE

10. PLEASE FURNISH QUOTATIONS TO THE ISSUING OFICE IN BLOCK 5a ON OR BEFORE CLOSE OF BUSINESS (Date)	IMPORTANT: This is a request for information, and quotations furnished are not officers. If you are unable to quote, please so indicate on this form and return it to the address in Block 5a. This request does not commit the Government to pay any costs incurred in the preparation of the submission of this quotation or to contract for supplies or service. Supplies are of domestic origin unless otherwise indicated by quoter. Any representations and/or certifications attached to this Request for Quotation must be completed by the quoter.

11. SCHEDULE (Include applicable Federal, State and local taxes)

ITEM NO. (a)	SUPPLIES/ SERVICES (b)	QUANTITY (c)	UNIT (d)	UNIT PRICE (e)	AMOUNT (f)

12. DISCOUNT FOR PROMPT PAYMENT ▶	a. 10 CALENDAR DAYS (%)	b. 20 CALENDAR DAYS (%)	c. 30 CALENDAR DAYS (%)	d. CALENDAR DAYS
				NUMBER	PERCENTAGE

NOTE: Additional provisions and representations ☐ are ☐ are not attached.

13. NAME AND ADDRESS OF QUOTER	14. SIGNATURE OF PERSON AUTHORIZED TO SIGN QUOTATION	15. DATE OF QUOTATION
a. NAME OF QUOTER		
b. STREET ADDRESS		16. SIGNER
c. COUNTY	a. NAME (Type or print)	b. TELEPHONE AREA CODE
d. CITY	e. STATE	f. ZIP CODE	c. TITLE (Type or print)	NUMBER

AUTHORIZED FOR LOCAL REPRODUCTION
Previous edition not usable

FormFlow/Delrina Inc.

STANDARD FORM 18 (REV. 6-95)
Prescribed by GSA-FAR (48 CFR) 53.215-1(a)

PART 53.3—ILLUSTRATION OF FORMS

53.301-24

Standard Form 24

BID BOND *(See instruction on reverse)*	DATE BOND EXECUTED *(Must not be later than bid opening date)*	OMB NO.: 9000-0045

Public reporting burden for this collection of information is estimated to average 25 minutes per response, including the time for reviewing instructions, searching existing data sources, gathering and maintaining the data needed, and completing and reviewing the collection of information. Send comments regarding this burden estimate or any other aspect of this collection of information, including suggestions for reducing this burden, to the FAR Secretariat (MVR), Federal Acquisition Policy Division, GSA, Washington, DC 20405.

PRINCIPAL *(Legal name and business address)*	TYPE OF ORGANIZATION *("X" one)*
	☐ INDIVIDUAL ☐ PARTNERSHIP
	☐ JOINT VENTURE ☐ CORPORATION
	STATE OF INCORPORATION

SURETY(IES) *(Name and business address)*

PENAL SUM OF BOND				BID IDENTIFICATION	
PERCENT OF BID PRICE	AMOUNT NOT TO EXCEED			BID DATE	INVITATION NO.
	MILLION(S)	THOUSAND(S)	HUNDRED(S)	CENTS	
					FOR *(Construction, Supplies, or Services)*

OBLIGATION:

We, the Principal and Surety(ies) are firmly bound to the United States of America (hereinafter called the Government) in the above penal sum. For payment of the penal sum, we bind ourselves, our heirs, executors, administrators, and successors, jointly and severally. However, where the Sureties are corporations acting as co-sureties, we, the Sureties, bind ourselves in such sum "jointly and severally" as well as "severally" only for the purpose of allowing a joint action or actions against any or all of us. For all other purposes, each Surety binds itself, jointly and severally with the Principal, for the payment of the sum shown opposite the name of the Surety. If no limit of liability is indicated, the limit of liability is the full amount of the penal sum.

CONDITIONS:

The Principal has submitted the bid identified above.

THEREFORE:

The above obligation is void if the Principal - (a) upon acceptance by the Government of the bid identified above, within the period specified therein for acceptance (sixty (60) days if no period is specified), executes the further contractual documents and gives the bond(s) required by the terms of the bid as accepted within the time specified (ten (10) days if no period is specified) after receipt of the forms by the principal; or (b) in the event of failure to execute such further contractual documents and give such bonds, pays the Government for any cost of procuring the work which exceeds the amount of the bid.

Each Surety executing this instrument agrees that its obligation is not impaired by any extension(s) of the time for acceptance of the bid that the Principal may grant to the Government. Notice to the surety(ies) of extension(s) are waived. However, waiver of the notice applies only to extensions aggregating not more than sixty (60) calendar days in addition to the period originally allowed for acceptance of the bid.

WITNESS:

The Principal and Surety(ies) executed this bid bond and affixed their seals on the above date.

	PRINCIPAL			
SIGNATURE(S)	1. (Seal)	2. (Seal)	3. (Seal)	Corporate Seal
NAME(S) & TITLE(S) *(Typed)*	1.	2.	3.	

	INDIVIDUAL SURETY(IES)	
SIGNATURE(S)	1. (Seal)	2. (Seal)
NAME(S) *(Typed)*	1.	2.

	CORPORATE SURETY(IES)			
SURETY A	NAME & ADDRESS		STATE OF INC.	LIABILITY LIMIT ($)
	SIGNATURE(S)	1.	2.	Corporate Seal
	NAME(S) & TITLE(S) *(Typed)*	1.	2.	

AUTHORIZED FOR LOCAL REPRODUCTION
Previous edition is usable

STANDARD FORM 24 (REV. 10-98)
Prescribed by GSA - FAR (48 CFR) 53.228(a)

Standard Form 24 (Back)

			STATE OF INC.	LIABILITY LIMIT ($)	
SURETY B	NAME & ADDRESS				Corporate Seal
	SIGNATURE(S)	1.	2.		
	NAME(S) & TITLE(S) *(Typed)*	1.	2.		
SURETY C	NAME & ADDRESS		STATE OF INC.	LIABILITY LIMIT ($)	Corporate Seal
	SIGNATURE(S)	1.	2.		
	NAME(S) & TITLE(S) *(Typed)*	1.	2.		
SURETY D	NAME & ADDRESS		STATE OF INC.	LIABILITY LIMIT ($)	Corporate Seal
	SIGNATURE(S)	1.	2.		
	NAME(S) & TITLE(S) *(Typed)*	1.	2.		
SURETY E	NAME & ADDRESS		STATE OF INC.	LIABILITY LIMIT ($)	Corporate Seal
	SIGNATURE(S)	1.	2.		
	NAME(S) & TITLE(S) *(Typed)*	1.	2.		
SURETY F	NAME & ADDRESS		STATE OF INC.	LIABILITY LIMIT ($)	Corporate Seal
	SIGNATURE(S)	1.	2.		
	NAME(S) & TITLE(S) *(Typed)*	1.	2.		
SURETY G	NAME & ADDRESS		STATE OF INC.	LIABILITY LIMIT ($)	Corporate Seal
	SIGNATURE(S)	1.	2.		
	NAME(S) & TITLE(S) *(Typed)*	1.	2.		

INSTRUCTIONS

1. This form is authorized for use when a bid guaranty is required. Any deviation from this form will require the written approval of the Administrator of General Services.

2. Insert the full legal name and business address of the Principal in the space designated "Principal" on the face of the form. An authorized person shall sign the bond. Any person signing in a representative capacity (e.g., an attorney-in-fact) must furnish evidence of authority if that representative is not a member of the firm, partnership, or joint venture, or an officer of the corporation involved.

3. The bond may express penal sum as a percentage of the bid price. In these cases, the bond may state a maximum dollar limitation (e.g., (e.g., 20% of the bid price but the amount not to exceed_____ dollars).

4. (a) Corporations executing the bond as sureties must appear on the Department of the Treasury's list of approved sureties and must act within the limitation listed therein. where more than one corporate surety is involved, their names and addresses shall appear in the spaces (Surety A, Surety B, etc.) headed "CORPORATE SURETY(IES)." In the space designed "SURETY(IES)" on the face of the form, insert only the letter identification of the sureties.

   (b) Where individual sureties are involved, a completed Affidavit of Individual surety (Standard Form 28), for each individual surety, shall accompany the bond. The Government may require the surety to furnish additional substantiating information concerning its financial capability.

5. Corporations executing the bond shall affix their corporate seals. Individuals shall execute the bond opposite the word "Corporate Seal"; and shall affix an adhesive seal if executed in Maine, New Hampshire, or any other jurisdiction requiring adhesive seals.

6. Type the name and title of each person signing this bond in the space provided.

7. In its application to negotiated contracts, the terms "bid" and "bidder" shall include "proposal" and "offeror."

STANDARD FORM 24 (REV. 10-98) BACK

Standard Form 25

PERFORMANCE BOND
(See instructions on reverse)

DATE BOND EXECUTED (Must be same or later than date of contract)

OMB Number: 9000-0045
Expiration Date: 6/30/2016

PAPERWORK REDUCTION ACT STATEMENT: Public reporting burden for this collection of information is estimated to average 60 minutes per response, including the time for reviewing instructions, searching existing data sources, gathering and maintaining the data needed, and completing and reviewing the collection of information. Send comments regarding this burden estimate or any other aspects of this collection of information, including suggestions for reducing this burden, to U.S. General Services Administration, Regulatory Secretariat (MVCB)/IC 9000-0045, Office of Governmentwide Acquisition Policy, 1800 F Street, NW, Washington, DC 20405.

PRINCIPAL (Legal name and business address)

TYPE OF ORGANIZATION ("X" one)
☐ INDIVIDUAL   ☐ PARTNERSHIP
☐ JOINT VENTURE   ☐ CORPORATION

STATE OF INCORPORATION

SURETY(IES) (Name(s) and business address(es))

PENAL SUM OF BOND
MILLION(S)	THOUSANDS	HUNDRED(S)	CENTS

CONTRACT DATE | CONTRACT NO.

OBLIGATION

We, the Principal and Surety(ies), are firmly bound to the United States of America (hereinafter called the Government) in the above penal sum. For payment of the penal sum, we bind ourselves, our heirs, executors, administrators, and successors, jointly and severally. However, where the Sureties are corporations acting as co-sureties, we the sureties bind ourselves in such sum "jointly and severally" as well as "severally" only for the purpose of allowing a joint action or actions against any or all of us. For all other purposes, each Surety binds itself, jointly and severally with the Principal, for the payment of the sum shown opposite the name of the Surety. If no limit of liability is indicated, the limit of liability is the full amount of the penal sum.

CONDITIONS

The Principal has entered into the contract identified above.

THEREFORE

The above obligation is void if the Principal-

(a)(1) Performs and fulfills all the undertaking, covenants, terms, conditions, and agreements of the contract during the original term of the contract and any extensions thereof that are granted by the Government, with or without notice of the Surety(ies) and during the life of any guaranty required under the contract, and (2) performs and fulfills all the undertakings, covenants, terms, conditions, and agreements of any and all duly authorized modifications of the contract that hereafter are made. Notice of those modifications to the Surety(ies) are waived.

(b) Pays to the Government the full amount of the taxes imposed by the Government, if the said contract is subject to 41 U.S.C. Chapter 31, Subchapter III, Bonds, which are collected, deducted, or withheld from wages paid by the Principal in carrying out the construction contract with respect to which this bond is furnished.

WITNESS

The Principal and Surety(ies) executed this performance bond and affixed their seals on the above date.

PRINCIPAL

SIGNATURE(S)	1. (Seal)	2. (Seal)	3. (Seal)	Corporate Seal
NAME(S) & TITLE(S) (Typed)	1.	2.	3.	

INDIVIDUAL SURETY(IES)

SIGNATURE(S)	1. (Seal)	2. (Seal)
NAME(S) (Typed)	1.	2.

CORPORATE SURETY(IES)

SURETY A	NAME & ADDRESS		STATE OF INC.	LIABILITY LIMIT ($)	
	SIGNATURE(S)	1.		2.	Corporate Seal
	NAME(S) & TITLE(S) (Typed)	1.		2.	

AUTHORIZED FOR LOCAL REPRODUCTION
Previous edition not usable

STANDARD FORM 25 (REV. 3/2013)
Prescribed by GSA-FAR (48 CFR) 53.228 (b)

Standard Form 25 (Back)

		CORPORATE SURETY(IES) *(Continued)*			
SURETY B	NAME & ADDRESS		STATE OF INC.	LIABILITY LIMIT ($)	Corporate Seal
	SIGNATURE(S)	1.	2.		
	NAME(S) & TITLE(S) *(Typed)*	1.	2.		
SURETY C	NAME & ADDRESS		STATE OF INC.	LIABILITY LIMIT ($)	Corporate Seal
	SIGNATURE(S)	1.	2.		
	NAME(S) & TITLE(S) *(Typed)*	1.	2.		
SURETY D	NAME & ADDRESS		STATE OF INC.	LIABILITY LIMIT ($)	Corporate Seal
	SIGNATURE(S)	1.	2.		
	NAME(S) & TITLE(S) *(Typed)*	1.	2.		
SURETY E	NAME & ADDRESS		STATE OF INC.	LIABILITY LIMIT ($)	Corporate Seal
	SIGNATURE(S)	1.	2.		
	NAME(S) & TITLE(S) *(Typed)*	1.	2.		
SURETY F	NAME & ADDRESS		STATE OF INC.	LIABILITY LIMIT ($)	Corporate Seal
	SIGNATURE(S)	1.	2.		
	NAME(S) & TITLE(S) *(Typed)*	1.	2.		
SURETY G	NAME & ADDRESS		STATE OF INC.	LIABILITY LIMIT ($)	Corporate Seal
	SIGNATURE(S)	1.	2.		
	NAME(S) & TITLE(S) *(Typed)*	1.	2.		

BOND PREMIUM ▶	RATE PER THOUSAND ($)	TOTAL ($)

INSTRUCTIONS

1. This form is authorized for use in connection with Government contracts. Any deviation from this form will require the written approval of the Administrator of General Services.

2. Insert the full legal name and business address of the Principal in the space designated "Principal" on the face of the form. An authorized person shall sign the bond. Any person signing in a representative capacity (e.g., an attorney-in-fact) must furnish evidence of authority if that representative is not a member of the firm, partnership, or joint venture, or an officer of the corporation involved.

3. (a) Corporations executing the bond as sureties must appear on the Department of the Treasury's list of approved sureties and must act within the limitation listed therein. Where more than one corporate surety is involved, their names and addresses shall appear in the spaces (Surety A, Surety B, etc.) headed "CORPORATE SURETY(IES)." In the space designated "SURETY(IES)" on the face of the form, insert only the letter identification of the sureties.

(b) Where individual sureties are involved, a completed Affidavit of Individual Surety (Standard Form 28) for each individual surety, shall accompany the bond. The Government may require the surety to furnish additional substantiating information concerning their financial capability.

4. Corporations executing the bond shall affix their corporate seals. Individuals shall execute the bond opposite the words "Corporate Seal", and shall affix an adhesive seal if executed in Maine, New Hampshire, or any other jurisdiction requiring adhesive seals.

5. Type the name and title of each person signing this bond in the space provided.

STANDARD FORM 25 (REV. 3/2013) **BACK**

FAC 2005–73 MAY 29, 2014

PART 53.3—ILLUSTRATION OF FORMS   53.301-25A

Standard Form 25A

PAYMENT BOND
(See instructions on reverse)

DATE BOND EXECUTED (Must be same or later than date of contract)

OMB Number: **9000-0045**
Expiration Date: **6/30/2016**

PAPERWORK REDUCTION ACT STATEMENT: Public reporting burden for this collection of information is estimated to average 60 minutes per response, including the time for reviewing instructions, searching existing data sources, gathering and maintaining the data needed, and completing and reviewing the collection of information. Send comments regarding this burden estimate or any other aspects of this collection of information, including suggestions for reducing this burden, to U.S. General Services Administration, Regulatory Secretariat (MVCB)/IC 9000-0045, Office of Governmentwide Acquisition Policy,1800 F Street, NW, Washington, DC 20405.

PRINCIPAL (Legal name and business address)

TYPE OF ORGANIZATION ("X" one)
☐ INDIVIDUAL   ☐ PARTNERSHIP
☐ JOINT VENTURE   ☐ CORPORATION

STATE OF INCORPORATION

SURETY(IES) (Name(s) and business address(es))

PENAL SUM OF BOND
MILLION(S)	THOUSAND(S)	HUNDRED(S)	CENTS

CONTRACT DATE   CONTRACT NO.

OBLIGATION:

We, the Principal and Surety(ies), are firmly bound to the United States of America (hereinafter called the Government) in the above penal sum. For payment of the penal sum, we bind ourselves, our heirs, executors, administrators, and successors, jointly and severally. However, where the Sureties are corporations acting as co-sureties, we, the Sureties, bind ourselves in such sum "jointly and severally" as well as "severally" only for the purpose of allowing a joint action or actions against any or all of us. For all other purposes, each Surety binds itself, jointly and severally with the Principal, for the payment of the sum shown opposite the name of the Surety. If no limit is indicated, the limit of liability is the full amount of the penal sum.

CONDITIONS:

The above obligation is void if the Principal promptly makes payment to all persons having a direct relationship with the Principal or a subcontractor of the Principal for furnishing labor, material or both in the prosecution of the work provided for in the contract identified above, and any authorized modifications of the contract that subsequently are made. Notice of those modifications to the Surety(ies) are waived.

WITNESS:

The Principal and Surety(ies) executed this payment bond and affixed their seals on the above date.

PRINCIPAL

SIGNATURE(S)	1. (Seal)	2. (Seal)	3. (Seal)	Corporate Seal
NAME(S) & TITLE(S) (Typed)	1.	2.	3.	

INDIVIDUAL SURETY(IES)

SIGNATURE(S)	1. (Seal)	2. (Seal)
NAME(S) (Typed)	1.	2.

CORPORATE SURETY(IES)

SURETY A	NAME & ADDRESS		STATE OF INC.	LIABILITY LIMIT $	
	SIGNATURE(S)	1.	2.		Corporate Seal
	NAME(S) & TITLE(S) (Typed)	1.	2.		

AUTHORIZED FOR LOCAL REPRODUCTION
Previous edition is usable

STANDARD FORM 25A (REV. 3/2013)
Prescribed by GSA-FAR (48 CFR) 53.2228(c)

Standard Form 25A (Back)

		CORPORATE SURETY(IES) *(Continued)*			
SURETY B	NAME & ADDRESS		STATE OF INC.	LIABILITY LIMIT $	Corporate Seal
	SIGNATURE(S)	1.	2.		
	NAME(S) & TITLE(S) *(Typed)*	1.	2.		
SURETY C	NAME & ADDRESS		STATE OF INC.	LIABILITY LIMIT $	Corporate Seal
	SIGNATURE(S)	1.	2.		
	NAME(S) & TITLE(S) *(Typed)*	1.	2.		
SURETY D	NAME & ADDRESS		STATE OF INC.	LIABILITY LIMIT $	Corporate Seal
	SIGNATURE(S)	1.	2.		
	NAME(S) & TITLE(S) *(Typed)*	1.	2.		
SURETY E	NAME & ADDRESS		STATE OF INC.	LIABILITY LIMIT $	Corporate Seal
	SIGNATURE(S)	1.	2.		
	NAME(S) & TITLE(S) *(Typed)*	1.	2.		
SURETY F	NAME & ADDRESS		STATE OF INC.	LIABILITY LIMIT $	Corporate Seal
	SIGNATURE(S)	1.	2.		
	NAME(S) & TITLE(S) *(Typed)*	1.	2.		
SURETY G	NAME & ADDRESS		STATE OF INC.	LIABILITY LIMIT $	Corporate Seal
	SIGNATURE(S)	1.	2.		
	NAME(S) & TITLE(S) *(Typed)*	1.	2.		

INSTRUCTIONS

1. This form, for the protection of persons supplying labor and material, is used when a payment bond is required under 40 U.S.C. Chapter 31, Subchapter III, Bonds. Any deviation from this form will require the written approval of the Administrator of General Services.

2. Insert the full legal name and business address of the Principal in the space designated "Principal" on the face of the form. An authorized person shall sign the bond. Any person signing in a representative capacity (e.g., an attorney-in-fact) must furnish evidence of authority if that representative is not a member of the firm, partnership, or joint venture, or an officer of the corporation involved.

3. (a) Corporations executing the bond as sureties must appear on the Department of the Treasury's list of approved sureties and must act within the limitation listed therein. Where more than one corporate surety is involved, their names and addresses shall appear in the spaces (Surety A, Surety B, etc.) headed "CORPORATE SURETY(IES)."

In the space designated "SURETY(IES)" on the face of the form, insert only the letter identification of the sureties.

(b) Where individual sureties are involved, a completed Affidavit of Individual Surety (Standard Form 28) for each individual surety, shall accompany the bond. The Government may require the surety to furnish additional substantiating information concerning their financial capability.

4. Corporations executing the bond shall affix their corporate seals. Individuals shall execute the bond opposite the words "Corporate Seal", and shall affix an adhesive seal if executed in Maine, New Hampshire, or any other jurisdiction requiring adhesive seals.

5. Type the name and title of each person signing this bond in the space provided.

STANDARD FORM 25A (REV. 3/2013) BACK

Standard Form 25B

CONTINUATION SHEET
(For Standard Forms 24, 25, and 25A)

NAME OF PRINCIPAL *(Legal name and business address)*

TYPE OF BOND
- [ ] BID
- [ ] PERFORMANCE
- [ ] PAYMENT

FURNISHED IN CONNECTION WITH -
- [ ] BID
- [ ] CONTRACT

DATED -

CORPORATE SURETY(IES)

			STATE OF INC.	LIABILITY LIMIT $	
SURETY H	Name & Address				Corporate Seal
	Signature(s)	1.	2.		
	Name(s) & Title(s) (Typed)	1.	2.		
SURETY I	Name & Address		STATE OF INC.	LIABILITY LIMIT $	Corporate Seal
	Signature(s)	1.	2.		
	Name(s) & Title(s) (Typed)	1.	2.		
SURETY J	Name & Address		STATE OF INC.	LIABILITY LIMIT $	Corporate Seal
	Signature(s)	1.	2.		
	Name(s) & Title(s) (Typed)	1.	2.		
SURETY K	Name & Address		STATE OF INC.	LIABILITY LIMIT $	Corporate Seal
	Signature(s)	1.	2.		
	Name(s) & Title(s) (Typed)	1.	2.		
SURETY L	Name & Address		STATE OF INC.	LIABILITY LIMIT $	Corporate Seal
	Signature(s)	1.	2.		
	Name(s) & Title(s) (Typed)	1.	2.		
SURETY M	Name & Address		STATE OF INC.	LIABILITY LIMIT $	Corporate Seal
	Signature(s)	1.	2.		
	Name(s) & Title(s) (Typed)	1.	2.		
SURETY N	Name & Address		STATE OF INC.	LIABILITY LIMIT $	Corporate Seal
	Signature(s)	1.	2.		
	Name(s) & Title(s) (Typed)	1.	2.		
SURETY O	Name & Address		STATE OF INC.	LIABILITY LIMIT $	Corporate Seal
	Signature(s)	1.	2.		
	Name(s) & Title(s) (Typed)	1.	2.		

AUTHORIZED FOR LOCAL REPRODUCTION
PREVIOUS EDITION USABLE

STANDARD FORM 25B (REV. 10-83)
Prescribed by GSA - FAR (48 CFR) 53.228(d)

Standard Form 25B (Back)

		CORPORATE SURETY(IES) *(Continued)*			
SURETY P	Name & Address		STATE OF INC.	LIABILITY LIMIT $	Corporate Seal
	Signature(s)	1.	2.		
	Name(s) & Title(s) *(Typed)*	1.	2.		
SURETY Q	Name & Address		STATE OF INC.	LIABILITY LIMIT $	Corporate Seal
	Signature(s)	1.	2.		
	Name(s) & Title(s) *(Typed)*	1.	2.		
SURETY R	Name & Address		STATE OF INC.	LIABILITY LIMIT $	Corporate Seal
	Signature(s)	1.	2.		
	Name(s) & Title(s) *(Typed)*	1.	2.		
SURETY S	Name & Address		STATE OF INC.	LIABILITY LIMIT $	Corporate Seal
	Signature(s)	1.	2.		
	Name(s) & Title(s) *(Typed)*	1.	2.		
SURETY T	Name & Address		STATE OF INC.	LIABILITY LIMIT $	Corporate Seal
	Signature(s)	1.	2.		
	Name(s) & Title(s) *(Typed)*	1.	2.		
SURETY U	Name & Address		STATE OF INC.	LIABILITY LIMIT $	Corporate Seal
	Signature(s)	1.	2.		
	Name(s) & Title(s) *(Typed)*	1.	2.		
SURETY V	Name & Address		STATE OF INC.	LIABILITY LIMIT $	Corporate Seal
	Signature(s)	1.	2.		
	Name(s) & Title(s) *(Typed)*	1.	2.		
SURETY W	Name & Address		STATE OF INC.	LIABILITY LIMIT $	Corporate Seal
	Signature(s)	1.	2.		
	Name(s) & Title(s) *(Typed)*	1.	2.		
SURETY X	Name & Address		STATE OF INC.	LIABILITY LIMIT $	Corporate Seal
	Signature(s)	1.	2.		
	Name(s) & Title(s) *(Typed)*	1.	2.		
SURETY Y	Name & Address		STATE OF INC.	LIABILITY LIMIT $	Corporate Seal
	Signature(s)	1.	2.		
	Name(s) & Title(s) *(Typed)*	1.	2.		

STANDARD FORM 25B BACK (REV. 10-83)

Standard Form 26

AWARD/CONTRACT	1. THIS CONTRACT IS A RATED ORDER UNDER DPAS (15 CFR 700)	RATING	PAGE	OF	PAGES

2. CONTRACT (Proc. Inst. Ident.) NO.	3. EFFECTIVE DATE	4. REQUISITION/PURCHASE REQUEST/PROJECT NO.

5. ISSUED BY	CODE	6. ADMINISTERED BY (If other than Item 5)	CODE

7. NAME AND ADDRESS OF CONTRACTOR (No., street, county, State and ZIP Code)	8. DELIVERY
	☐ FOB ORIGIN ☐ OTHER (See below)
	9. DISCOUNT FOR PROMPT PAYMENT
	10. SUBMIT INVOICES (4 copies unless otherwise specified) TO THE ADDRESS SHOWN IN ITEM
CODE FACILITY CODE	

11. SHIP TO/MARK FOR	CODE	12. PAYMENT WILL BE MADE BY	CODE

13. AUTHORITY FOR USING OTHER THAN FULL AND OPEN COMPETITION:	14. ACCOUNTING AND APPROPRIATION DATA
☐ 10 U.S.C. 2304(c)( ) ☐ 41 U.S.C. 3304(a)( )	

15A. ITEM NO.	15B. SUPPLIES/SERVICES	15C. QUANTITY	15D. UNIT	15E. UNIT PRICE	15F. AMOUNT
			15G. TOTAL AMOUNT OF CONTRACT ▶		$

16. TABLE OF CONTENTS

(X)	SEC.	DESCRIPTION	PAGE(S)	(X)	SEC.	DESCRIPTION	PAGE(S)
		PART I - THE SCHEDULE				PART II - CONTRACT CLAUSES	
	A	SOLICITATION/CONTRACT FORM			I	CONTRACT CLAUSES	
	B	SUPPLIES OR SERVICES AND PRICES/COSTS				PART III - LIST OF DOCUMENTS, EXHIBITS AND OTHER ATTACH.	
	C	DESCRIPTION/SPECS./WORK STATEMENT			J	LIST OF ATTACHMENTS	
	D	PACKAGING AND MARKING				PART IV - REPRESENTATIONS AND INSTRUCTIONS	
	E	INSPECTION AND ACCEPTANCE			K	REPRESENTATIONS, CERTIFICATIONS AND OTHER STATEMENTS OF OFFERORS	
	F	DELIVERIES OR PERFORMANCE					
	G	CONTRACT ADMINISTRATION DATA			L	INSTRS., CONDS., AND NOTICES TO OFFERORS	
	H	SPECIAL CONTRACT REQUIREMENTS			M	EVALUATION FACTORS FOR AWARD	

CONTRACTING OFFICER WILL COMPLETE ITEM 17 (SEALED-BID OR NEGOTIATED PROCUREMENT) OR 18 (SEALED-BID PROCUREMENT) AS APPLICABLE

17. ☐ CONTRACTOR'S NEGOTIATED AGREEMENT (Contractor is required to sign this document and return _____ copies to issuing office.) Contractor agrees to furnish and deliver all items or perform all the services set forth or otherwise identified above and on any continuation sheets for the consideration stated herein. The rights and obligations of the parties to this contract shall be subject to and governed by the following documents: (a) this award/contract, (b) the solicitation, if any, and (c) such provisions, representations, certifications, and specifications, as are attached or incorporated by reference herein. (Attachments are listed herein.)	18. ☐ SEALED-BID AWARD (Contractor is not required to sign this document.) Your bid on Solicitation Number _____ including the additions or changes made by you which additions or changes are set forth in full above, is hereby accepted as to the terms listed above and on any continuation sheets. This award consummates the contract which consists of the following documents: (a) the Government's solicitation and your bid, and (b) this award/contract. No further contractual document is necessary. (Block 18 should be checked only when awarding a sealed-bid contract.)

19A. NAME AND TITLE OF SIGNER (Type or Print)	20A. NAME OF CONTRACTING OFFICER

19B. NAME OF CONTRACTOR	19C. DATE SIGNED	20B. UNITED STATES OF AMERICA	20C. DATE SIGNED
BY _____ (Signature of person authorized to sign)		BY _____ (Signature of Contracting Officer)	

AUTHORIZED FOR LOCAL REPRODUCTION
Previous edition is NOT usable

STANDARD FORM 26 (REV. 3/2013)
Prescribed by GSA - FAR (48 CFR) 53.214(a)

PART 53.3—ILLUSTRATION OF FORMS

53.301-28

Standard Form 28

AFFIDAVIT OF INDIVIDUAL SURETY
(See instructions on reverse)

OMB No.: 9000-0001

Public reporting burden for this collection of information is estimated to average 3 hours per response, including the time for reviewing instructions, searching existing data sources, gathering and maintaining the data needed, and completing and reviewing the collection of information. Send comments regarding this burden estimate or any other aspect of this collection of information, including suggestions for reducing this burden, to the Regulatory Secretariat (MVA), Office of Acquisition Policy, GSA, Washington, DC 20405.

STATE OF

COUNTY OF   SS.

I, the undersigned, being duly sworn, depose and say that I am: (1) the surety to the attached bond(s); (2) a citizen of the United States; and of full age and legally competent. I also depose and say that, concerning any stocks or bonds included in the assets listed below, that there are no restrictions on the resale of these securities pursuant to the registration provisions of Section 5 of the Securities Act of 1933. I recognize that statements contained herein concern a matter within the jurisdiction of an agency of the United States and the making of a false, fictitious or fraudulent statement may render the maker subject to prosecution under Title 18, United States Code Sections 1001 and 494. This affidavit is made to induce the United States of America to accept me as surety on the attached bond.

1. NAME *(First, Middle, Last) (Type or Print)*

2. HOME ADDRESS *(Number, Street, City, State, ZIP Code)*

3. TYPE AND DURATION OF OCCUPATION

4. NAME AND ADDRESS OF EMPLOYER *(If Self-employed, so State)*

5. NAME AND ADDRESS OF INDIVIDUAL SURETY BROKER USED *(If any)*
   (Number, Street, City, State, ZIP Code)

6. TELEPHONE NUMBER

   HOME -

   BUSINESS -

7. THE FOLLOWING IS A TRUE REPRESENTATION OF THE ASSETS I HAVE PLEDGED TO THE UNITED STATES IN SUPPORT OF THE ATTACHED BOND:

   (a) Real estate *(Include a legal description, street address and other identifying description; the market value; attach supporting certified documents including recorded lien; evidence of title and the current tax assessment of the property. For market value approach, also provide a current appraisal.)*

   (b) Assets other than real estate *(describe the assets, the details of the escrow account, and attach certified evidence thereof).*

8. IDENTIFY ALL MORTGAGES, LIENS, JUDGEMENTS, OR ANY OTHER ENCUMBRANCES INVOLVING SUBJECT ASSETS INCLUDING REAL ESTATE TAXES DUE AND PAYABLE.

9. IDENTIFY ALL BONDS, INCLUDING BID GUARANTEES, FOR WHICH THE SUBJECT ASSETS HAVE BEEN PLEDGED WITHIN 3 YEARS PRIOR TO THE DATE OF EXECUTION OF THIS AFFIDAVIT.

DOCUMENTATION OF THE PLEDGED ASSET MUST BE ATTACHED.

10. SIGNATURE

11. BOND AND CONTRACT TO WHICH THIS AFFIDAVIT RELATES *(Where appropriate)*

12. SUBSCRIBED AND SWORN TO BEFORE ME AS FOLLOWS:

a. DATE OATH ADMINISTERED
   MONTH   DAY   YEAR

b. CITY AND STATE *(Or other jurisdiction)*

c. NAME AND TITLE OF OFFICIAL ADMINISTERING OATH
   (Type or print)

d. SIGNATURE

e. MY COMMISSION EXPIRES

Official Seal

AUTHORIZED FOR LOCAL REPRODUCTION
Previous edition is not usable

STANDARD FORM 28 (REV. 6/2003)
Prescribed by GSA-FAR (48 CFR) 53.228(e)

Standard Form 28 (Back)

INSTRUCTIONS

1. Individual sureties on bonds executed in connection with Government contracts must complete and submit this form with the bond. (See 48 CFR 28.203, 53.228(e).) The surety must have the completed form notarized.

2. No corporation, partnership, or other unincorporated association or firm, as such, is acceptable as an individual surety. Likewise, members of a partnership are not acceptable as sureties on bonds that a partnership or an association, or any co-partner or member thereof, is the principal obligor. However, stockholders of corporate principals are acceptable provided (a) their qualifications are independent of their stockholdings or financial interest therein, and (b) that the fact is expressed in the affidavit of justification. An individual surety will not include any financial interest in assets connected with the principal on the bond that this affidavit supports.

3. United States citizenship is a requirement for individual sureties for contracts and bonds when the contract is awarded in the United States. However, when the Contracting Officer is located in an outlying area or a foreign country, the individual surety is only required to be a permanent resident of the area or country in which the contracting officer is located.

4. All signatures of the affidavit submitted must be originals. Affidavits bearing reproduced signatures are not acceptable. An authorized person must sign the bond. Any person signing in a representative capacity (e.g., an attorney-in-fact) must furnish evidence of authority if that representative is not a member of a firm, partnership, or joint venture, or an officer of the corporation involved.

STANDARD FORM 28 (REV. 6/2003) BACK

Standard Form 30

AMENDMENT OF SOLICITATION/MODIFICATION OF CONTRACT	1. CONTRACT ID CODE	PAGE	OF	PAGES
2. AMENDMENT/MODIFICAITON NO.	3. EFFECTIVE DATE	4. REQUISITION/PURCHASE REQ. NO.	5. PROJECT NO. (If applicble)	
6. ISSUED BY CODE		7. ADMINISTERED BY (If other than Item 6) CODE		

8. NAME AND ADDRESS OF CONTRACTOR (No., street, county, State and ZIP Code)	(X)	9A. AMENDMENT OF SOLICIATION NO.
		9B. DATED (SEE ITEM 11)
		10A. MODIFICATION OF CONTRACT/ORDER NO.
		10B. DATED (SEE ITEM 11)
CODE	FACILITY CODE	

11. THIS ITEM ONLY APPLIES TO AMENDMENTS OF SOLICITATIONS

☐ The above numbered solicitation is amended as set forth in Item 14. The hour and date specified for receipt of Offers ☐ is extended, ☐ is not extended.

Offers must acknowledge receipt of this amendment prior to the hour and date specified in the solicitation or as amended, by one of the following methods:

(a) By completing items 8 and 15, and returning _____ copies of the amendment; (b) By acknowledging receipt of this amendment on each copy of the offer submitted; or (c) By separate letter or telegram which includes a reference to the solicitation and amendment numbers. FAILURE OF YOUR ACKNOWLEDGMENT TO BE RECEIVED AT THE PLACE DESIGNATED FOR THE RECEIPT OF OFFERS PRIOR TO THE HOUR AND DATE SPECIFIED MAY RESULT IN REJECTION OF YOUR OFFER. If by virtue of this amendment your desire to change an offer already submitted, such change may be made by telegram or letter, provided each telegram or letter makes reference to the solicitation and this amendment, and is received prior to the opening hour and date specified.

12. ACCOUNTING AND APPROPRIATION DATA (If required)

**13. THIS ITEM ONLY APPLIES TO MODIFICATION OF CONTRACTS/ORDERS.
IT MODIFIES THE CONTRACT/ORDER NO. AS DESCRIBED IN ITEM 14.**

CHECK ONE		
	A.	THIS CHANGE ORDER IS ISSUED PURSUANT TO: (Specify authority) THE CHANGES SET FORTH IN ITEM 14 ARE MADE IN THE CONTRACT ORDER NO. IN ITEM 10A.
	B.	THE ABOVE NUMBERED CONTRACT/ORDER IS MODIFIED TO REFLECT THE ADMINISTRATIVE CHANGES (such as changes in paying office, appropriation date, etc.) SET FORTH IN ITEM 14, PURSUANT TO THE AUTHORITY OF FAR 43.103(b).
	C.	THIS SUPPLEMENTAL AGREEMENT IS ENTERED INTO PURSUANT TO AUTHORITY OF:
	D.	OTHER (Specify type of modification and authority)

E. IMPORTANT: Contractor ☐ is not, ☐ is required to sign this document and return _____ copies to the issuing office.

14. DESCRIPTION OF AMENDMENT/MODIFICATION (Organized by UCF section headings, including solicitation/contract subject matter where feasible.)

Except as provided herein, all terms and conditions of the document referenced in Item 9A or 10A, as heretofore changed, remains unchanged and in full force and effect.

15A. NAME AND TITLE OF SIGNER (Type or print)	16A. NAME AND TITLE OF CONTRACTING OFFICER (Type or print)	
15B. CONTRACTOR/OFFEROR	15C. DATE SIGNED	16B. UNITED STATES OF AMERICA	16C. DATE SIGNED
(Signature of person authorized to sign)		(Signature of Contracting Officer)	

NSN 7540-01-152-8070
Previous edition unusable

STANDARD FORM 30 (REV. 10-83)
Prescribed by GSA FAR (48 CFR) 53.243

Standard Form 30 (Back)

INSTRUCTIONS

Instructions for items other than those that are self-explanatory, are as follows:

(a) Item 1 (Contract ID Code). Insert the contract type identification code that appears in the title block of the contract being modified.

(b) Item 3 (Effective date).

   (1) For a solicitation amendment, change order, or administrative change, the effective date shall be the issue date of the amendment, change order, or administrative change.

   (2) For a supplemental agreement, the effective date shall be the date agreed to by the contracting parties.

   (3) For a modification issued as an initial or confirming notice of termination for the convenience of the Government, the effective date and the modification number of the confirming notice shall be the same as the effective date and modification number of the initial notice.

   (4) For a modification converting a termination for default to a termination for the convenience of the Government, the effective date shall be the same as the effective date of the termination for default.

   (5) For a modification confirming the contacting officer's determination of the amount due in settlement of a contract termination, the effective date shall be the same as the effective date of the initial decision.

(c) Item 6 (Issued By). Insert the name and address of the issuing office. If applicable, insert the appropriate issuing office code in the code block.

(d) Item 8 (Name and Address of Contractor). For modifications to a contract or order, enter the contractor's name, address, and code as shown in the original contract or order, unless changed by this or a previous modification.

(e) Item 9, (Amendment of Solicitation No. - Dated), and 10, (Modification of Contract/Order No. - Dated). Check the appropriate box and in the corresponding blanks insert the number and date of the original solicitation, contract, or order.

(f) Item 12 (Accounting and Appropriation Data). When appropriate, indicate the impact of the modification on each affected accounting classification by inserting one of the following entries.

   (1) Accounting classification _____
       Net increase $ _____

   (2) Accounting classification _____
       Net decrease $ _____

NOTE: If there are changes to multiple accounting classifications that cannot be placed in block 12, insert an asterisk and the words "See continuation sheet".

(g) Item 13. Check the appropriate box to indicate the type of modification. Insert in the corresponding blank the authority under which the modification is issued. Check whether or not contractor must sign this document. (See FAR 43.103.)

(h) Item 14 (Description of Amendment/Modification).

   (1) Organize amendments or modifications under the appropriate Uniform Contract Format (UCF) section headings from the applicable solicitation or contract. The UCF table of contents, however, shall not be set forth in this document

   (2) Indicate the impact of the modification on the overall total contract price by inserting one of the following entries:

      (i) Total contract price increased by $ _____

      (ii) Total contract price decreased by $ _____

      (iii) Total contract price unchanged.

   (3) State reason for modification.

   (4) When removing, reinstating, or adding funds, identify the contract items and accounting classifications.

   (5) When the SF 30 is used to reflect a determination by the contracting officer of the amount due in settlement of a contract terminated for the convenience of the Government, the entry in Item 14 of the modification may be limited to --

      (i) A reference to the letter determination; and

      (ii) A statement of the net amount determined to be due in settlement of the contract.

   (6) Include subject matter or short title of solicitation/contract where feasible.

(i) Item 16B. The contracting officer's signature is not required on solicitation amendments. The contracting offier's signature is normally affixed last on supplemental agreements.

STANDARD FORM 30 (REV. 10-83) BACK

Standard Form 33

SOLICITATION, OFFER AND AWARD	1. THIS CONTRACT IS A RATED ORDER UNDER DPAS (15 CFR 700)	RATING	PAGE	OF	PAGES

2. CONTRACT NUMBER	3. SOLICITATION NUMBER	4. TYPE OF SOLICITATION ☐ SEALED BID (IFB) ☐ NEGOTIATED (RFP)	5. DATE ISSUED	6. REQUISITION/PURCHASE NUMBER

7. ISSUED BY	CODE	8. ADDRESS OFFER TO (If other than Item 7)

NOTE: In sealed bid solicitations "offer" and "offeror" mean "bid" and "bidder".

SOLICITATION

9. Sealed offers in original and _____ copies for furnishing the supplies or services in the Schedule will be received at the place specified in Item 8, or if handcarried, in the depository located in _____ until _____ local time _____
(Hour) (Date)

CAUTION - LATE Submissions, Modifications, and Withdrawals: See Section L, Provision No. 52.214-7 or 52.215-1. All offers are subject to all terms and conditions contained in this solicitation.

10. FOR INFORMATION CALL:	A. NAME	B. TELEPHONE (NO COLLECT CALLS) AREA CODE	NUMBER	EXT.	C. E-MAIL ADDRESS

11. TABLE OF CONTENTS

(X)	SEC.	DESCRIPTION	PAGE(S)	(X)	SEC.	DESCRIPTION	PAGE(S)
		PART I - THE SCHEDULE				PART II - CONTRACT CLAUSES	
	A	SOLICITATION/CONTRACT FORM			I	CONTRACT CLAUSES	
	B	SUPPLIES OR SERVICES AND PRICES/COSTS				PART III - LIST OF DOCUMENTS, EXHIBITS AND OTHER ATTACH.	
	C	DESCRIPTION/SPECS./WORK STATEMENT			J	LIST OF ATTACHMENTS	
	D	PACKAGING AND MARKING				PART IV - REPRESENTATIONS AND INSTRUCTIONS	
	E	INSPECTION AND ACCEPTANCE			K	REPRESENTATIONS, CERTIFICATIONS AND OTHER STATEMENTS OF OFFERORS	
	F	DELIVERIES OR PERFORMANCE					
	G	CONTRACT ADMINISTRATION DATA			L	INSTRS., CONDS., AND NOTICES TO OFFERORS	
	H	SPECIAL CONTRACT REQUIREMENTS			M	EVALUATION FACTORS FOR AWARD	

OFFER (Must be fully completed by offeror)

NOTE: Item 12 does not apply if the solicitation includes the provisions at 52.214-16, Minimum Bid Acceptance Period.

12. In compliance with the above, the undersigned agrees, if this offer is accepted within _____ calendar days (60 calendar days unless a different period is inserted by the offeror) from the date for receipt of offers specified above, to furnish any or all items upon which prices are offered at the price set opposite each item, delivered at the designated point(s), within the time specified in the schedule.

13. DISCOUNT FOR PROMPT PAYMENT (See Section I, Clause No. 52.232-8)	10 CALENDAR DAYS (%)	20 CALENDAR DAYS (%)	30 CALENDAR DAYS (%)	CALENDAR DAYS (%)

14. ACKNOWLEDGMENT OF AMEND-MENTS (The offeror acknowledges receipt of amendments to the SOLICITATION for offerors and related documents numbered and dated):	AMENDMENT NO.	DATE	AMENDMENT NO.	DATE

15A. NAME AND ADDRESS OF OFFER-OR	CODE	FACILITY	16. NAME AND TITLE OF PERSON AUTHORIZED TO SIGN OFFER (Type or print)

15B. TELEPHONE NUMBER AREA CODE	NUMBER	EXT.	15C. CHECK IF REMITTANCE ADDRESS IS DIFFERENT FROM ABOVE - ENTER SUCH ADDRESS IN SCHEDULE.	17. SIGNATURE	18. OFFER DATE

AWARD (To be completed by Government)

19. ACCEPTED AS TO ITEMS NUMBERED	20. AMOUNT	21. ACCOUNTING AND APPROPRIATION

22. AUTHORITY FOR USING OTHER THAN FULL AND OPEN COMPETITION: ☐ 10 U.S.C. 2304(c)( ) ☐ 41 U.S.C. 253(c)( )	23. SUBMIT INVOICES TO ADDRESS SHOWN IN (4 copies unless otherwise specified)	ITEM

24. ADMINISTERED BY (If other than Item 7)	CODE	25. PAYMENT WILL BE MADE BY	CODE

26. NAME OF CONTRACTING OFFICER (Type or print)	27. UNITED STATES OF AMERICA (Signature of Contracting Officer)	28. AWARD DATE

IMPORTANT - Award will be made on this Form, or on Standard Form 26, or by other authorized official written notice.

AUTHORIZED FOR LOCAL REPRODUCTION
Previous edition is unusable

STANDARD FORM 33 (REV. 9-97)
Prescribed by GSA - FAR (48 CFR) 53.214(c)

PART 53.3—ILLUSTRATION OF FORMS

Standard Form 34

ANNUAL BID BOND
(See instructions on reverse)

DATE BOND EXECUTED

OMB No.: 9000-0045
Expires: 12/31/92

Public reporting burden for this collection of information is estimated to average 25 minutes per response, including the time for reviewing instructions, searching existing data sources, gathering and maintaining the data needed, and completing and reviewing the collection of information. Send comments regarding this burden estimate or any other aspect of this collection of information, including suggestions for reducing this burden, to the FAR Secretariat (VRS), Office of Federal Acquisition Policy, GSA, Washington, DC 20405; and to the Office of Management and Budget, Paperwork Reduction Project (9000-0045), Washington, DC 20503.

PRINCIPAL *(Legal name and business address)*

TYPE OF ORGANIZATION *("X" one)*
☐ INDIVIDUAL   ☐ PARTNERSHIP
☐ JOINT   ☐ CORPORATION

STATE OF INCORPORATION

SURETY(IES) *(Name, business address, and State of Incorporation)*

AGENCY TO WHICH BIDS ARE TO BE SUBMITTED

BIDS TO BE SUBMITTED DURING FISCAL YEAR ENDING
September 30, 19 _____

OBLIGATION:

We, the Principal and surety(ies), are firmly bound to the United States of America (hereinafter called the Government) in the penal sum or sums that is sufficient to indemnify the Government in case of the default of the principal as provided herein. For payment of the penal sum or sums, we bind ourselves, our heirs, executors, administrators, and successors, jointly and severally.

CONDITION:

The Principal contemplates submitting bids from time to time during the fiscal year shown above to the department or agency named above for furnishing supplies or services to the Government. The Principal desires that all of those bids submitted for opening during the fiscal year be covered by a single bond instead of by a separate bid bond for each bid.

THEREFORE:

The above obligation is void and of no effect if the principal - (a) upon acceptance by the Government of any such bid within the period specified therein for acceptance (sixty (60) days if no period is specified), executes the further contractual documents and gives the bond(s) required by the terms of the bid as accepted within the time specified (ten (10) days if no period is specified) after receipt of forms by him/her; or (b) in the event of failure to execise the further contractual documents and give the bond(s), pays the Government for any cost of acquiring the work which exceeds the amount of the bid.

WITNESS:

The Principal and Surety(ies) executed this bid bond and affixed their seals on the above date.

SIGNATURES	NAMES AND TITLES *(Typed)*	
PRINCIPAL		
1. (Seal)	1.	
2. (Seal)	2.	Corporate Seal
3. (Seal)	3.	
INDIVIDUAL SURETIES		
1. (Seal)	1.	
2. (Seal)	2.	
CORPORATE SURETY		
1.	1.	
2.	2.	Corporate Seal

AUTHORIZED FOR LOCAL REPRODUCTION
Previous edition is usable

STANDARD FORM 34 (REV. 1-90)
Prescribed by GSA - FAR (48 CFR) 53.228(f)

Standard Form 34 (Back)

INSTRUCTIONS

1. This form is authorized for use in the acquisition of supplies and services, excluding construction, in lieu of Standard Form 24 (Bid Bond). Any deviation from this form will require the written approval of the Administrator of General Services.

2. Insert the full legal name and business address of the Principal in the space designed "Principal" on the face of the form. An authorized person shall sign the bond. Any person signing in a representative capacity (e.g., an attorney-in-fact) must furnish evidence of authority if that representative is not a member of the firm, partnership, or joint venture, or an officer of the corporation involved.

3. (a) Corporations executing the bond as sureties must appear on the Department of the Treasury's list of approved sureties and must act within the limitation listed therein.

   (b) Where individual sureties are involved, a completed Affidavit of Individual Surety (Standard Form 28), for each individual surety, shall accompany the bond. The Government may require the surety to furnish additional substantiating information concerning its financial capability.

4. Corporations executing the bond shall affix their corporate seals. Individuals shall execute the bond opposite the word "Corporate Seal", and shall affix an adhesive seal if executed in Maine, New Hampshire, or any other jurisdiction requiring adhesive seals.

5. Type the name and title of each person signing this bond in the space provided.

6. In its application to negotiated contracts, the terms "bid" and "bidder" shall include "proposal" and "offeror."

STANDARD FORM 34 (REV. 1-90) **BACK**

Standard Form 35

ANNUAL PERFORMANCE BOND (See Instructions on reverse)	DATE BOND EXECUTED	OMB NO.: 9000-0045 Expires: 09/30/98

Public reporting burden for this collection of information is estimated to average 25 minutes per response, including the time for reviewing instructions, searching existing data sources, gathering and maintaining the data needed, and completing and reviewing the collection of information. Send comments regarding this burden estimate or any other aspect of this collection of information, including suggestions for reducing this burden, to the FAR Secretariat (VRS), Office of Federal Acquisition Policy, GSA, Washington, DC 20405; and to the Office of Management and Budget, Paperwork Reduction Project (9000-0045), Washington, DC 20503.

PRINCIPAL (Legal name and business address)

TYPE OF ORGANIZATION ("X" one)
☐ INDIVIDUAL ☐ PARTNERSHIP
☐ JOINT VENTURE ☐ CORPORATION

STATE OF INCORPORATION

SURETY(IES) (Name(s) and business address(es))

PENAL SUM OF BOND

MILLION(S)	THOUSAND(S)	HUNDRED(S)	CENTS

FISCAL YEAR ENDING

September 30, 19____

AGENCY REPRESENTING THE GOVERNMENT

OBLIGATION:
We, the Principal and Surety(ies) are firmly bound to the United States of America (hereinafter called the Government) in the above penal sum. For payment of the penal sum, we bind ourselves, our heirs, executors, adminsitrators, and successors, jointly and severally.

CONDITIONS:
The Princiapl contemplates entering into contracts, from time to time during the fiscal year shown above, with the Government department or agency shown above, for furnishing supplies or services to the Government. The Principal desires that all of those contracts be covered by one bond instead of by a separate performance bond for each contract.

THEREFORE:
The above obligation is void if the Principal - (a) performs and fulfills all the undertakings, covenants, terms, conditions, and agreements of any and all of those contracts entered into during the original term and any extensions granted by the Government with or without notice to the surety(ies) and during the life of any guaranty required under the contracts; and (b) performs and fulfills all the undertakings, covenants, terms, conditions, and agreements of any and all duly authorized modifications of those contracts, that subsequently are made. Notice of those modifications to the surety(ies) is waived.

WITNESS:
The Principal and Surety(ies) executed this performance bond and affixed their seals on the above date.

SIGNATURES	NAMES AND TITLES (Typed)	
PRINCIPAL		
1. (Seal)	1.	
2. (Seal)	2.	Corporate Seal
3. (Seal)	3.	
INDIVIDUAL SURETIES		
1. (Seal)	1.	
2. (Seal)	2.	
CORPORATE SURETY		
1.	1.	Corporate Seal
2.	2.	

AUTHORIZED FOR LOCAL REPRODUCTION
Previous edition not usable

STANDARD FORM 35 (REV. 1-90)
Prescribed by GSA - FAR (48 CFR) 53.228(g)

Standard Form 35 (Back)

INSTRUCTIONS

1. This form is authorized for use in the acquisition of supplies and services, excluding construction, in lieu of Standard Form 25 (Performance Bond). Any deviation from this form will require the written approval of the Administrator of General Services.

2. Insert the full legal name and business address of the Principal in the space designated "Principal" on the face of the form. An authorized person shall sign the bond. Any person signing in a representative capacity (e.g., an attorney-in-fact) must furnish evidence of authority if that representative is not a member of the firm, partnership, or joint venture, or an officer of the corporation involved.

3. (a) Corporations executing the bond as sureties must appear on the Department of the Treasury's list of approved sureties and must act within the limitation listed therein.

   (b) Where individual sureties are involved, a completed Affidavit of Individual Surety (Standard Form 28), for each individual surety, shall accompany the bond. The Government may require the surety to furnish additional substantiating information concerning its financial capability.

4. Corporations executing the bond shall affix their corporate seals. Individuals shall execute the bond opposite the word "Corporate Seal"; and shall affix an adhesive seal if executed in Maine, New Hampshire, or any other jurisdiction requiring adhesive seals.

5. Type the name and title of each person signing this bond in the space provided.

6. In its application to negotiated contracts, the terms "bid" and "bidder" shall include "proposal" or "offeror".

STANDARD FORM 35 (REV. 1-90) BACK

Standard Form 44

U.S. GOVERNMENT

PURCHASE ORDER—INVOICE—VOUCHER

Anyone who finds this booklet, please notify:

OFFICE:

TELEPHONE NUMBER:

SPECIMEN

NSN 7540-01-152-8068
PREVIOUS EDITION USABLE
44-108

STANDARD FORM 44 (Rev. 10-83)
PRESCRIBED BY GSA,
FAR (48 CFR) 53.213(c)

Standard Form 44a

INSTRUCTIONS

(This form is for official Government use only)

1. Filling in the Form

(a) All copies of the form must be legible. To insure legibility, indelible pencil or ball-point pen should be used. SELLER'S NAME AND ADDRESS MUST BE PRINTED.

(b) Items ordered will be individually listed. General descriptions such as "hardware" are not acceptable. Show discount terms.

(c) Enter project reference or other identifying description in space captioned "PURPOSE." Also, enter proper accounting information, if known.

2. Distributing Copies

Copy No. 1—Give to seller for use as the invoice or as an attachment to his commercial invoice.

Copy No. 2—Give to seller for use as a record of the order.

Copy No. 3—

(1) On over-the-counter transactions where delivery has been made, complete receiving report section and forward this copy to the proper administrative office.

(2) On other than completed over-the-counter transactions, forward this copy to location specified for delivery. (Upon delivery, receiving report section is to be completed and this copy then forwarded to the proper administrative office.)

Copy No. 4—Retain in the book, unless otherwise instructed.

3. When Paying Cash at Time of Purchase

(a) Enter the amount of cash paid and obtain seller's signature in the space provided in the Seller section of Copy No. 1. If seller prefers to provide a commercial cash receipt, attach it to Copy No. 1 and check the "paid in cash" block at the bottom of the form.

(b) Distribution of copies when payment is by cash is the same as described above, except that Copy No. 1 is retained by Government representative when cash payment is made. Copy No. 1 is used thereafter in accordance with agency instructions pertaining to handling receipts for cash payment.

PART 53.3—ILLUSTRATION OF FORMS 53.301-44B & C

Standard Form 44b & c

53.3-27

# Standard Form 44d

Standard Form 98

[Standard Form 98 has been removed.]

Standard Form 98a

[Standard Form 98a has been removed.]

Standard Form 99

[Standard Form 99 has been removed.]

Standard Form 120

STANDARD FORM 120 REV. APRIL 1957 GEN. SERV. ADMIN. FPMR (41 CFR) 101-43.311	REPORT OF EXCESS PERSONAL PROPERTY	1. REPORT NO.	2. DATE MAILED	3. TOTAL COST $

PAGE 1 OF

| 4. TYPE OF REPORT | (Check one only of "a," "b," "c," or "d") | ☐ a. ORIGINAL ☐ b. CORRECTED | ☐ c. PARTIAL ☐ d. TOTAL W/D | (Also check "e" and/or "f" if appropriate) | ☐ e. OVERSEAS ☐ f. CONTRACTORS INV |

5. TO *(Name and Address of Agency to which report is made)* THRU

6. APPROPR. OR FUND TO BE REIMBURSED *(If any)*

7. FROM *(Name and Address of Reporting Agency)*

8. REPORT APPROVED BY *(Name and Title)*

9. FOR FURTHER INFORMATION CONTACT *(Title, Address and Telephone No.)*

10. AGENCY APPROVAL *(If applicable)*

11. SEND PURCHASE ORDERS OR DISPOSAL INSTRUCTIONS TO *(Title, Address and Telephone No.)*

12. GSA CONTROL NO.

| 13. FSC GROUP NO. | 14. LOCATION OF PROPERTY *(If location is to be abandoned, give date)* | 15. REIM.REQD YES / NO | 16. AGENCY CONTROL NO. | 17. SURPLUS RELEASE DATE |

EXCESS PROPERTY LIST

ITEM NO. (a)	DESCRIPTION (b)	COND (c)	UNIT (d)	NUMBER OF UNITS (e)	ACQUISITION COST		FAIR VALUE % (h)
					PER UNIT (f)	TOTAL (g)	

STANDARD FORM 120 REV. APRIL 1957 EDITION
(Use Standard Form 120A for Continuation Sheets)
NSN 7540-00-634-4074
PREVIOUS EDITION USABLE

Standard Form 120A

STANDARD FORM 120-A APRIL 1957 GEN. SERV. ADMIN. FPRM (41 CFR) 101-43.311	CONTINUATION SHEET (Report of Excess Personal Property)				PAGE _____		
FROM (Name and Address of Reporting Agency)				REPORT NO.	AGENCY CONTROL NO.		
EXCESS PROPERTY LIST (Continued)							
ITEM NO. (a)	DESCRIPTION (b)	COND (c)	UNIT (d)	NUMBER OF UNITS (e)	ACQUISITION COST		FAIR VALUE % (h)
					PER UNIT (f)	TOTAL (g)	

STANDARD FORM 120A
APRIL 1957 EDITION

PART 53.3—ILLUSTRATION OF FORMS

Standard Form 126

REPORT OF PERSONAL PROPERTY FOR SALE		PAGE	OF
1. FROM *(NAME, ADDRESS AND ZIP CODE OF OWNING AGENCY)*	2. REPORT NO.	3. DATE	
	4. FSC GROUP	5. TOTAL ACQUISITION COST	
6. PUBLIC MAY INSPECT PROPERTY BY CONTACTING *(NAME, ADDRESS, ZIP CODE AND TELEPHONE NO.)*	7. PROPERTY LOCATED AT		
8. TO • General Services Administration •	9. LOADING BY GOV'T	a. ACTIVITY WILL LOAD FOR PURCHASER ☐ (1) YES ☐ (2) NO	
		b. EXTENT *(IF CHECKED "YES")*	
	10. PROPERTY IS EXCHANGE/SALE ☐ a. YES ☐ b. NO	11. PROPERTY IS REIMBURSABLE ☐ a. YES ☐ b. NO	
12. SEND EXECUTED SALES DOCUMENTS TO *(NAME, ADDRESS AND ZIP CODE)*	13. DEPOSIT PROCEEDS TO *(APPROPRIATE FUND SYMBOL AND TITLE)*		
	14. STATION DEPOSIT SYMBOL OR STATION ACCOUNT NUMBER		
15. UTILIZATION AND DONATION SCREENING REQUIREMENTS COMPLETED. PROPERTY IS AVAILABLE FOR SALE	BY *(SIGNATURE AND TITLE)* ▶		

16. **PROPERTY LIST** *(USE CONTINUATION SHEET, IF NECESSARY)*

ITEM NO. (a)	ITEM NO. ASSIGNED BY GSA (b)	COMMERCIAL DESCRIPTION AND CONDITION (c)	UNIT (d)	NUMBER OF UNITS (e)	ACQUISITION COST	
					PER UNIT (f)	TOTAL (g)

17. RECEIPT OF PROPERTY AT GSA SALES SITE OR CENTER ACKNOWLEDGED		18. RECEIPT OF REPORTS IS HEREBY ACKNOWLEDGED	
SIGNATURE AND TITLE	DATE	SIGNATURE AND TITLE	DATE

FOR GSA INTERNAL USE ONLY

19. SALE NO.	20. TYPE OF SALE	21. INSPECTION DATES	22. BID OPENING DATE AND TIME

STANDARD FORM 126 (REV. 7-78)
Prescribed by GSA, FPMR (41 CFR)
101-45.303

53.301-126A　　　　　　　　　　　　　　　　　　　　FEDERAL ACQUISITION REGULATION

Standard Form 126A

Standard Form 126-A February 1965 Prescribed by General Services Administration FPMR (41 CFR) 101-45.303	REPORT OF PERSONAL PROPERTY FOR SALE (CONTINUATION SHEET)		PAGE　OF　PAGES	
1. FROM *(Name and adress of owning agency. Please include ZIP Code)*		FSC GROUP	REPORT NO.	

		PROPERTY LIST				
ITEM NO. (a)	ITEM NO. ASSIGNED BY GSA (b)	COMMERCIAL DESCRIPTION AND CONDITION (c)	UNIT (d)	NUMBER OF UNITS (e)	ACQUISITION COST	
					PER UNIT (f)	TOTAL (g)

53.3-38

Standard Form 252

ARCHITECT-ENGINEER CONTRACT

1. CONTRACT NO.

2. DATE OF CONTRACT

3a. NAME OF ARCHITECT-ENGINEER

3b. TELEPHONE NO. *(Include Area Code)*

3c. ADDRESS OF ARCHITECT-ENGINEER *(Include ZIP Code)*

4. DEPARTMENT OR AGENCY AND ADDRESS *(Include ZIP Code)*

5. PROJECT TITLE AND LOCATION

6. CONTRACT FOR *(General description of services to be provided)*

7. CONTRACT AMOUNT *(Express in words and figures)*

8. NEGOTIATION AUTHORITY

9. ADMINISTRATIVE, APPROPRIATION, AND ACCOUNTING DATA

NSN 7540-00-181-8326
PREVIOUS EDITION NOT USABLE

STANDARD FORM 252 (REV. 10-83)
Prescribed by GSA - FAR (48 CFR) 53.236-2(a)

Standard Form 252 (Back)

10. The United States of America (called the Government) represented by the Contracting Officer executing this contract, and the Architect-Engineer agree to perform this contract in strict accordance with the clauses and the documents identified as follows, all of which are made a part of this contract:

If the parties to this contract are comprised of more than one legal entity, each entity shall be jointly and severally liable under this conract. The parties hereto have executed this contract as of the date recorded in Item 2.

	SIGNATURES	NAMES AND TITLES *(Typed)*
	11. ARCHITECT-ENGINEER OR OTHER PROFESSIONAL SERVICES CONTRACTOR	
A		
B		
C		
D		
	12. THE UNITED STATES OF AMERICA	
		Contracting Officer

STANDARD FORM 252 (REV. 10-83) **BACK**

Standard Form 273

REINSURANCE AGREEMENT FOR A BONDS STATUTE PERFORMANCE BOND
(See instructions on reverse)

OMB Number: 9000-0045
Expiration Date: 6/30/2016

PAPERWORK REDUCTION ACT STATEMENT: Public reporting burden for this collection of information is estimated to average 60 minutes per response, including the time for reviewing instructions, searching existing data sources, gathering and maintaining the data needed, and completing and reviewing the collection of information. Send comments regarding this burden estimate or any other aspects of this collection of information, including suggestions for reducing this burden, to U.S. General Services Administration, Regulatory Secretariat (MVCB)/IC 9000-0045, Office of Governmentwide Acquisition Policy, 1800 F Street, NW, Washington, DC 20405.

1. DIRECT WRITING COMPANY*

1A. DATE DIRECT WRITING COMPANY EXECUTES THIS AGREEMENT

1B. STATE OF INCORPORATION

2. REINSURING COMPANY*

2A. AMOUNT OF THIS REINSURANCE ($)

2B. DATE REINSURING COMPANY EXECUTES THIS AGREEMENT

2C. STATE OF INCORPORATION

3. DESCRIPTION OF CONTRACT

3A. AMOUNT OF CONTRACT

3B. CONTRACT DATE

3C. CONTRACT NO.

3D. DESCRIPTION OF CONTRACT

3E. CONTRACTING AGENCY

4. DESCRIPTION OF BOND

4A. PENAL SUM OF BOND

4B. DATE OF BOND

4C. BOND NO.

4D. PRINCIPAL*

4E. STATE OF INCORPORATION (If Corporate Principal)

AGREEMENT:

(a) The Direct Writing Company named above is bound as surety to the United States of America on the performance bond described above, wherein the above described is the principal, for the protection of the United States on the contract described above. The contract is for the construction, alteration, or repair of a public building or public work of the United States, and the performance bond was furnished to the United States under 40 U.S.C. chapter 31, subchapter III, Bonds, known as the Bonds Statute. The Direct Writing Company has applied to the Reinsuring Company named above to be reinsured and countersecured in the amount shown opposite the name of the Reinsuring Company (referred to as the "Amount of this Reinsurance"), or for whatever amount less than the "Amount of this Reinsurance" the Direct Writing Company is liable to pay under or by virtue of the performance bond.

(b) For a sum mutually agreed upon, paid by the Direct Writing Company to the Reinsuring Company which acknowledges its receipt, the parties to this Agreement covenant and agree to the terms and conditions of the agreement.

TERMS AND CONDITIONS:

(a) The purpose and intent of this agreement is to guarantee and indemnify the United States against loss under the performance and to the extent of the "Amount of this Reinsurance," or any sum less than the "Amount of this Reinsurance" that is owing and unpaid by the Direct Writing Company to the United States under the performance bond.

(b) If the Direct Writing Company fails to pay any default under the performance bond equal to or in excess of the "Amount of this Reinsurance," the Reinsuring Company covenants and agrees to pay to the United States, the obligee on the performance bond, the "Amount of this Reinsurance." If the Direct Writing Company fails to pay to the United States any default for a sum less than the "Amount of this Reinsurance" the Reinsuring Company covenants and agrees to pay to the United States the full amount of the default, or so much thereof that is not paid to the United States by the Direct Writing Company.

(c) If there is a default on the performance bond for the "Amount of this Reinsurance," or more, the Reinsuring Company and the Direct Writing Company hereby covenant and agree that the United States may bring suit against the Reinsuring Company for the "Amount of this Reinsurance" or, in case the amount of the default is for less than the "Amount of this Reinsurance," for the full amount of the default.

WITNESS:

The Direct Writing Company and the Reinsuring Company, respectively, have caused this Agreement to be signed and impressed with their respective corporate seals by officers possessing power to sign this instrument, and to be duly attested by officers empowered thereto, on the day and date above written opposite their respective names.

*Items 1, 2, 4D - Furnish legal name, business address and ZIP Code.   (Over)

AUTHORIZED FOR LOCAL REPRODUCTION
Previous edition is usable

STANDARD FORM 273 (REV. 4-2013)
Prescribed by GSA - FAR (48 CFR) 53.228(h)

Standard Form 273 (Back)

	5. DIRECT WRITING COMPANY	
5A(1) SIGNATURE	(2) ATTEST: SIGNATURE	Corporate Seal
5B(1) NAME AND TITLE *(Typed)*	(2) NAME AND TITLE *(Typed)*	

	6. REINSURING COMPANY	
6A(1) SIGNATURE	(2) ATTEST: SIGNATURE	Corporate Seal
6B(1) NAME AND TITLE *(Typed)*	(2) NAME AND TITLE *(Typed)*	

INSTRUCTIONS

This form is to be used in cases where it is desired to cover the excess of a Direct Writing Company's underwriting limitation by reinsurance instead of co-insurance on Bonds Statute performance bonds running to the United States. See FAR (48 CFR) 28.202-1 and 53.228(h).

Execute and file this form as follows:

Original and copies (as specified by the bond-approving officer), signed and sealed, shall accompany the bond or be filed within the time period shown in the bid or proposal.

One copy, signed and sealed, shall accompany the Direct Writing Company's quarterly Schedule of Excess Risks filed with the Department of the Treasury.

Other copies may be prepared for the use of the Direct Writing Company and Reinsuring Company. Each Reinsuring Company should use a separate form.

STANDARD FORM 273 (REV. 4/2013) BACK

Standard Form 274

REINSURANCE AGREEMENT FOR A BONDS STATUTE PAYMENT BOND
(See instruction on reverse)

OMB Control Number: 9000-0045
Expiration Date: 6/30/2016

PAPERWORK REDUCTION ACT STATEMENT: Public reporting burden for this collection of information is estimated to average 60 minutes per response, including the time for reviewing instructions, searching existing data sources, gathering and maintaining the data needed, and completing and reviewing the collection of information. Send comments regarding this burden estimate or any other aspects of this collection of information, including suggestions for reducing this burden, to U.S. General Services Administration, Regulatory Secretariat (MVCB)/IC 9000-0045, Office of Governmentwide Acquisition Policy, 1800 F Street, NW, Washington, DC 20405.

1. DIRECT WRITING COMPANY*

1A. DATE DIRECT WRITING COMPANY EXECUTES THIS AGREEMENT

1B. STATE OF INCORPORATION

2. REINSURING COMPANY*

2A. AMOUNT OF THIS REINSURANCE
$

2B. DATE REINSURING COMPANY EXECUTES THIS AGREEMENT

2C. STATE OF INCORPORATION

3. DESCRIPTION OF CONTRACT

3A. AMOUNT OF CONTRACT

3B. CONTRACT DATE

3C. CONTRACT NO.

3D. DESCRIPTION OF CONTRACT

3E. CONTRACTING AGENCY

4. DESCRIPTION OF BOND

4A. PENAL SUM OF BOND

4B. DATE OF BOND

4C. BOND NO.

4D. PRINCIPAL*

4E. STATE OF INCORPORATION *(If Corporate Principal)*

AGREEMENT:

(a) The Direct Writing Company named above is bound as a surety on the payment bond described above, wherein the above described is the principal, for the protection of all persons supplying labor and material on the contract described above, which is for the construction, alteration, or repair of a public building or public work of the United States. The payment bond is for the use of persons supplying labor or material, and is furnished to the United States under 40 U.S.C. chapter 31, subchapter III, Bonds, known as the Bonds Statute. The Direct Writing Company has applied to the Reinsuring Company named above to be reinsured and countersecured in the amount above opposite the name of the Reinsuring Company (referred to as "Amount of this Reinsurance"), or for whatever amount less than the "Amount of this Reinsurance" the Direct Writing Company is liable to pay under or by virtue of the payments bond.

(b) For a sum mutually agreed upon, paid by the Direct Writing Company to the Reinsuring Company which acknowledges its receipt, the parties to this Agreement covenant and agree to the terms and conditions of this agreement.

TERMS AND CONDITIONS:

The purpose and intent of this agreement is (a) to guarantee and indemnify the persons who have furnished or supplied labor or material in the prosecution of the work provided for in the contract referred to above (hereinafter referred to as "laborers and materialmen," the term "materialmen" including persons having a direct contractual relation with a subcontractor but no contractual relationship expressed or implied with the contractor who has furnished the said payment bond) against loss under the payment bond to the extent of the "Amount of this Reinsurance," or for any sum less than the "Amount of this Reinsurance," that is owing and unpaid by the Direct Writing Company to the "laborers and materialmen" on the payment bond; and (b) to make the "laborers and materialmen" obligees under this Reinsurance Agreement to the same extent as if their respective names were written herein.

THEREFORE:

1. The Reinsuring Company covenants and agrees -

(a) To pay the "Amount of this Reinsurance" to the "laborers and materialmen" in the event of the Direct Writing Company's failure to pay to the "laborers and materialmen" any default under the payment bond equal to or in excess of the "Amount of this Reinsurance;" and

(b) To pay (1) the full amount to the "laborers and materialmen," or (2) the amount not paid to them by the Direct Writing Company; in case the Direct Writing Company fails to pay the "laborers and materialmen" any default under the payment bond less than the "Amount of this Reinsurance."

*Items 1, 2 ,4D - furnished legal name, business address and ZIP Code.   *(Over)*

AUTHORIZED FOR LOCAL REPRODUCTION
Previous edition is usable

STANDARD FORM 274 (REV. 4-2013)
Prescribed by GSA - FAR (48 CFR) 53.228(i)

Standard Form 274 (Back)

2. The Reinsuring Company and the Direct Writing Company covenant and agree that, in the case of default on the payment bond for the "Amount of this Reinsurance," or more, the persons given a "right of action" or a "right to sue" on the payment bond by 40 U.S.C. 3133 may bring suit against the Reinsuring Company in the United States District Court for the district in which the contract described above is to be performed and executed for the "Amount of this Reinsurance" or, if the amount of the default is for less than the "Amount of this Reinsurance," for whatever the full amount of the default may be. The Reinsuring Company further covenants and agrees to comply with all requirements necessary to give such court jurisdiction, and to consent to determination of matters arising under this Reinsurance Agreement in accordance with the law and practice of the court. It is expressly understood by the parties that the rights, powers, and privileges given in this paragraph to persons are in addition to or supplemental to or in accordance with other rights, powers, and privileges which they might have under the statutes of the United States, any States, or the other laws of either, and should not be construed as limitations.

3. The Reinsuring Company and the Direct Writing Company further covenant and agree that the Reinsuring Company designates the process agent, appointed by the Direct Writing Company in the district in which the contract is to be performed and executed, as an agent to accept service of process in any suit instituted on this Reinsurance Agreement, and that the process agent shall send, by registered mail, to the Reinsuring Company at its principal place of business shown above, a copy of the process.

4. The Reinsuring Company and the Direct Writing Company further covenant and agree that this Reinsurance Agreement is an integral part of the payment bond.

WITNESS:

The Direct Writing Company and the Reinsuring Company, respectively, have caused this Agreement to be signed and impressed with their respective corporate seals by officers possessing the power to sign this instrument, and to be duly attested to by officers empowered thereto, on the day and date in Item 1A written opposite their respective names.

5. DIRECT WRITING COMPANY		
5A. (1) SIGNATURE	(2) ATTEST SIGNATURE	Corporate Seal
5B. (1) NAME AND TITLE *(Typed)*	(2) NAME AND TITLE *(Typed)*	

6. REINSURING COMPANY		
6A. (1) SIGNATURE	(2) ATTEST SIGNATURE	Corporate Seal
6B. (1) NAME AND TITLE *(Typed)*	(2) NAME AND TITLE *(Typed)*	

INSTRUCTIONS

This form is to be used in cases where it is desired to cover the excess of a Direct Writing Company's underwriting limitation by reinsurance instead of co-insurance on Bonds Statute payment bonds running to the United States. See FAR (48 CFR) 28.202-1 and 53.228(i).

Execute and file this form as follows:

  Original and copies (as specified by the bond-approving officer), signed and sealed, shall accompany the bond or be filed within the time period shown in bid or proposal.

  One copy, signed and sealed, shall accompany the Direct Writing Company's quarterly Schedule of Excess Risks filled with the Department of Treasury.

  Other copies may be prepared for the use of the Direct Writing Company and Reinsuring Company. Each Reinsuring Company should use a separate form.

STANDARD FORM 274 (REV. 4-2013) BACK

Standard Form 275

REINSURANCE AGREEMENT IN FAVOR OF THE UNITED STATES
(See instructions on reverse)

OMB No.: 9000-0045

Public reporting burden for this collection of information is estimated to average 25 minutes per response, including the time for reviewing instructions, searching existing data sources, gathering and maintaining the data needed, and completing and reviewing the collection of information. Send comments regarding this burden estimate or any other aspect of this collection of information, including suggestions for reducing this burden, to the FAR Secretariat (MVR), Federal Acquisition Policy Division, GSA, Washington, DC 20405.

1. DIRECT WRITING COMPANY*

1A. DATE DIRECT WRITING COMPANY EXECUTES THIS AGREEMENT

1B. STATE OF INCORPORATION

2. REINSURING COMPANY*

2A. AMOUNT OF THIS REINSURANCE ($)

2B. DATE REINSURING COMPANY EXECUTES THIS AGREEMENT

2C. STATE OF INCORPORATION

3. DESCRIPTION OF BOND

3A. DESCRIPTION OF BOND *(Type, purpose etc.) (If associated with contract number, date, amount, etc., include name of Government agency involved.)*

3B. PENAL SUM OF BOND
$

3C. DATE OF BOND

3D. BOND NO.

3E. PRINCIPAL*

3F. STATE OF INCORPORATION *(If Corporate Principal)*

AGREEMENT:

    (a) The Direct Writing Company named above is bound as surety to the United States of America, on the bond described above, wherein the above-named is the principal. The bond is given for the protection of the United States and the Direct Writing Company has applied to the above Reinsuring Company to be reinsured and counter-secured in the amount shown opposite the name of the Reinsuring Company (referred to as the "Amount of this Reinsurance"), or for whatever amount less than the "Amount of this Reinsurance" the Direct Writing Company is liable to pay under or by virtue of the bond.

    (b) For a sum mutually agreed upon, paid by the Direct Writing Company to the Reinsuring Company which acknowledges its receipt, the parties to this Agreement covenant and agree to the terms and conditions of this agreement.

TERMS AND CONDITIONS:

    The purpose and intent of this agreement is to guarantee and indemnify the United States against loss under the bond to the extent of the "Amount of this Reinsurance," or for any less sum than the "Amount of this Reinsurance," that is owing and unpaid by the Direct Writing Company to the United States.

THEREFORE:

    1. If the Direct Writing Company fails to pay any default under the bond equal to or in excess of the "Amount of this Reinsurance," the Reinsuring Company covenants and agrees to pay to the United States, the obligee on the bond, the "Amount of this Reinsurance." If the Direct Writing Company fails to pay to the United States any default for a sum less than the "Amount of this Reinsurance," the Reinsuring Company covenants and agrees to pay to the United States the full amount of the default, or so much thereof that is not paid to the United States by the Direct Writing Company.

    2. The Reinsuring Company further covenants and agrees that in case of default on the bond for the "Amount of this Reinsurance," or more, the United States may sue the Reinsuring Company for the "Amount of this Reinsurance" or for the full amount of the default when the default is less than the "Amount of this Reinsurance."

WITNESS

    The Direct Writing Company and the Reinsuring Company, respectively, have caused this Agreement to be signed and impressed with their respective corporate seals by officers possessing power to sign this instrument, and to be duly attested to by officers empowered thereto, on the day and date above -- written opposite their respective names.

(Over)

*Items 1, 2, 3E - Furnish legal name, business address and ZIP Code.

AUTHORIZED FOR LOCAL REPRODUCTION
Previous edition usable

STANDARD FORM 275 REV. 10-98)
Prescribed by GSA-FAR (48 CFR) 53.228(j)

Standard Form 275 (Back)

4. DIRECT WRITING COMPANY		
4A.(1). SIGNATURE	(2). ATTEST: SIGNATURE	Corporate Seal
4B.(1) NAME AND TITLE *(Typed)*	4B.(2). NAME AND TITLE *(Typed)*	
5. REINSURING COMPANY		
5A.(1). SIGNATURE	(2). ATTEST: SIGNATURE	Corporate Seal
5B.(1). NAME AND TITLE *(Typed)*	5B.(2). NAME AND TITLE *(Typed)*	

INSTRUCTIONS

This form is to be used in cases where it is desired to cover the excess of a Direct Writing Company's underwriting limitation by reinsurance instead of co-insurance on bonds running to the United States except Miller Act Performance and Payment Bonds. See FAR (48 CFR) 28.202-1 and 53.228(j) and 31 CFR 223.11(b)(1). If this form is used to reinsure a bid bond, the "Penal Sum of Bond" and "Amount of this Reinsurance" may be expressed as percentage of the bid provided the actual amounts will not exceed the companies' respective underwriting limitations.

Execute and file this form as follows:

Original and copies (as specified by the bond-approving officer), signed and sealed, shall accompany the bond or be filed within the time period shown in the bid or proposal.

One carbon copy, signed and sealed, shall accompany the Direct Writing Company's quarterly Schedule of Excess Risks filed with the Department of Treasury.

Other copies may be prepared for the use of the Direct Writing Company and Reinsuring Company. Each Reinsuring Company should use a separate form.

STANDARD FORM 275 (REV. 10-98) BACK

Standard Form 294

[Go to *http://www.gsa.gov/forms* to access form.]

Standard Form 295

[Standard Form 295 has been removed.]

Standard Form 295

[Standard Form 295 has been removed.]

FAC 2005–19 SEPTEMBER 17, 2007

PART 53.3—ILLUSTRATION OF FORMS

53.301-298

Standard Form 298

REPORT DOCUMENTATION PAGE	Form Approved OMB No. 0704-0188

The public reporting burden for this collection of information is estimated to average 1 hour per response, including the time for reviewing instructions, searching existing data sources, gathering and maintaining the data needed, and completing and reviewing the collection of information. Send comments regarding this burden estimate or any other aspect of this collection of information, including suggestions for reducing the burden, to Department of Defense, Washington Headquarters Services, Directorate for Information Operations and Reports (0704-0188), 1215 Jefferson Davis Highway, Suite 1204, Arlington, VA 22202-4302. Respondents should be aware that notwithstanding any other provision of law, no person shall be subject to any penalty for failing to comply with a collection of information if it does not display a currently valid OMB control number.
PLEASE DO NOT RETURN YOUR FORM TO THE ABOVE ADDRESS.

1. REPORT DATE *(DD-MM-YYYY)*	2. REPORT TYPE	3. DATES COVERED *(From - To)*
4. TITLE AND SUBTITLE		5a. CONTRACT NUMBER
		5b. GRANT NUMBER
		5c. PROGRAM ELEMENT NUMBER
6. AUTHOR(S)		5d. PROJECT NUMBER
		5e. TASK NUMBER
		5f. WORK UNIT NUMBER
7. PERFORMING ORGANIZATION NAME(S) AND ADDRESS(ES)		8. PERFORMING ORGANIZATION REPORT NUMBER
9. SPONSORING/MONITORING AGENCY NAME(S) AND ADDRESS(ES)		10. SPONSOR/MONITOR'S ACRONYM(S)
		11. SPONSOR/MONITOR'S REPORT NUMBER(S)
12. DISTRIBUTION/AVAILABILITY STATEMENT			
13. SUPPLEMENTARY NOTES			
14. ABSTRACT			
15. SUBJECT TERMS			

16. SECURITY CLASSIFICATION OF:			17. LIMITATION OF ABSTRACT	18. NUMBER OF PAGES	19a. NAME OF RESPONSIBLE PERSON
a. REPORT	b. ABSTRACT	c. THIS PAGE			
					19b. TELEPHONE NUMBER *(Include area code)*

Standard Form 298 (Rev. 8/98)
Prescribed by ANSI Std. Z39.18

Standard Form 298 (Back)

INSTRUCTIONS FOR COMPLETING SF 298

1. REPORT DATE. Full publication date, including day, month, if available. Must cite at least the year and be Year 2000 compliant, e.g. 30-06-1998; xx-06-1998; xx-xx-1998.

2. REPORT TYPE. State the type of report, such as final, technical, interim, memorandum, master's thesis, progress, quarterly, research, special, group study, etc.

3. DATES COVERED. Indicate the time during which the work was performed and the report was written, e.g., Jun 1997 - Jun 1998; 1-10 Jun 1996; May - Nov 1998; Nov 1998.

4. TITLE. Enter title and subtitle with volume number and part number, if applicable. On classified documents, enter the title classification in parentheses.

5a. CONTRACT NUMBER. Enter all contract numbers as they appear in the report, e.g. F33615-86-C-5169.

5b. GRANT NUMBER. Enter all grant numbers as they appear in the report, e.g. AFOSR-82-1234.

5c. PROGRAM ELEMENT NUMBER. Enter all program element numbers as they appear in the report, e.g. 61101A.

5d. PROJECT NUMBER. Enter all project numbers as they appear in the report, e.g. 1F665702D1257; ILIR.

5e. TASK NUMBER. Enter all task numbers as they appear in the report, e.g. 05; RF0330201; T4112.

5f. WORK UNIT NUMBER. Enter all work unit numbers as they appear in the report, e.g. 001; AFAPL30480105.

6. AUTHOR(S). Enter name(s) of person(s) responsible for writing the report, performing the research, or credited with the content of the report. The form of entry is the last name, first name, middle initial, and additional qualifiers separated by commas, e.g. Smith, Richard, J, Jr.

7. PERFORMING ORGANIZATION NAME(S) AND ADDRESS(ES). Self-explanatory.

8. PERFORMING ORGANIZATION REPORT NUMBER. Enter all unique alphanumeric report numbers assigned by the performing organization, e.g. BRL-1234; AFWL-TR-85-4017-Vol-21-PT-2.

9. SPONSORING/MONITORING AGENCY NAME(S) AND ADDRESS(ES). Enter the name and address of the organization(s) financially responsible for and monitoring the work.

10. SPONSOR/MONITOR'S ACRONYM(S). Enter, if available, e.g. BRL, ARDEC, NADC.

11. SPONSOR/MONITOR'S REPORT NUMBER(S). Enter report number as assigned by the sponsoring/ monitoring agency, if available, e.g. BRL-TR-829; -215.

12. DISTRIBUTION/AVAILABILITY STATEMENT. Use agency-mandated availability statements to indicate the public availability or distribution limitations of the report. If additional limitations/ restrictions or special markings are indicated, follow agency authorization procedures, e.g. RD/FRD, PROPIN, ITAR, etc. Include copyright information.

13. SUPPLEMENTARY NOTES. Enter information not included elsewhere such as: prepared in cooperation with; translation of; report supersedes; old edition number, etc.

14. ABSTRACT. A brief (approximately 200 words) factual summary of the most significant information.

15. SUBJECT TERMS. Key words or phrases identifying major concepts in the report.

16. SECURITY CLASSIFICATION. Enter security classification in accordance with security classification regulations, e.g. U, C, S, etc. If this form contains classified information, stamp classification level on the top and bottom of this page.

17. LIMITATION OF ABSTRACT. This block must be completed to assign a distribution limitation to the abstract. Enter UU (Unclassified Unlimited) or SAR (Same as Report). An entry in this block is necessary if the abstract is to be limited.

Standard Form 298 Back (Rev. 8/98)

Standard Form 308

Request For Wage Determination And Response To Request
(Construction Wage Rate Requirements Statute and Related Statutes)

U.S. Department of Labor
Wage and Hour Division

Mail Your Request To:
U.S. Department of Labor
Wage and Hour Division
Branch of Construction Contract Wage Determinations
Washington, D.C. 20210

Requesting Officer *(Typed name and signature)*

Department, Agency, or Bureau

Phone Number

Date of Request

Estimated Advertising Date

Estimated Bid Opening Date

Prior Decision Number (if any)

Estimated $ Value of Contract
☐ Under 1/2 Mil   ☐ 1 to 5 Mil
☐ 1/2 to 1 Mil   ☐ Over 5 Mil

Type of Work
☐ Bldg.   ☐ Highway
☐ Resid.   ☐ Heavy

Address to which wage determination should be mailed. *(Print or type)*

Location of Project *(City, County, State, Zip Code)*

Description of Work *(Be specific) (Print or type)*

CHECK OR LIST CRAFTS NEEDED
(Attach continuation sheet if needed)

Asbestos workers
Boilermakers
Bricklayers
Carpenters
Cement masons
Electricians
Glaziers
Ironworkers
Laborers *(Specify classes)*

Lathers
Marble & tile setters, terrazzo workers
Painters
Piledrivermen
Plasterers
Plumbers
Roofers
Sheet metal workers
Soft floor layers
Steamfitters
Welders-rate for craft
Truck drivers
Power equipment operators
(Specify types)

Other Crafts

Response To Request

FOR DEPARTMENT OF LABOR USE

☐ Use area determination issued for this area

☐ The attached decision noted below is applicable to this project

Decision Number

Date of Decision

Expires

Supersedes Decision Number

Approved

Standard Form 308 (Rev. 2/2013)
U.S. Department of Labor -29 CFR Part 1

Standard Form 330

ARCHITECT-ENGINEER QUALIFICATIONS

OMB No.: 9000-0157
Expires: 10/31/2014

PAPERWORK REDUCTION ACT STATEMENT: Public reporting burden for this collection of information is estimated to average 29 hours (25 hours for part 1 and 4 hours for Part 2) per response, including the time for reviewing instructions, searching existing data sources, gathering and maintaining the data needed, and completing and reviewing the collection of information. Send comments regarding this burden estimate or any other aspects of this collection of information, including suggestions for reducing this burden, to U.S. General Services Administration, Regulatory Secretariat (MVCB)/IC 9000-0157, Office of Governmentwide Acquisition Policy, 1800 F Street, NW, Washington, DC 20405.

PURPOSE

Federal agencies use this form to obtain information from architect-engineer (A-E) firms about their professional qualifications. Federal agencies select firms for A-E contracts on the basis of professional qualifications as required by 40 U.S.C. chapter 11, Selection of Architects Engineers, and Part 36 of the Federal Acquisition Regulation (FAR).

The Selection of Architects and Engineers statute requires the public announcement of requirements for A-E services (with some exceptions provided by other statutes), and the selection of at least three of the most highly qualified firms based on demonstrated competence and professional qualifications according to specific criteria published in the announcement. The Act then requires the negotiation of a contract at a fair and reasonable price starting first with the most highly qualified firm.

The information used to evaluate firms is from this form and other sources, including performance evaluations, any additional data requested by the agency, and interviews with the most highly qualified firms and their references.

GENERAL INSTRUCTIONS

Part I presents the qualifications for a specific contract.

Part II presents the general qualifications of a firm or a specific branch office of a firm. Part II has two uses:

1. An A-E firm may submit Part II to the appropriate central, regional or local office of each Federal agency to be kept on file. A public announcement is not required for certain contracts, and agencies may use Part II as a basis for selecting at least three of the most highly qualified firms for discussions prior to requesting submission of Part I. Firms are encouraged to update Part II on file with agency offices, as appropriate, according to FAR Part 36. If a firm has branch offices, submit a separate Part II for each branch office seeking work.

2. Prepare a separate Part II for each firm that will be part of the team proposed for a specific contract and submitted with Part I. If a firm has branch offices, submit a separate Part II for each branch office that has a key role on the team.

INDIVIDUAL AGENCY INSTRUCTIONS

Individual agencies may supplement these instructions. For example, they may limit the number of projects or number of pages submitted in Part I in response to a public announcement for a particular project. Carefully comply with any agency instructions when preparing and submitting this form. Be as concise as possible and provide only the information requested by the agency.

DEFINITIONS

Architect-Engineer Services: Defined in FAR 2.101.

Branch Office: A geographically distinct place of business or subsidiary office of a firm that has a key role on the team.

Discipline: Primary technical capabilities of key personnel, as evidenced by academic degree, professional registration, certification, and/or extensive experience.

Firm: Defined in FAR 36.102.

Key Personnel: Individuals who will have major contract responsibilities and/or provide unusual or unique expertise.

SPECIFIC INSTRUCTIONS

Part I - Contract-Specific Qualifications

Section A. Contract Information.

1. Title and Location. Enter the title and location of the contract for which this form is being submitted, exactly as shown in the public announcement or agency request.

2. Public Notice Date. Enter the posted date of the agency's notice on the Federal Business Opportunity website (FedBizOpps), other form of public announcement or agency request for this contract.

3. Solicitation or Project Number. Enter the agency's solicitation number and/or project number, if applicable, exactly as shown in the public announcement or agency request for this contract.

Section B. Architect-Engineer Point of Contact.

4-8. Name, Title, Name of Firm, Telephone Number, Fax (Facsimile) Number and E-mail (Electronic Mail) Address. Provide information for a representative of the prime contractor or joint venture that the agency can contact for additional information.

AUTHORIZED FOR LOCAL REPRODUCTION

STANDARD FORM 330 (REV. 3/2013) PAGE 1 OF INSTRUCTIONS
Prescribed by GSA - FAR (48 CFR) 53.236-2(b)

Standard Form 330 (Page 2 of Instructions)

Section C. Proposed Team.

9-11. Firm Name, Address, and Role in This Contract. Provide the contractual relationship, name, full mailing address, and a brief description of the role of each firm that will be involved in performance of this contract. List the prime contractor or joint venture partners first. If a firm has branch offices, indicate each individual branch office that will have a key role on the team. The named subcontractors and outside associates or consultants must be used, and any change must be approved by the contracting officer. (See FAR Part 52 Clause "Subcontractors and Outside Associates and Consultants (Architect-Engineer Services)".) Attach an additional sheet in the same format as Section C if needed.

Section D. Organizational Chart of Proposed Team.

As an attachment after Section C, present an organizational chart of the proposed team showing the names and roles of all key personnel listed in Section E and the firm they are associated with as listed in Section C.

Section E. Resumes of Key Personnel Proposed for This Contract.

Complete this section for each key person who will participate in this contract. Group by firm, with personnel of the prime contractor or joint venture partner firms first. The following blocks must be completed for each resume:

12. Name. Self-explanatory.

13. Role in This Contract. Self-explanatory.

14. Years Experience. Total years of relevant experience (block 14a), and years of relevant experience with current firm, but not necessarily the same branch office (block 14b).

15. Firm Name and Location. Name, city and state of the firm where the person currently works, which must correspond with one of the firms (or branch office of a firm, if appropriate) listed in Section C.

16. Education. Provide information on the highest relevant academic degree(s) received. Indicate the area(s) of specialization for each degree.

17. Current Professional Registration. Provide information on current relevant professional registration(s) in a State or possession of the United States, Puerto Rico, or the District of Columbia according to FAR Part 36.

18. Other Professional Qualifications. Provide information on any other professional qualifications relating to this contract, such as education, professional registration, publications, organizational memberships, certifications, training, awards, and foreign language capabilities.

19. Relevant Projects. Provide information on up to five projects in which the person had a significant role that demonstrates the person's capability relevant to her/his proposed role in this contract. These projects do not necessarily have to be any of the projects presented in Section F for the project team if the person was not involved in any of those projects or the person worked on other projects that were more relevant than the team projects in Section F. Use the check box provided to indicate if the project was performed with any office of the current firm. If any of the professional services or construction projects are not complete, leave Year Completed blank and indicate the status in Brief Description and Specific Role (block (3)).

Section F. Example Projects Which Best Illustrate Proposed Team's Qualifications for This Contract.

Select projects where multiple team members worked together, if possible, that demonstrate the team's capability to perform work similar to that required for this contract. Complete one Section F for each project. Present ten projects, unless otherwise specified by the agency. Complete the following blocks for each project:

20. Example Project Key Number. Start with "1" for the first project and number consecutively.

21. Title and Location. Title and location of project or contract. For an indefinite delivery contract, the location is the geographic scope of the contract.

22. Year Completed. Enter the year completed of the professional services (such as planning, engineering study, design, or surveying), and/or the year completed of construction, if applicable. If any of the professional services or the construction projects are not complete, leave Year Completed blank and indicate the status in Brief Description of Project and Relevance to This Contract (block 24).

23a. Project Owner. Project owner or user, such as a government agency or installation, an institution, a corporation or private individual.

23b. Point of Contact Name. Provide name of a person associated with the project owner or the organization which contracted for the professional services, who is very familiar with the project and the firm's (or firms') performance.

23c. Point of Contact Telephone Number Self-explanatory.

24. Brief Description of Project and Relevance to This Contract. Indicate scope, size, cost, principal elements and special features of the project. Discuss the relevance of the example project to this contract. Enter any other information requested by the agency for each example project.

Standard Form 330 (Page 3 of Instructions)

25. **Firms from Section C Involved with This Project.** Indicate which firms (or branch offices, if appropriate) on the project team were involved in the example project, and their roles. List in the same order as Section C.

Section G. Key Personnel Participation in Example Projects.

This matrix is intended to graphically depict which key personnel identified in Section E worked on the example projects listed in Section F. Complete the following blocks (see example below).

26. and 27. **Names of Key Personnel and Role in This Contract.** List the names of the key personnel and their proposed roles in this contract in the same order as they appear in Section E.

28. **Example Projects Listed in Section F.** In the column under each project key number (see block 29) and for each key person, place an "X" under the project key number for participation in the same or similar role.

29. **Example Projects Key.** List the key numbers and titles of the example projects in the same order as they appear in Section F.

Section H. Additional Information.

30. Use this section to provide additional information specifically requested by the agency or to address selection criteria that are not covered by the information provided in Sections A-G.

Section I. Authorized Representative.

31. and 32. **Signature of Authorized Representative and Date.** An authorized representative of a joint venture or the prime contractor must sign and date the completed form. Signing attests that the information provided is current and factual, and that all firms on the proposed team agree to work on the project. Joint ventures selected for negotiations must make available a statement of participation by a principal of each member of the joint venture.

33. **Name and Title.** Self-explanatory.

SAMPLE ENTRIES FOR SECTION G (MATRIX)

26. NAMES OF KEY PERSONNEL (From Section E, Block 12)	27. ROLE IN THIS CONTRACT (From Section E, Block 13)	28. EXAMPLE PROJECTS LISTED IN SECTION F (Fill in "Example Projects Key" section below first, before completing table. Place "X" under project key number for participation in same or similar role.)									
		1	2	3	4	5	6	7	8	9	10
Jane A. Smith	Chief Architect	X		X							
Joseph B. Williams	Chief Mech. Engineer	X	X	X	X						
Tara C. Donovan	Chief Elec. Engineer	X	X		X						

29. EXAMPLE PROJECTS KEY

NO.	TITLE OF EXAMPLE PROJECT (FROM SECTION F)	NO.	TITLE OF EXAMPLE PROJECT (FROM SECTION F)
1	Federal Courthouse, Denver, CO	6	XYZ Corporation Headquarters, Boston, MA
2	Justin J. Wilson Federal Building, Baton Rouge, LA	7	Founder's Museum, Newport RI

Standard Form 330 (Page 4 of Instructions)

Part II - General Qualifications

See the "**General Instructions**" on page 1 for firms with branch offices. Prepare Part II for the specific branch office seeking work if the firm has branch offices.

1. Solicitation Number. If Part II is submitted for a specific contract, insert the agency's solicitation number and/or project number, if applicable, exactly as shown in the public announcement or agency request.

2a-2e. Firm (or Branch Office) Name and Address. Self-explanatory.

3. Year Established. Enter the year the firm (or branch office, if appropriate) was established under the current name.

4. DUNS Number. Insert the Data Universal Numbering System number issued by Dun and Bradstreet Information Services. Firms must have a DUNS number. See FAR Part 4.6.

5. Ownership.

a. Type. Enter the type of ownership or legal structure of the firm (sole proprietor, partnership, corporation, joint venture, etc.).

b. Small Business Status. Refer to the North American Industry Classification System (NAICS) code in the public announcement, and indicate if the firm is a small business according to the current size standard for that NAICS code (for example, Engineering Services (part of NAICS 541330), Architectural Services (NAICS 541310), Surveying and Mapping Services (NAICS 541370)). The small business categories and the internet website for the NAICS codes appear in FAR Part 19. Contact the requesting agency for any questions. Contact your local U.S. Small Business Administration office for any questions regarding Business Status.

6a-6c. Point of Contact. Provide this information for a representative of the firm that the agency can contact for additional information. The representative must be empowered to speak on contractual and policy matters.

7. Name of Firm. Enter the name of the firm if Part II is prepared for a branch office.

8a-8c. Former Firm Names. Indicate any other previous names for the firm (or branch office) during the last six years. Insert the year that this corporate name change was effective and the associated DUNS Number. This information is used to review past performance on Federal contracts.

9. Employees by Discipline. Use the relevant disciplines and associated function codes shown at the end of these instructions and list in the same numerical order. After the listed disciplines, write in any additional disciplines and leave the function code blank. List no more than 20 disciplines. Group remaining employees under "Other Employees" in column b. Each person can be counted only once according to his/her primary function. If Part II is prepared for a firm (including all branch offices), enter the number of employees by disciplines in column c(1). If Part II is prepared for a branch office, enter the number of employees by discipline in column c(2) and for the firm in column c(1).

10. Profile of Firm's Experience and Annual Average Revenue for Last 5 Years. Complete this block for the firm or branch office for which this Part II is prepared. Enter the experience categories which most accurately reflect the firm's technical capabilities and project experience. Use the relevant experience categories and associated profile codes shown at the end of these instructions, and list in the same numerical order. After the listed experience categories, write in any unlisted relevant project experience categories and leave the profile codes blank. For each type of experience, enter the appropriate revenue index number to reflect the professional services revenues received annually (averaged over the last 5 years) by the firm or branch office for performing that type of work. A particular project may be identified with one experience category or it may be broken into components, as best reflects the capabilities and types of work performed by the firm. However, do not double count the revenues received on a particular project.

11. Annual Average Professional Services Revenues of Firm for Last 3 Years. Complete this block for the firm or branch office for which this Part II is prepared. Enter the appropriate revenue index numbers to reflect the professional services revenues received annually (averaged over the last 3 years) by the firm or branch office. Indicate Federal work (performed directly for the Federal Government, either as the prime contractor or subcontractor), non-Federal work (all other domestic and foreign work, including Federally-assisted projects), and the total. If the firm has been in existence for less than 3 years, see the definition for "Annual Receipts" under FAR 19.101.

12. Authorized Representative. An authorized representative of the firm or branch office must sign and date the completed form. Signing attests that the information provided is current and factual. Provide the name and title of the authorized representative who signed the form.

STANDARD FORM 330 (REV. 3/2013) PAGE 4 OF INSTRUCTIONS

Standard Form 330 (Page 5 of Instructions)

List of Disciplines (Function Codes)

Code	Description	Code	Description
01	Acoustical Engineer	32	Hydraulic Engineer
02	Administrative	33	Hydrographic Surveyor
03	Aerial Photographer	34	Hydrologist
04	Aeronautical Engineer	35	Industrial Engineer
05	Archeologist	36	Industrial Hygienist
06	Architect	37	Interior Designer
07	Biologist	38	Land Surveyor
08	CADD Technician	39	Landscape Architect
09	Cartographer	40	Materials Engineer
10	Chemical Engineer	41	Materials Handling Engineer
11	Chemist	42	Mechanical Engineer
12	Civil Engineer	43	Mining Engineer
13	Communications Engineer	44	Oceanographer
14	Computer Programmer	45	Photo Interpreter
15	Construction Inspector	46	Photogrammetrist
16	Construction Manager	47	Planner: Urban/Regional
17	Corrosion Engineer	48	Project Manager
18	Cost Engineer/Estimator	49	Remote Sensing Specialist
19	Ecologist	50	Risk Assessor
20	Economist	51	Safety/Occupational Health Engineer
21	Electrical Engineer	52	Sanitary Engineer
22	Electronics Engineer	53	Scheduler
23	Environmental Engineer	54	Security Specialist
24	Environmental Scientist	55	Soils Engineer
25	Fire Protection Engineer	56	Specifications Writer
26	Forensic Engineer	57	Structural Engineer
27	Foundation/Geotechnical Engineer	58	Technician/Analyst
28	Geodetic Surveyor	59	Toxicologist
29	Geographic Information System Specialist	60	Transportation Engineer
30	Geologist	61	Value Engineer
31	Health Facility Planner	62	Water Resources Engineer

STANDARD FORM 330 (REV. 3/2013) PAGE 5 OF INSTRUCTIONS

Standard Form 330 (Page 6 of Instructions)

List of Experience Categories (Profile Codes)

Code	Description	Code	Description
A01	Acoustics, Noise Abatement	E01	Ecological & Archeological Investigations
A02	Aerial Photography; Airborne Data and Imagery Collection and Analysis	E02	Educational Facilities; Classrooms
		E03	Electrical Studies and Design
A03	Agricultural Development; Grain Storage; Farm Mechanization	E04	Electronics
A04	Air Pollution Control	E05	Elevators; Escalators; People-Movers
A05	Airports; Navaids; Airport Lighting; Aircraft Fueling	E06	Embassies and Chanceries
		E07	Energy Conservation; New Energy Sources
A06	Airports; Terminals and Hangars; Freight Handling	E08	Engineering Economics
A07	Arctic Facilities	E09	Environmental Impact Studies, Assessments or Statements
A08	Animal Facilities		
A09	Anti-Terrorism/Force Protection	E10	Environmental and Natural Resource Mapping
A10	Asbestos Abatement		
A11	Auditoriums & Theaters	E11	Environmental Planning
A12	Automation; Controls; Instrumentation	E12	Environmental Remediation
		E13	Environmental Testing and Analysis
B01	Barracks; Dormitories		
B02	Bridges	F01	Fallout Shelters; Blast-Resistant Design
		F02	Field Houses; Gyms; Stadiums
C01	Cartography	F03	Fire Protection
C02	Cemeteries *(Planning & Relocation)*	F04	Fisheries; Fish ladders
C03	Charting: Nautical and Aeronautical	F05	Forensic Engineering
C04	Chemical Processing & Storage	F06	Forestry & Forest products
C05	Child Care/Development Facilities	G01	Garages; Vehicle Maintenance Facilities; Parking Decks
C06	Churches; Chapels		
C07	Coastal Engineering	G02	Gas Systems (Propane; Natural, Etc.)
C08	Codes; Standards; Ordinances	G03	Geodetic Surveying: Ground and Air-borne
C09	Cold Storage; Refrigeration and Fast Freeze	G04	Geographic Information System Services: Development, Analysis, and Data Collection
C10	Commercial Building *(low rise)* ; Shopping Centers		
C11	Community Facilities	G05	Geospatial Data Conversion: Scanning, Digitizing, Compilation, Attributing, Scribing, Drafting
C12	Communications Systems; TV; Microwave		
C13	Computer Facilities; Computer Service		
C14	Conservation and Resource Management	G06	Graphic Design
C15	Construction Management		
C16	Construction Surveying	H01	Harbors; Jetties; Piers, Ship Terminal Facilities
C17	Corrosion Control; Cathodic Protection; Electrolysis	H02	Hazardous Materials Handling and Storage
C18	Cost Estimating; Cost Engineering and Analysis; Parametric Costing; Forecasting	H03	Hazardous, Toxic, Radioactive Waste Remediation
C19	Cryogenic Facilities	H04	Heating; Ventilating; Air Conditioning
		H05	Health Systems Planning
D01	Dams *(Concrete; Arch)*	H06	Highrise; Air-Rights-Type Buildings
D02	Dams *(Earth; Rock)*; Dikes; Levees	H07	Highways; Streets; Airfield Paving; Parking Lots
D03	Desalinization *(Process & Facilities)*		
D04	Design-Build - Preparation of Requests for Proposals	H08	Historical Preservation
D05	Digital Elevation and Terrain Model Development	H09	Hospital & Medical Facilities
D06	Digital Orthophotography	H10	Hotels; Motels
D07	Dining Halls; Clubs; Restaurants	H11	Housing *(Residential, Multi-Family; Apartments; Condominiums)*
D08	Dredging Studies and Design	H12	Hydraulics & Pneumatics
		H13	Hydrographic Surveying

STANDARD FORM 330 (REV. 3/2013) PAGE 6 OF INSTRUCTIONS

Standard Form 330 (Page 7 of Instructions)

List of Experience Categories (Profile Codes)

Code	Description	Code	Description
I01	Industrial Buildings; Manufacturing Plants	P09	Product, Machine Equipment Design
I02	Industrial Processes; Quality Control	P10	Pneumatic Structures, Air-Support Buildings
I03	Industrial Waste Treatment	P11	Postal Facilities
I04	Intelligent Transportation Systems	P12	Power Generation, Transmission, Distribution
I05	Interior Design; Space Planning	P13	Public Safety Facilities
I06	Irrigation; Drainage	R01	Radar; Sonar; Radio & Radar Telescopes
J01	Judicial and Courtroom Facilities	R02	Radio Frequency Systems & Shieldings
L01	Laboratories; Medical Research Facilities	R03	Railroad; Rapid Transit
L02	Land Surveying	R04	Recreation Facilities (Parks, Marinas, Etc.)
L03	Landscape Architecture	R05	Refrigeration Plants/Systems
L04	Libraries; Museums; Galleries	R06	Rehabilitation (Buildings; Structures; Facilities)
L05	Lighting (Interior; Display; Theater, Etc.)	R07	Remote Sensing
L06	Lighting (Exteriors; Streets; Memorials; Athletic Fields, Etc.)	R08	Research Facilities
		R09	Resources Recovery; Recycling
M01	Mapping Location/Addressing Systems	R10	Risk Analysis
M02	Materials Handling Systems; Conveyors; Sorters	R11	Rivers; Canals; Waterways; Flood Control
M03	Metallurgy	R12	Roofing
M04	Microclimatology; Tropical Engineering	S01	Safety Engineering; Accident Studies; OSHA Studies
M05	Military Design Standards		
M06	Mining & Mineralogy	S02	Security Systems; Intruder & Smoke Detection
M07	Missile Facilities (Silos, Fuels, Transport)	S03	Seismic Designs & Studies
M08	Modular Systems Design; Pre-Fabricated Structures or Components	S04	Sewage Collection, Treatment and Disposal
		S05	Soils & Geologic Studies; Foundations
		S06	Solar Energy Utilization
N01	Naval Architecture; Off-Shore Platforms	S07	Solid Wastes; Incineration; Landfill
N02	Navigation Structures; Locks	S08	Special Environments; Clean Rooms, Etc.
N03	Nuclear Facilities; Nuclear Shielding	S09	Structural Design; Special Structures
O01	Office Buildings; Industrial Parks	S10	Surveying; Platting; Mapping; Flood Plain Studies
O02	Oceanographic Engineering		
O03	Ordnance; Munitions; Special Weapons	S11	Sustainable Design
		S12	Swimming Pools
P01	Petroleum Exploration; Refining	S13	Storm Water Handling & Facilities
P02	Petroleum and Fuel (Storage and Distribution)	T01	Telephone Systems (Rural; Mobile; Intercom, Etc.)
P03	Photogrammetry		
P04	Pipelines (Cross-Country - Liquid & Gas)	T02	Testing & Inspection Services
P05	Planning (Community, Regional, Areawide and State)	T03	Traffic & Transportation Engineering
P06	Planning (Site, Installation, and Project)	T04	Topographic Surveying and Mapping
P07	Plumbing & Piping Design	T05	Towers (Self-Supporting & Guyed Systems)
P08	Prisons & Correctional Facilities	T06	Tunnels & Subways

Standard Form 330 (Page 8 of Instructions)

List of Experience Categories (Profile Codes)

Code	Description
U01	Unexploded Ordnance Remediation
U02	Urban Renewals; Community Development
U03	Utilities (Gas and Steam)
V01	Value Analysis; Life-Cycle Costing
W01	Warehouses & Depots
W02	Water Resources; Hydrology; Ground Water
W03	Water Supply; Treatment and Distribution
W04	Wind Tunnels; Research/Testing Facilities Design
Z01	Zoning; Land Use Studies

STANDARD FORM 330 (REV. 3/2013) PAGE 8 OF INSTRUCTIONS

Standard Form 330 (Page 1)

ARCHITECT - ENGINEER QUALIFICATIONS

PART I - CONTRACT-SPECIFIC QUALIFICATIONS

A. CONTRACT INFORMATION

1. TITLE AND LOCATION *(City and State)*

2. PUBLIC NOTICE DATE

3. SOLICITATION OR PROJECT NUMBER

B. ARCHITECT-ENGINEER POINT OF CONTACT

4. NAME AND TITLE

5. NAME OF FIRM

6. TELEPHONE NUMBER

7. FAX NUMBER

8. E-MAIL ADDRESS

C. PROPOSED TEAM
(Complete this section for the prime contractor and all key subcontractors.)

(Check) PRIME / J-V PARTNER / SUBCONTRACTOR	9. FIRM NAME	10. ADDRESS	11. ROLE IN THIS CONTRACT
a.	☐ CHECK IF BRANCH OFFICE		
b.	☐ CHECK IF BRANCH OFFICE		
c.	☐ CHECK IF BRANCH OFFICE		
d.	☐ CHECK IF BRANCH OFFICE		
e.	☐ CHECK IF BRANCH OFFICE		
f.	☐ CHECK IF BRANCH OFFICE		

D. ORGANIZATIONAL CHART OF PROPOSED TEAM   ☐ (Attached)

AUTHORIZED FOR LOCAL REPRODUCTION   STANDARD FORM 330 (REV. 3/2013) PAGE 1

Standard Form 330 (Page 2)

E. RESUMES OF KEY PERSONNEL PROPOSED FOR THIS CONTRACT
(Complete one Section E for each key person.)

12. NAME	13. ROLE IN THIS CONTRACT	14. YEARS EXPERIENCE	
		a. TOTAL	b. WITH CURRENT FIRM

15. FIRM NAME AND LOCATION *(City and State)*

16. EDUCATION *(DEGREE AND SPECIALIZATION)*	17. CURRENT PROFESSIONAL REGISTRATION *(STATE AND DISCIPLINE)*

18. OTHER PROFESSIONAL QUALIFICATIONS *(Publications, Organizations, Training, Awards, etc.)*

19. RELEVANT PROJECTS

a.
(1) TITLE AND LOCATION *(City and State)*	(2) YEAR COMPLETED	
	PROFESSIONAL SERVICES	CONSTRUCTION *(If applicable)*
(3) BRIEF DESCRIPTION *(Brief scope, size, cost, etc.)* AND SPECIFIC ROLE	☐ Check if project performed with current firm	

b.
(1) TITLE AND LOCATION *(City and State)*	(2) YEAR COMPLETED	
	PROFESSIONAL SERVICES	CONSTRUCTION *(If applicable)*
(3) BRIEF DESCRIPTION *(Brief scope, size, cost, etc.)* AND SPECIFIC ROLE	☐ Check if project performed with current firm	

c.
(1) TITLE AND LOCATION *(City and State)*	(2) YEAR COMPLETED	
	PROFESSIONAL SERVICES	CONSTRUCTION *(If applicable)*
(3) BRIEF DESCRIPTION *(Brief scope, size, cost, etc.)* AND SPECIFIC ROLE	☐ Check if project performed with current firm	

d.
(1) TITLE AND LOCATION *(City and State)*	(2) YEAR COMPLETED	
	PROFESSIONAL SERVICES	CONSTRUCTION *(If applicable)*
(3) BRIEF DESCRIPTION *(Brief scope, size, cost, etc.)* AND SPECIFIC ROLE	☐ Check if project performed with current firm	

e.
(1) TITLE AND LOCATION *(City and State)*	(2) YEAR COMPLETED	
	PROFESSIONAL SERVICES	CONSTRUCTION *(If applicable)*
(3) BRIEF DESCRIPTION *(Brief scope, size, cost, etc.)* AND SPECIFIC ROLE	☐ Check if project performed with current firm	

Standard Form 330 (Page 3)

F. EXAMPLE PROJECTS WHICH BEST ILLUSTRATE PROPOSED TEAM'S QUALIFICATIONS FOR THIS CONTRACT (Present as many projects as requested by the agency, or 10 projects, if not specified. Complete one Section F for each project.)		20. EXAMPLE PROJECT KEY NUMBER
21. TITLE AND LOCATION *(City and State)*	22. YEAR COMPLETED	
	PROFESSIONAL SERVICES	CONSTRUCTION *(If applicable)*

23. PROJECT OWNER'S INFORMATION		
a. PROJECT OWNER	b. POINT OF CONTACT NAME	c. POINT OF CONTACT TELEPHONE NUMBER

24. BRIEF DESCRIPTION OF PROJECT AND RELEVANCE TO THIS CONTRACT *(Include scope, size, and cost)*

25. FIRMS FROM SECTION C INVOLVED WITH THIS PROJECT		
a. (1) FIRM NAME	(2) FIRM LOCATION *(City and State)*	(3) ROLE
b. (1) FIRM NAME	(2) FIRM LOCATION *(City and State)*	(3) ROLE
c. (1) FIRM NAME	(2) FIRM LOCATION *(City and State)*	(3) ROLE
d. (1) FIRM NAME	(2) FIRM LOCATION *(City and State)*	(3) ROLE
e. (1) FIRM NAME	(2) FIRM LOCATION *(City and State)*	(3) ROLE
f. (1) FIRM NAME	(2) FIRM LOCATION *(City and State)*	(3) ROLE

STANDARD FORM 330 (REV. 3/2013) PAGE 3

Standard Form 330 (Page 4)

G. KEY PERSONNEL PARTICIPATION IN EXAMPLE PROJECTS

26. NAMES OF KEY PERSONNEL (From Section E, Block 12)	27. ROLE IN THIS CONTRACT (From Section E, Block 13)	28. EXAMPLE PROJECTS LISTED IN SECTION F (Fill in "Example Projects Key" section below before completing table. Place "X" under project key number for participation in same or similar role.)									
		1	2	3	4	5	6	7	8	9	10

29. EXAMPLE PROJECTS KEY

NO.	TITLE OF EXAMPLE PROJECT (FROM SECTION F)	NO.	TITLE OF EXAMPLE PROJECT (FROM SECTION F)
1		6	
2		7	
3		8	
4		9	
5		10	

STANDARD FORM 330 (REV. 3/2013) PAGE 4

Standard Form 330 (Page 5)

H. ADDITIONAL INFORMATION

30. PROVIDE ANY ADDITIONAL INFORMATION REQUESTED BY THE AGENCY. ATTACH ADDITIONAL SHEETS AS NEEDED.

I. AUTHORIZED REPRESENTATIVE
The foregoing is a statement of facts.

31. SIGNATURE

32. DATE

33. NAME AND TITLE

STANDARD FORM 330 (REV. 3/2013) PAGE 5

Standard Form 330 (Page 6)

ARCHITECT-ENGINEER QUALIFICATIONS

1. SOLICITATION NUMBER *(If any)*

PART II - GENERAL QUALIFICATIONS
(If a firm has branch offices, complete for each specific branch office seeking work.)

2a. FIRM (OR BRANCH OFFICE) NAME	3. YEAR ESTABLISHED	4. DUNS NUMBER

2b. STREET

5. OWNERSHIP
a. TYPE

2c. CITY	2d. STATE	2e. ZIP CODE

b. SMALL BUSINESS STATUS

6a. POINT OF CONTACT NAME AND TITLE

7. NAME OF FIRM *(If block 2a is a branch office)*

6b. TELEPHONE NUMBER	6c. E-MAIL ADDRESS

8a. FORMER FIRM NAME(S) *(If any)*	8b. YR. ESTABLISHED	8c. DUNS NUMBER

9. EMPLOYEES BY DISCIPLINE

a. Function Code	b. Discipline	c. No. of Employees	
		(1) FIRM	(2) BRANCH

10. PROFILE OF FIRM'S EXPERIENCE AND ANNUAL AVERAGE REVENUE FOR LAST 5 YEARS

a. Profile Code	b. Experience	c. Revenue Index Number *(see below)*

Other Employees / Total

11. ANNUAL AVERAGE PROFESSIONAL SERVICES REVENUES OF FIRM FOR LAST 3 YEARS
(Insert revenue index number shown at right)

a. Federal Work
b. Non-Federal Work
c. Total Work

PROFESSIONAL SERVICES REVENUE INDEX NUMBER

1. Less than $100,000
2. $100,00 to less than $250,000
3. $250,000 to less than $500,000
4. $500,000 to less than $1 million
5. $1 million to less than $2 million
6. $2 million to less than $5 million
7. $5 million to less than $10 million
8. $10 million to less than $25 million
9. $25 million to less than $50 million
10. $50 million or greater

12. AUTHORIZED REPRESENTATIVE
The foregoing is a statement of facts.

a. SIGNATURE

b. DATE

c. NAME AND TITLE

AUTHORIZED FOR LOCAL REPRODUCTION

STANDARD FORM 330 (REV. 3/2013) PAGE 6

Standard Form 1034

Standard Form 1034 Revised October 1987 Department of the Treasury 1 TFM 4-2000	**PUBLIC VOUCHER FOR PURCHASES AND SERVICES OTHER THAN PERSONAL**		VOUCHER NO.
U.S. DEPARTMENT, BUREAU, OR ESTABLISHMENT AND LOCATION	DATE VOUCHER PREPARED		SCHEDULE NO.
	CONTRACT NUMBER AND DATE		PAID BY
	REQUISITION NUMBER AND DATE		

PAYEE'S NAME AND ADDRESS

DATE INVOICE RECEIVED

DISCOUNT TERMS

PAYEE'S ACCOUNT NUMBER

SHIPPED FROM — TO — WEIGHT — GOVERNMENT B/L NUMBER

NUMBER AND DATE OF ORDER	DATE OF DELIVERY OR SERVICE	ARTICLES OR SERVICES (Enter description, item number of contract or Federal supply schedule, and other information deemed necessary)	QUAN-TITY	UNIT PRICE		AMOUNT
				COST	PER	(1)

(Use continuation sheet(s) if necessary)   (Payee must NOT use the space below)   TOTAL

PAYMENT:
- [ ] PROVISIONAL
- [ ] COMPLETE
- [ ] PARTIAL
- [ ] FINAL
- [ ] PROGRESS
- [ ] ADVANCE

APPROVED FOR ___ = $ ___   EXCHANGE RATE ___ = $1.00   BY 2

DIFFERENCES

Amount verified; correct for
(Signature or initials)

Pursuant to authority vested in me, I certify that this voucher is correct and proper for payment.

_____   _____   _____
(Date)   (Authorized Certifying Officer) 2   (Title)

ACCOUNTING CLASSIFICATION

PAID BY:
CHECK NUMBER ___ ON ACCOUNT OF U.S. TREASURY   CHECK NUMBER ___ ON (Name of bank)
CASH $ ___   DATE ___   PAYEE 3
PER
TITLE

1 When stated in foreign currency, insert name of currency.
2 If the ability to certify and authority to approve are combined in one person, one signature only is necessary; otherwise the approving officer will sign in the space provided, over his official title.
3 When a voucher is receipted in the name of a company or corporation, the name of the person writing the company or corporate name, as well as the capacity in which he signs, must appear. For example: "John Doe Company, per John

Previous edition usable.   NSN 7540-00-900-2234

PRIVACY ACT STATEMENT

The information requested on this form is required under the provisions of 31 U.S.C. 82b and 82c, for the purpose of disbursing Federal money. The information requested is to identify the particular creditor and the amounts to be paid. Failure to furnish this information will hinder discharge of the payment obligation.

Standard Form 1034A

Standard Form 1034A Revised October 1987 Department of the Treasury 1 TFM 4-2000	PUBLIC VOUCHER FOR PURCHASES AND SERVICES OTHER THAN PERSONAL		VOUCHER NO.
U.S. DEPARTMENT, BUREAU, OR ESTABLISHMENT AND LOCATION	DATE VOUCHER PREPARED		SCHEDULE NO.
	CONTRACT NUMBER AND DATE		PAID BY
	REQUISITION NUMBER AND DATE		

PAYEE'S NAME AND ADDRESS

DATE INVOICE RECEIVED

DISCOUNT TERMS

PAYEE'S ACCOUNT NUMBER

SHIPPED FROM	TO	WEIGHT	GOVERNMENT B/L NUMBER

NUMBER AND DATE OF ORDER	DATE OF DELIVERY OR SERVICE	ARTICLES OR SERVICES (Enter description, item number of contract or Federal supply schedule, and other information deemed necessary)	QUAN-TITY	UNIT PRICE		AMOUNT
				COST	PER	(1)

(Use continuation sheet(s) if necessary)   (Payee must NOT use the space below)   **TOTAL**

PAYMENT:
- [ ] PROVISIONAL
- [ ] COMPLETE
- [ ] PARTIAL
- [ ] FINAL
- [ ] PROGRESS
- [ ] ADVANCE

DIFFERENCES

Amount verified; correct for
(Signature or initials)

MEMORANDUM

ACCOUNTING CLASSIFICATION

PAID BY	CHECK NUMBER	ON ACCOUNT OF U.S. TREASURY	CHECK NUMBER	ON *(Name of bank)*
	CASH $	DATE		

Previous edition usable

PRIVACY ACT STATEMENT

The information requested on this form is required under the provisions of 31 U.S.C. 82b and 82c, for the purpose of disbursing Federal money. The information requested is to identify the particular creditor and the amounts to be paid. Failure to furnish this information will hinder discharge of the payment obligation.

Standard Form 1035

Standard Form 1035 (EG) September 1973 4 Treasury FRM 2000 1035-110	PUBLIC VOUCHER FOR PURCHASES AND SERVICES OTHER THAN PERSONAL *CONTINUATION SHEET*	VOUCHER NO.
		SCHEDULE NO.
		SHEET NO.

U.S.. DEPARTMENT, BUREAU, OR ESTABLISHMENT

NUMBER AND DATE OF ORDER	DATE OF DELIVERY OR SERVICE	ARTICLES OR SERVICES *(Enter description, item number of contract or Federal supply schedule, and other information deemed necessary)*	QUAN-TITY	UNIT PRICE		AMOUNT
				COST	PER	

Designed using Perform Pro, WHS/DIOR, Aug 96

Standard Form 1035A

Standard Form No. 1035-A September 1973 4 Treasury FRM 2000 1035-209-01	PUBLIC VOUCHER FOR PURCHASES AND SERVICES OTHER THAN PERSONAL **MEMORANDUM** *CONTINUATION SHEET*				VOUCHER NO. SCHEDULE NO. SHEET NO.	
U.S. DEPARTMENT, BUREAU, OR ESTABLISHMENT						
NUMBER AND DATE OF ORDER	DATE OF DELIVERY OR SERVICE	ARTICLES OR SERVICES *(Enter description, item number of contract or Federal supply schedule, and other information deemed necessary)*	QUAN-TITY	UNIT PRICE COST	PER	AMOUNT

Standard Form 1093

SCHEDULE OF WITHHOLDINGS UNDER THE CONSTRUCTION WAGE RATE REQUIREMENTS STATUTE (40 U.S.C. CHAPTER 31, SUBCHAPTER IV, §3144)
AND/OR
THE CONTRACT WORK HOURS AND SAFETY STANDARDS STATUTE (40 U.S.C. CHAPTER 37, §3703)

U.S. GOVERNMENT ACCOUNTABILITY OFFICE
Office of General Counsel
Davis-Bacon Group
WASHINGTON, DC 20548

Contractor or subcontractor charged with violations _____

Prime contractor _____

Contract No. _____ , _____
(Date)

Report concerning irregularities transmitted to--

_____ , _____
(Date)

Deducted from amounts otherwise due the contractor, for deposit to the account "05X6022," covering wages due the employees whose names, social security numbers, and current addresses are listed on the attached schedule, are withholdings pursuant to the following laws:

Construction Wage Rate Requirements Statute _____ $ _____
Contract Work Hours and Safety Standards Statute _____ $ _____
Total _____ $ _____

Forwarded herewith is check No. _____ , dated _____
for $ _____

_____
(Disbursing officer or other administrative official)

STANDARD FORM 1093 (REV. 2/2013)

Standard Form 1094

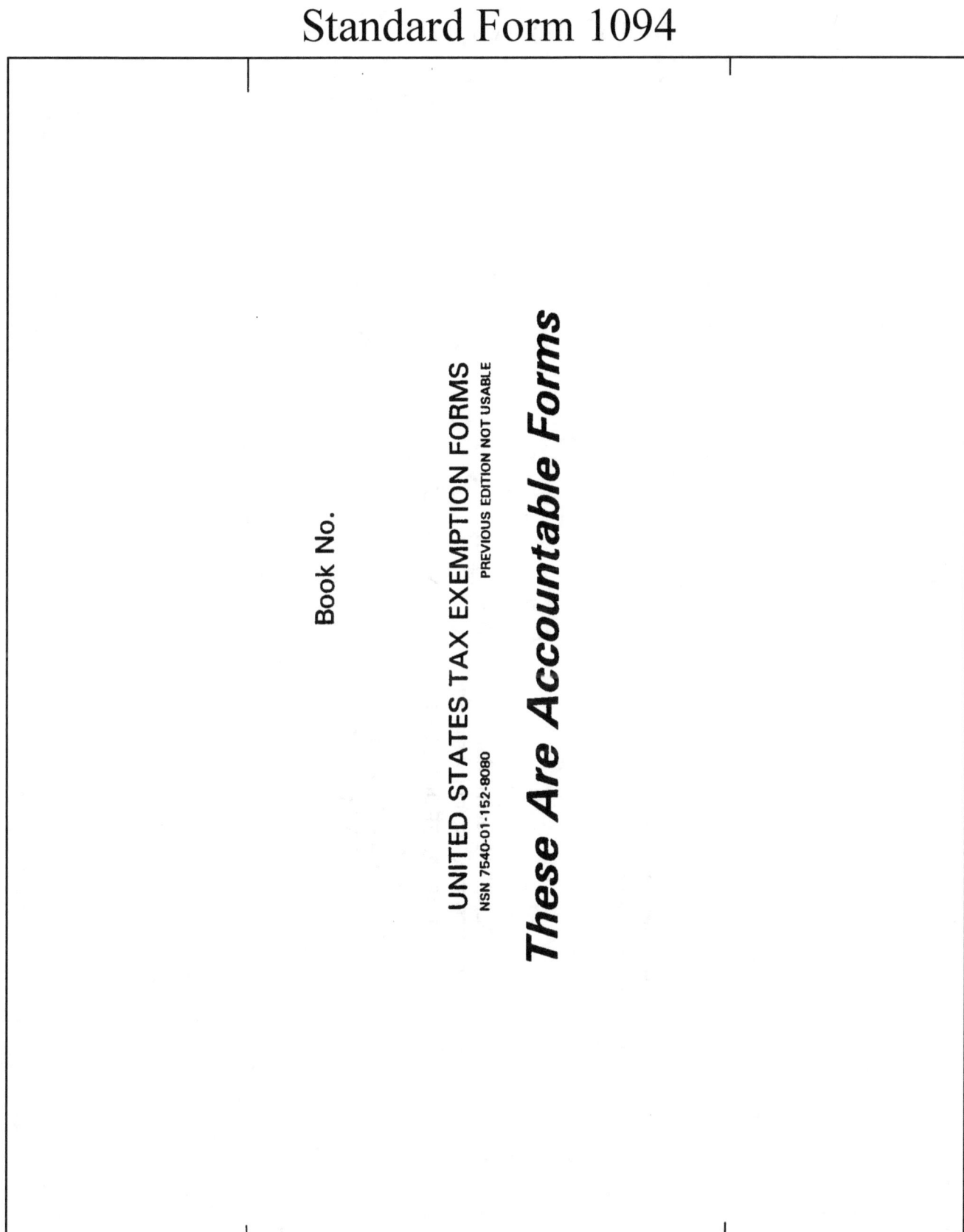

Standard Form 1094

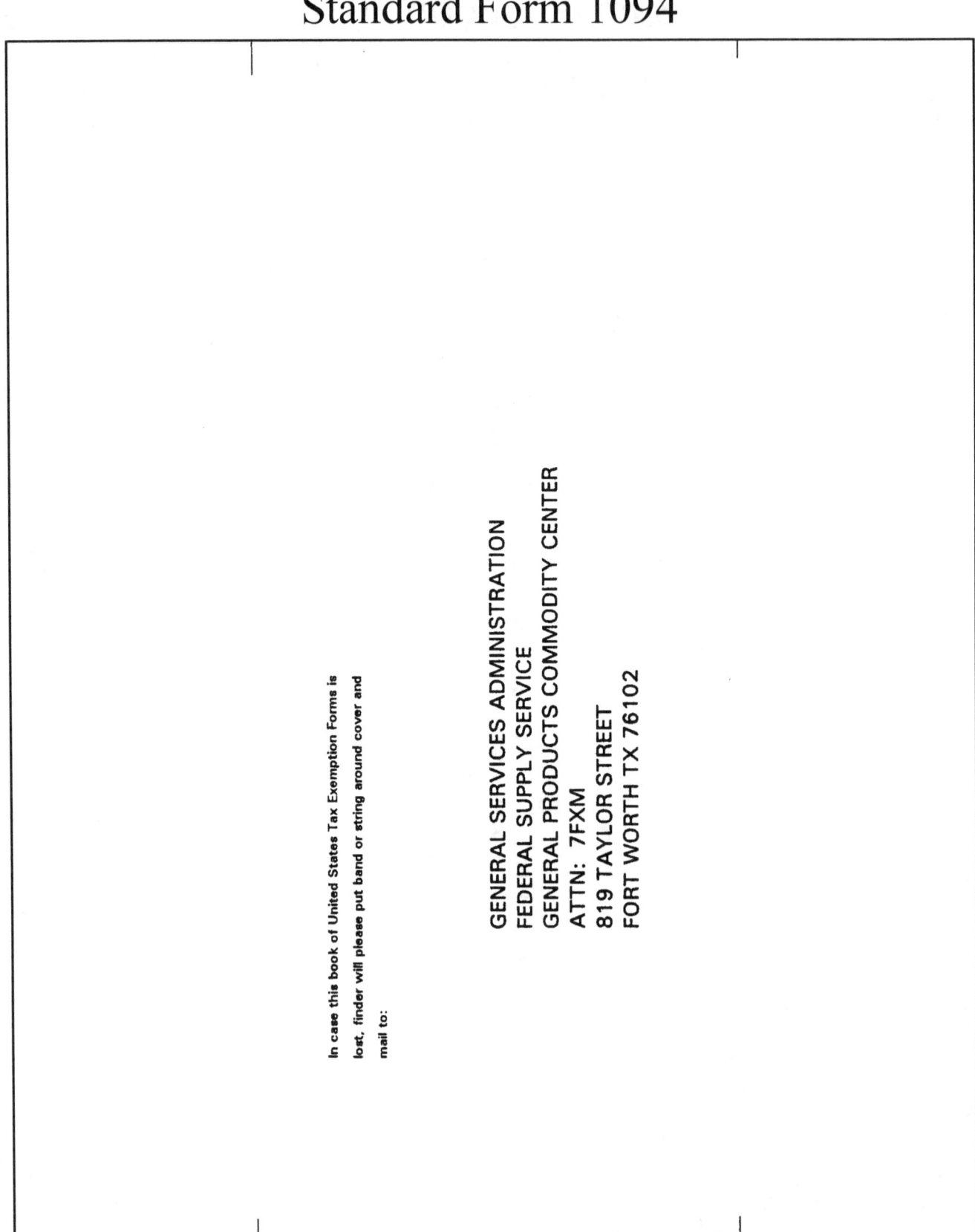

Standard Form 1094

Standard Form 1094 (Back)

INSTRUCTIONS

1. This form will be used to establish the Government's exemption or immunity from State or Local taxes whenever no other evidence is available.

2. This form shall NOT be used for:
   (a) Purchases of quarters or subsistence made by employees in travel status.
   (b) Expenses incident to use of a privately owned motor vehicle for which a mileage allowance has been authorized, or
   (c) Merchandise purchased which is subject only to Federal Tax.

3. If the spaces provided on the face of this form are inadequate, attach a separate statement containing the required information.

4. If both State and local taxes are involved, use a separate form for each tax. The form will be provided to the vendor when the prices exclude State or local tax.

5. The serial number of each form prepared will be shown on the payment voucher.

THE FRAUDULENT USE OF THIS FORM FOR THE PURPOSE OF OBTAINING EXCEPTION FROM OR ADJUSTMENT OF TAXES IS PROHIBITED.

STANDARD FORM 1094 (REV.12-96) BACK

Standard Form 1094A

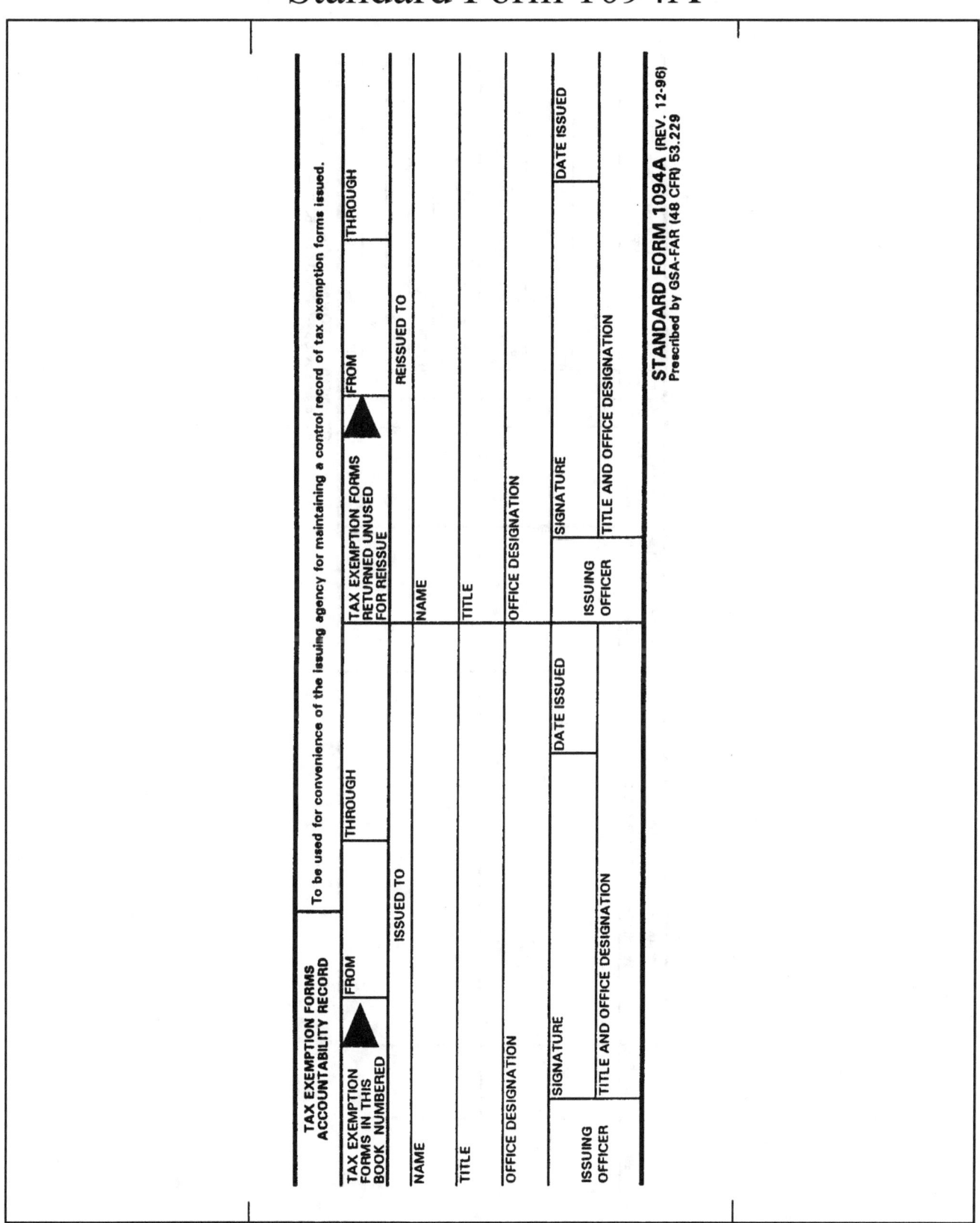

Standard Form 1094A (Back)

FORM		Mark "X" in appropriate column to indicate type of tax		TAX EXCLUDED (Amount $)	STATE	LOCAL	TRANSACTION REFERENCE
NO.	DATE	VENDOR NAME AND ADDRESS	ITEM PURCHASED				
							Voucher No.: Voucher Date: PO/Cont. No.:
							Voucher No.: Voucher Date: PO/Cont. No.:
							Voucher No.: Voucher Date: PO/Cont. No.:
							Voucher No.: Voucher Date: PO/Cont. No.:

STANDARD FORM 1094A (REV. 12-96) BACK
Prescribed by GSA-FAR (48 CFR) 53.229

PART 53.3—ILLUSTRATION OF FORMS

Standard Form 1165

Standard Form 1165
GAO 5100
1165-105

RECEIPT FOR CASH—SUBVOUCHER

(To be used when invoice is not available)

Subvoucher No. _____

Date _____

Received in cash from _____ and _____ ($ _____) for the following:
100

QUANTITY	ARTICLES OR SERVICES	AMOUNT

By _____
(Signature of Vendor/Agent)

Title _____
(DO NOT SIGN IN DUPLICATE)

Vendor _____

Address _____

Purpose (Project, etc.) _____

APPROPRIATION AND ACCOUNTING CLASSIFICATION

INTERIM RECEIPT FOR CASH

Date _____

Received of Imprest Fund Cashier $ _____ for which I hold myself accountable to the United States.

_____
(Signature)

NOTE TO SIGNER

Be sure this receipt is marked "VOID" and returned to you when the transaction is completed or the funds returned to the Cashier.

Standard Form 1402

CERTIFICATION OF APPOINTMENT

Under authority vested in the undersigned and in conformance with Subpart 1.6 of the Federal Acquisition Regulation

_____ is appointed

Contracting Officer

for the

United States of America

Subject to the limitations contained in the Federal Acquisition Regulation and to the following:

Unless sooner terminated, this appointment is effective as long as the appointee is assigned to:

_____
(Organization)

_____
(Agency/Department)

_____
(Signature and Title)

_____
(Date)

_____
(No.)

NSN 7540-01-152-5812

STANDARD FORM 1402 (10-83)
Prescribed by GSA - FAR (48 CFR) 53.201-1

Standard Form 1403

PREAWARD SURVEY OF PROSPECTIVE CONTRACTOR (GENERAL)

1. SERIAL NO. *(For surveying activity use)*

OMB NO.: **9000-0011**
Expires: 10/31/97

Public reporting burden for this collection of information is estimated to average 24 hours per response, including the time for reviewing instructions, searching existing datasources, gathering and maintaining the data needed, and completing and reviewing the collection of information. Send comments regarding this burden estimate or any other aspect of this collection of information, including suggestions for reducing this burden, to the FAR Secretariat (VRS), Office of Federal Acquisition and Regulatory Policy, GSA, Washington, DC 20405; and to the Office of Management and Budget, Paperwork Reduction Project (9000-0011), Washington, DC 20503.

SECTION I - REQUEST *(For Completion by Contracting Office)*

2. NAME AND ADDRESS OF SURVEYING ACTIVITY
3. SOLICITATION NO.
4. TOTAL OFFERED PRICE $
5. TYPE OF CONTRACT
6A. NAME AND ADDRESS OF SECONDARY SURVEY ACTIVITY *(For surveying activity use)*
7A. NAME AND ADDRESS OF PROSPECTIVE CONTRACTOR
6B. TELEPHONE NO. *(Include AUTOVON, WATS, or FTS, if available)*
7B. FIRM'S CONTACT
7C. TELEPHONE NO. *(with area code)*
8. WILL CONTRACTING OFFICE PARTICIPATE IN SURVEY? ☐ YES ☐ NO
13. NAME AND ADDRESS OF PARENT COMPANY *(If applicable)*
9. DATE OF REQUEST
10. DATE REPORT REQUIRED
11. PROSPECTIVE CONTRACTOR REPRESENT THAT IT ☐ IS, ☐ IS NOT A SMALL BUSINESS CONCERN.
12. WALSH-HEALY CON ACT *(Check applicable box(es))*
  A. IS NOT APPLICABLE
  B. IS APPLICABLE AND PROSPECTIVE CONTRACTOR REPRESENTS HIS CLASSIFICATION AS:
  ☐ MANUFACTURER ☐ REGULAR DEALER
  ☐ OTHER *(Specify)*
14A. PLANT AND LOCATION *(If different from Item 7, above)*
15A. NAME OF REQUESTING ACTIVITY CONTRACTING OFFICER
14B. POINT OF CONTACT
14C. TELEPHONE NO. *(with area code)*
15B. SIGNATURE
16A. NAME OF CONTACT POINT AT REQUESTING ACTIVITY *(If different from Item 15A)*
15C. TELEPHONE NO. *(Include AUTOVAN, WATS or FTS, if available)*
17. RETURN PREAWARD SURVEY TO THIS ADDRESS:
16B. TELEPHONE NO. *(Include AUTOVON, WATS, or FTS, if available)*

ATTN:

SECTION II - DATA *(For Completion by Conracting Office)*

18A. ITEM NO.	18B. NATIONAL STOCK NUMBER (NEW) AND NOMENCLATURE		18C. TOTAL QUANTITY	18D. UNIT PRICE	18E. DELIVERY SCHEDULE				
					(a)	(b)	(c)	(d)	(e)
		SOLICITED							
		OFFERED		$					
		SOLICITED							
		OFFERED		$					
		SOLICITED							
		OFFERED		$					
		SOLICITED							
		OFFERED		$					
		SOLICITED							
		OFFERED		$					
		SOLICITED							
		OFFERED		$					
		SOLICITED							
		OFFERED		$					

AUTHORIZATION FOR LOCAL REPRODUCTION
Previous edition is usable.

STANDARD FORM 1403 (REV. 9-88)
Prescribed by GSA FAR (48 CFR) 53.209-1(a)

Standard Form 1403 (Back)

SECTION III - FACTORS TO BE INVESTIGATED

19. MAJOR FACTORS	CHK. (a)	SAT. (b)	UN-SAT. (c)	20. OTHER FACTORS *(Provide specific requirements in Remarks)*	CHK. (a)	SAT. (b)	UN-SAT. (c)
A. TECHNICAL CAPABILITY				A. GOVERNMENT PROPERTY CONTROL			
B. PRODUCTION CAPABILITY				B. TRANSPORTATION			
C. QUALITY ASSURANCE CAPABILITY				C. PACKAGING			
D. FINANCIAL CAPABILITY				D. SECURITY			
E. ACCOUNTING SYSTEM				E. SAFETY			
21. IS THIS A SHORT FORM PREAWARD REPORT? *(For completion by surveying activity)* ☐ YES ☐ NO				F. ENVIRONMENTAL/ENERGY CONSIDERATION			
				G. FLIGHT OPERATIONS/FLIGHT SAFETY			
22. IS A FINANCIAL ASSISTANCE PAYMENT PROVISION IN THE SOLICITATION? *(For completion by contracting activity)* ☐ YES ☐ NO				H. OTHER *(Specify)*			

23. REMARKS *(For Contracting Activity Use)*

SECTION IV - SURVEYING ACTIVITY RECOMMENDATIONS

24. RECOMMEND	25A. NAME AND TITLE OF SURVEY APPROVING OFFICIAL	25B. TELEPHONE NO.
☐ A. COMPLETE AWARD ☐ B. PARTIAL AWARD (Quantity _____) ☐ C. NO AWARD	25C. SIGNATURE	25D. DATE

STANDARD FORM 1403 (REV. 9-88) BACK

Standard Form 1404

PREAWARD SURVEY OF PROSPECTIVE CONTRACTOR TECHNICAL

SERIAL NO. *(For surveying activity use)*

PROSPECTIVE CONTRACTOR

OMB NO.: **9000-0011**
Expires: 10/31/97

Public reporting burden for this collection of information is estimated to average 24 hours per response, including the time for reviewing instructions, searching existing data sources, gathering and maintaining the data needed, and completing and reviewing the collection of information. Send comments regarding this burden estimate or any other aspect of this collection of information, including suggestions for reducing this burden, to the FAR Secretariat (VRS), Office of Federal Acquisition and Regulatory Policy, GSA, Washington, DC 20405; and to the Office of Management and Budget, Paperwork Reduction Project (9000-0011), Washington, DC 20503.

1. RECOMMENDED
☐ a. COMPLETE AWARD ☐ b. PARTIAL AWARD (Quantity: _____) ☐ c. NO AWARD

2. NARRATIVE *(Include the following information concerning key personnel who will be involved with the prospective contract: (1) Names, qualifications/experience and length of affiliation with prospective contractor; (2) Evaluate technical capabilities with respect to the requirements of the proposed contract or item classifications); (3) Description of any technical capabilities which the prospective contractor lacks. Comment on the prospective contractor's efforts to obtain the needed technical capabilities.)*

IF CONTINUATION SHEETS ATTACHED - MARK HERE ☐

3. FIRM HAS AND/OR UNDERSTANDS *(Give explanation for any items marked "NO" in 2. Narrative)*

a. SPECIFICATIONS	☐ YES ☐ NO	b. EXHIBITS	☐ YES ☐ NO
c. DRAWINGS	☐ YES ☐ NO	d. TECHNICAL DATA REQUIREMENTS	☐ YES ☐ NO

	a. SIGNATURE AND OFFICE *(Include typed or printed name)*	b. TELEPHONE NO. *(include area code)*	c. DATE SIGNED
4. SURVEY MADE BY			
5. SURVEY REVIEWING OFFICIAL	a. SIGNATURE AND OFFICE *(Include typed or printed name)*	b. TELEPHONE NO. *(include area code)*	c. DATE REVIEWED

AUTHORIZED FOR LOCAL REPRODUCTION
Previous edition is usable.

STANDARD FORM 1404 (REV. 9-88)
Prescribed by GSA - FAR (48 CFR) 53.209-1(b)

PART 53.3—ILLUSTRATION OF FORMS 53.301-1405

Standard Form 1405

PREAWARD SURVEY OF PROSPECTIVE CONTRACTOR PRODUCTION	SERIAL NO. *(For surveying activity use)*	OMB No.: **9000-0011** Expires: 09/30/91
	PROSPECTIVE CONTRACTOR	

Public reporting burden for this collection of information is estimated to average 24 hours per response, including the time for reviewing instructions, searching existing data sources, gathering and maintaining the data needed, and completing and reviewing the collection of information. Send comments regarding this burden estimate or any other aspect of this collection of information, including suggestions for reducing this burden, to the FAR Secretariat (VRS), Office of Federal Acquisition and Regulatory Policy, GSA, Washington, DC 20405; and to the Office of Management and Budget, Paperwork Reduction Project (9000-0011), Washington, DC 20503.

SECTION I - RECOMMENDATION

1. RECOMMENDED
   ☐ COMPLETE AWARD   ☐ b. PARTIAL AWARD *(Quantity: _____)*   ☐ c. NO AWARD

2. NARRATIVE *(Cite those sections of this report which substantiate the recommendations. List any other backup information in this space or on attached sheet if necessary. Identify any formal systems reviews and state results.)*

IF CONTINUATION SHEETS ATTACHED - MARK HERE ☐

	a. SIGNATURE AND OFFICE *(Include typed or printed name)*	b. TELEPHONE NUMBER *(Include are code)*	c. DATE SIGNED
3. SURVEY MADE BY			
4. SURVEY REVIEWING OFFICIAL	a. SIGNATURE AND OFFICE *(Include typed or printed name)*	b. TELEPHONE NUMBER *(Include are code)*	c. DATE REVIEWED

AUTHORIZED FOR LOCAL REPRODUCTION
Previous edition not usable

STANDARD FORM 1405 (REV. 9-88)
Prescribed by GSA-FAR (48 CFR) 53.209-1(c)

53.3-91

Standard Form 1405 (Page 2)

SECTION II - PLANT FACILITIES

1. SIZE OF TRACT		4. DESCRIPTION AND TYPE OF BUILDING(S)
2. SQUARE FEET UNDER ROOF	3. NO. OF BUILDINGS	☐ OWNED ☐ LEASED *(Give expiration date)*

5. SPACE					6. MISCELLANEOUS PLANT OBSERVATIONS *(Explain any items marked "NO" on an attached sheet.)*	YES	NO
	TYPE	SQUARE FEET	ADE-QUATE	INADE-QUATE			
MANUFAC-TURING	a. TOTAL MANUFACTURING SPACE				a. GOOD HOUSEKEEPING MAINTAINED		
	b. SPACE AVAILABLE FOR OFFERED ITEM				b. POWER AND FUEL SUPPLY ADEQUATE TO MEET PRODUCTION		
					c. ALTERNATE POWER AND FUEL SOURCE AVAILABLE		
STORAGE	c. TOTAL STORAGE SPACE				d. ADEQUATE MATERIAL HANDLING EQUIPMENT AVAILABLE		
	d. FOR INSPECTION LOTS				e. TRANSPORTATION FACILITIES AVAILABLE FOR SHIPPING PRODUCT		
	e. FOR SHIPPING QUANTITIES						
	f. SPACE AVAILABLE FOR OFFERED ITEM				**OTHER** *(Specify)* f. _____ g. _____ h. _____		
	g. AMOUNT OF STORAGE THAT CAN BE CONVERTED FOR MANUFAC-TURING, IF REQUIRED						

SECTION III - PRODUCTION EQUIPMENT

	LIST MAJOR EQUIPMENT REQUIRED *(Include GFP and annotate it as such)* (a)	QUANTITY REQUIRED FOR PROPOSED CONTRACT (b)	TOTAL QTY. REQD. DURING LIFE OF PROPOSED CONTRACT (c)	QUANTITY ON HAND (d)	CONDI-TION (e) G | F | P	QUANTITY SHORT* *(Col. (c) minus (d))* (f)	SOURCE, IF NOT ON HAND (g)	VERIFIED DELIVERY DATE (h)
1. **MANUFACTURING**								
2. **SPECIAL TOOLING**								
3. **SPECIAL TEST**								

*Coordinate shortage information for financial implications.

STANDARD FORM 1405 (REV. 9-88) PAGE 2

Standard Form 1405 (Page 3)

SECTION IV - MATERIALS, PURCHASED PARTS AND SUBCONTRACTS

1. PARTS/MATERIALS/SUBCONTRACTS WITH LONGEST LEAD TIME OR CRUCIAL ITEMS

DESCRIPTION (a)	SOURCE (b)	VERIFIED DELIVERY DATE TO MEET PROD. (c)

2. DESCRIBE THE MATERIAL CONTROL SYSTEM, INDICATING WHETHER IT IS CURRENTLY OPERATIONAL, AND EVALUATE ITS ABILITY TO MEET THE NEEDS OF THE PROPOSED ACQUISITION.

SECTION V - PERSONNEL

1. NUMBER AND SOURCE OF EMPLOYEES					
TYPE OF EMPLOYEES	NO. ON BOARD	ADD. NO. REQUIRED	AVAIL. YES	AVAIL. NO	SOURCE
a. SKILLED PRODUCTION					
b. UNSKILLED PRODUCTION					
c. ENGINEERING					
d. ADMINISTRATIVE					
e. TOT. (Lines A thru D)					

2. SHIFTS ON WHICH WORK IS TO BE PERFORMED
☐ FIRST ☐ SECOND ☐ THIRD

3. UNION AFFILIATION

AGREEMENT EXPIRATION DATE ▶

4. RELATIONSHIP WITH LABOR INDICATES PROBLEMS AFFECTING TIMELY PERFORMANCE OF PROPOSED CONTRACT (If "Yes," explain on attached sheet)
☐ YES ☐ NO

SECTION VI - DELIVERY PERFORMANCE RECORD

STANDARD FORM 1405 (REV. 9-88) PAGE 3

Standard Form 1405 (Page 4)

SECTION VII - RELATED PREVIOUS PRODUCTION (*Government*)							
PAST YEAR PRODUCTION		GOVERNMENT CONTRACT NUMBER* (c)	PERFORMANCE		QUANTITY (f)	DOLLAR VALUE ($000) (g)
ITEM NOMENCLATURE (a)	NATIONAL STOCK NO. (NSN) (b)		ON SCHED. (d)	DELIN- QUENT (e)		

* Identify identical items by an asterisk (*) after the Government contract number.

SECTION VIII - CURRENT PRODUCTION
(Government and civilian concurrent production schedule using same equipment and/or personnel as offered item)

ITEM(S) (Include Government Contract No., if applicable. Identify unsatisfactory performance with asterisk(*).)	MONTHLY SCHEDULE OF CONCURRENT DELIVERIES (*Quantity*)										
	1st	2nd	3rd	4th	5th	6th	7th	8th	9th	10th	BAL.
1. BEING PRODUCED											
2. PENDING AWARD											

SECTION IX - ORGANIZATION AND MANAGEMENT DATA

Provide the following information in SECTION NARRATIVE:

1. Describe the relationship between management production, and inspection. Attach an organization chart, if available.

2. Describe the prospective contractor's production control system. State whether or not it is operational.

3. Evaluate the prospective contractor's production control system in terms of (a) historical effectiveness, (b) the proposed contract, and (c) total production during performance of the proposed contract.

4. Comment on or evaluate other areas unique to this survey (include all special requests by the contracting office and any other information pertinent to the proposed contractor item classification).

STANDARD FORM 1405 (REV. 9-88) PAGE 4

Standard Form 1406

PREAWARD SURVEY OF PROSPECTIVE CONTRACTOR QUALITY ASSURANCE

SERIAL NO. *(For surveying activity use)*

PROSPECTIVE CONTRACTOR

OMB No.: **9000-0011**
Expires: 10/31/2000

Public reporting burden for this collection of information is estimated to average 24 hours per response, including the time for reviewing instructions, searching existing data sources, gathering and maintaining the data needed, and completing and reviewing the collection of information. Send comments regarding this burden estimate or any other aspect of this collection of information, including suggestions for reducing this burden, to the FAR Secretariat (MVR), Federal Acquisition Policy Division, GSA, Washington, DC 20405.

SECTION I - RECOMMENDATION

1. RECOMMEND: ☐ AWARD   ☐ NO AWARD *(Provide full substantiation for recommendation in 4. NARRATIVE)*

2. IF PROSPECTIVE CONTRACTOR RECEIVES AWARD, A POST AWARD CONFERENCE IS RECOMMENDED.   ☐ YES ☐ NO

3. AN ON-SITE SURVEY WAS PERFORMED.   ☐ YES ☐ NO

4. NARRATIVE

IF CONTINUATION SHEETS ATTACHED - MARK HERE ☐

5. SURVEY MADE BY			6. SURVEY REVIEWING OFFICIAL		
A. SIGNATURE		B. DATE SIGNED	A. SIGNATURE		B. DATE REVIEWED
C. NAME			C. NAME		
D. OFFICE			D. OFFICE		
E. AREA CODE	F. TELEPHONE NUMBER	G. EXT.	E. AREA CODE	F. TELEPHONE NUMBER	G. EXT.

AUTHORIZED FOR LOCAL REPRODUCTION
Previous edition is not usable.

STANDARD FORM 1406 (REV. 11-97)
Prescribed by GSA FAR (48 CFR) 53.209-1(d)

Standard Form 1406 (Back)

SECTION II - COMPANY AND SOLICITATION DATA

1. BRIEFLY DESCRIBE HOW QUALITY ASSURANCE RESPONSIBILITIES ARE ACCOMPLISHED.

2. QUALITY ASSURANCE OFFICIALS CONTACTED

A. NAME	B. TITLE	C. YEARS OF QUALITY ASSURANCE EXPERIENCE

3. APPLICABLE CONTRACT QUALITY REQUIREMENTS

A. NUMBER	B. TITLE	C. TAILORING (If any)

4. ☐ IDENTICAL OR ☐ SIMILAR ITEMS HAVE BEEN ☐ PRODUCED, ☐ SUPPLIED, OR ☐ SERVICED BY PROSPECTIVE CONTRACTOR

(If similar items, identify:)

SECTION III - EVALUATION CHECKLIST

STATEMENTS		YES	NO
1. These items (where applicable to the contract) are understood by the prospective contractor.	A. Exhibits, technical data, drawings, specifications, and approval requirements.		
	B. Preservation, packaging, packing, and marking requirements.		
	C. Other *(Specify)*		
2. Records available indicate that the prospective contractor has a satisfactory quality performance record during the past twelve (12) months for similar items.			
3. Used, reconditioned, or remanufactured material and former Government surplus material will be furnished by the prospective contractor. *(If Yes, explain in Section I NARRATIVE)*			
4. Prospective contractor will require unusual assistance from the Government. *(If Yes, explain in Section I NARRATIVE)*			
5. Did prospective contractor fulfill commitments to correct deficiencies, as proposed on previous surveys, when awarded that contract? *(If No, explain in Section I NARRATIVE)*			
6. Quality verification personnel	NUMBER SKILLED / NUMBER SEMI-SKILLED		
7. Quality verification to production personnel ratio.	RATIO		
THE FOLLOWING ARE AVAILABLE AND ADEQUATE. *(If not applicable, show "N/A" in "Yes" column.)*			
8. Inspection and test equipment, gauges, and instruments for first article and production *(including solicitation specified equipment).*			
9. Calibration/metrology program.			
10. Quality system procedures and controls.			
11. Control of specifications, drawings, changes and modifications, work/process instructions.			
12. System for determining inspection, test, and measurement requirements.			
13. Purchasing: Processes for selecting qualified suppliers and assuring the quality of purchased materials.			
14. Product identification, segregation, traceability, and maintenance.			
15. Government furnished property controls.			
16. Process controls.			
17. Nonconforming product: System for timely identification, disposition, correction of deficiencies, and corrective and preventative action.			
18. Preservation, storage, packaging, packing, marking, and delivery controls.			
19. Records *(such as: inspection, test, status, corrective actions, calibration, etc.)*			
20. Controls for investigation of customer complaints and correction of deficiencies.			
21. Design controls system.			
22. Computer software *(deliverable and/or non-deliverable)* quality assurance program.			
23. Management review and internal quality audits.			
24. Quality assurance training program.			
25. Installation and servicing quality assurance program.			
26. Statistical techniques.			

STANDARD FORM 1406 (REV. 11-97) BACK

PART 53.3—ILLUSTRATION OF FORMS 53.301-1407

Standard Form 1407

PREAWARD SURVEY OF PROSPECTIVE CONTRACTOR FINANCIAL CAPABILITY

SERIAL NO. *(For surveying activity use)*

OMB No.: 9000-0011
Expires: 09/30/91

PROSPECTIVE CONTRACTOR

Public reporting burden for this collection of information is estimated to average 24 hours per response, including the time for reviewing instructions, searching existing data sources, gathering and maintaining the data needed, and completing and reviewing the collection of information. Send comments regarding this burden estimate or any other aspect of this collection of information, including suggestions for reducing this burden, to the FAR Secretariat (VRS), Office Federal Acquisition and Regulatory Policy, GSA, Washington, DC 20405; and to the Office of Management and Budget, Paperwork Reduction Project (9000-0011), Washington, DC 20503.

SECTION I - RECOMMENDATION

1. RECOMMENDED
   ☐ a. COMPLETE AWARD   ☐ b. PARTIAL AWARD (Quantity: _____)   ☐ c. NO AWARD

2. TOTAL OFFERED PRICE

3. NARRATIVE *(Cite those sections of the report which substantiate the recommendation. Give any other backup information in this space or on an additional sheet, if necessary.)*

IF CONTINUATION SHEETS ATTACHED - MARK HERE ☐

4. SURVEY MADE BY	a. SIGNATURE	b. TELEPHONE NUMBER *(Include area code)*	c. DATE SIGNED
5. SURVEY REVIEWING OFFICIAL	a. SIGNATURE	b. TELEPHONE NUMBER *(Include area code)*	c. DATE REVIEWED

AUTHORIZED FOR LOCAL REPRODUCTION
Previous edition is usable.

STANDARD FORM 1407 (REV. 9-88)
Prescribed by GSA - FAR (48 CFR) 53.209-1(e)

Standard Form 1407 (Page 2)

SECTION II - GENERAL

1. TYPE OF COMPANY
- ☐ CORPORATION
- ☐ PARTNERSHIP
- ☐ SUBSIDIARY
- ☐ DIVISION
- ☐ PROPRIETORSHIP
- ☐ OTHER *(Specify)*

2. YEAR ESTABLISHED:

3. NAME AND ADDRESS OF:
a. PARENT CO.

b. SUBSIDIARIES

SECTION III - BALANCE SHEET/PROFIT AND LOSS STATEMENT

PART A - LATEST BALANCE SHEET

1. DATE
2. FILED WITH

3. FINANCIAL POSITION

a. Cash	$
b. Accounts Receivable	
c. Inventory	
d. Other Current Assets	
e. Total Current Assets	
f. Fixed Assets	
g. Current Liabilities	
h. Long Term Liabilities	
i. Total Liabilities	
j. Net Worth	

4. WORKING CAPITAL *(Current Assets less Current Liabilities)*

5. RATIOS

a. CURRENT ASSETS TO CURRENT LIABILITIES	b. ACID TEST *(Cash, temporary investments held in lieu of cash and current receivables to current liabilities)*	c. TOTAL LIABILITIES TO NET WORTH

PART B - LATEST PROFIT AND LOSS STATEMENT

1. CURRENT PERIOD — a. FROM / b. TO
2. FILED WITH

3. NET SALES
- a. CURRENT PERIOD $
- b. First prior fiscal year
- c. Second prior fiscal year

4. NET PROFITS BEFORE TAXES
- a. CURRENT PERIOD $
- b. First prior fiscal year
- c. Second prior fiscal year

PART C - OTHER

1. FISCAL YEAR ENDS *(Date)*: a. THROUGH *(Date)* b. BY *(Signature)*
2. BALANCE SHEETS AND PROFIT AND LOSS STATEMENTS HAVE BEEN CERTIFIED ▶
3. OTHER PERTINENT DATA

SECTION IV - PROSPECTIVE CONTRACTOR'S FINANCIAL ARRANGEMENTS

Mark "X" in appropriate column.

	YES	NO
1. USE OF OWN RESOURCES		
2. USE OF BANK CREDITS		
3. OTHER *(Specify)*		

4. INDEPENDENT ANALYSIS OF FINANCIAL POSITION SUPPORTS THE STATEMENTS SHOWN IN ITEMS 1, 2, AND 3 ☐ YES ☐ NO *(If "NO", explain)*

SECTION V - GOVERNMENT FINANCIAL AID

1. TO BE REQUESTED IN CONNECTION WITH PERFORMANCE OF PROPOSED CONTRACT

Mark "X" in appropriate column.

	YES	NO
a. PROGRESS PAYMENT(S)		
b. GUARANTEED LOAN		
c. ADVANCE PAYMENTS		

2. EXPLAIN ANY "YES" ANSWERS TO ITEMS 1a, b, AND c.

3. FINANCIAL AID CURRENTLY OBTAINED FROM THE GOVERNMENT
Complete items below only if Item a., is marked "YES."

a. PROSPECTIVE CONTRACTOR RECEIVES GOVERNMENT FINANCING AT PRESENT	b. IS LIQUIDATION CURRENT?	c. AMOUNT OF UNLIQUIDATED PROGRESS PAYMENTS OUTSTANDING	DOLLAR AMOUNTS	(a) AUTHORIZED	(b) IN USE
☐ YES ☐ NO	☐ YES ☐ NO	$	a. Guaranteed loans	$	$
			b. Advance payments	$	$

4. LIST THE GOVERNMENT AGENCIES INVOLVED

5. SHOW THE APPLICABLE CONTRACT NOS.

STANDARD FORM 1407 (REV. 9-88) PAGE 2

Standard Form 1407 (Page 3)

SECTION VI - BUSINESS AND FINANCIAL REPUTATION

1. COMMENTS OF PROSPECTIVE CONTRACTOR'S BANK

2. COMMENTS OF TRADE CREDITORS

3. COMMENTS AND REPORTS OF COMMERCIAL FINANCIAL SERVICES AND CREDIT ORGANIZATIONS *(Such as, Dun & Bradstreet, Standard and Poor, etc.)*

4. MOST RECENT CREDIT RATING ▶ a. DATE | b. BY

5. DOES PRICE APPEAR UNREALISTICALLY LOW? ☐ YES ☐ NO *(If Yes, explain in Section I NARRATIVE)*

6. DESCRIBE ANY OUTSTANDING LIENS OR JUDGMENTS

SECTION VII - SALES (000'S) FOR NEXT SIX QUARTERS

CATEGORY	1	2	3	4	5	6	TOTAL
1. CURRENT CONTRACT SALES (Backlog)	$	$	$	$	$	$	$
A. GOVERNMENT (Prime & Subcontractor)							
B. COMMERCIAL							
2. ANTICIPATED ADDITIONAL SALES							
A. GOVERNMENT (Prime & Subcontractor)							
B. COMMERCIAL							
3. TOTALS							

STANDARD FORM 1407 (REV. 9-88) PAGE 3

Standard Form 1408

PREAWARD SURVEY OF PROSPECTIVE CONTRACTOR ACCOUNTING SYSTEM	SERIAL NO. *(For surveying activity use)*	OMB No.: **9000-0011** Expires: 10/31/97
	PROSPECTIVE CONTRACTOR	

Public reporting burden for this collection of information is estimated to average 24 hours per response, including the time for reviewing instructions, searching existing data sources, gathering and maintaining the data needed, and completing and reviewing the collection of information. Send comments regarding this burden estimate or any other aspect of this collection of information, including suggestions for reducing this burden, to FAR Secretariat (VRS), Office of Federal Acquisition and Regulatory Policy, GSA, Washington, DC 20405; and to the Office of Management and Budget, Paperwork Reduction Project (9000-0011), Washington, DC 20503.

SECTION I - RECOMMENDATION

1. PROSPECTIVE CONTRACTOR'S ACCOUNTING SYSTEM IS ACCEPTABLE FOR AWARD OF PROSPCTIVE CONTRACT

☐ YES   ☐ NO *(Explain in 2. NARRATIVE)*

☐ YES, WITH A RECOMMENDATION THAT A FOLLOW ON ACCOUNTING SYSTEM REVIEW BE PERFORMED AFTER CONTRACT AWARD *(Explain in 2. NARRATIVE)*

2. NARRATIVE *(Clarification of deficiencies, and other pertinent comments,. If additional space is required, continue on plain sheets of paper.)*

IF CONTINUATION SHEETS ATTACHED - MARK HERE ☐

	a. SIGNATURE AND OFFICE *(Include typed or printed name)*	b. TELEPHONE NO. *(include area code)*	c. DATE SIGNED
3. SURVEY MADE BY			
4. SURVEY REVIEWING OFFICIAL	a. SIGNATURE AND OFFICE *(Include typed or printed name)*	b. TELEPHONE NO. *(include area code)*	c. DATE REVIEWED

AUTHORIZED FOR LOCAL REPRODUCTION
Previous edition usable

STANDARD FORM **1408** (REV. 9-88)
Prescribed by GSA
FAR (48 CFR) 53.209-1(f)

Standard Form 1408 (Back)

SECTION II - EVALUATION CHECKLIST			
MARK "X" IN THE APPROPRIATE COLUMN *(Explain any deficiencies in SECTION I NARRATIVE)*	YES	NO	NOT APPLIC-CABLE
1. EXCEPT AS STATED IN SECTION I NARRATIVE, IS THE ACCOUNTING SYSTEM IN ACCORD WITH GENERALLY ACCEPTED ACCOUNTING PRINCIPLES APPLICABLE IN THE CIRCUMSTANCES?			
2. ACCOUNTING SYSTEM PROVIDES FOR:			
a. Proper segregation of direct costs from indirect costs.			
b. Identification and accumulation of direct costs by contract.			
c. A logical and consistent method for the allocation of indirect costs to intermediate and final cost objectives. (A contract is a final cost objective.)			
d. Accumlation of costs under general ledger control.			
e. A timekeeping system that identifies employees' labor by intermediate or final cost objectives.			
f. A labor distribution system that charges direct and indirect labor to the appropriate cost objectives.			
g. Interim (at least monthly) determination of costs charged to a contract through routine posting of books of account.			
h. Exclusion from costs charged to government contracts of amounts which are not allowable in terms of FAR 31, Contract Cost Principles and Procedures, or other contract provisions.			
i. Identification of costs by contract line item and by units (as if each unit or line item were a separate contract) if required by the proposed contract.			
j. Segregation of preproduction costs from production costs.			
3. ACCOUNTING SYSTEM PROVIDES FINANCIAL INFORMATION:			
a. Required by contract clauses concerning limitation of cost (FAR 52.232-20 and 21) or limitation on payments (FAR 52.216-16).			
b. Required to support requests for progress payments.			
4. IS THE ACCOUNTING SYSTEM DESIGNED, AND ARE THE RECORDS MAINTAINED IN SUCH A MANNER THAT ADEQUATE, RELIABLE DATA ARE DEVELOPED FOR USE IN PRICING FOLLOW-ON ACQUISITONS?			
5. IS THE ACCOUNTING SYSTEM CURRENTLY IN FULL OPERATION? (If not, describe in Section I Narrative which portions are (1) in operation, (2) set up, but not yet in operation, (3) anticipated, or (4) nonexistent.)			

GSA FORM 1408 (REV. 9-88) BACK

Standard Form 1409

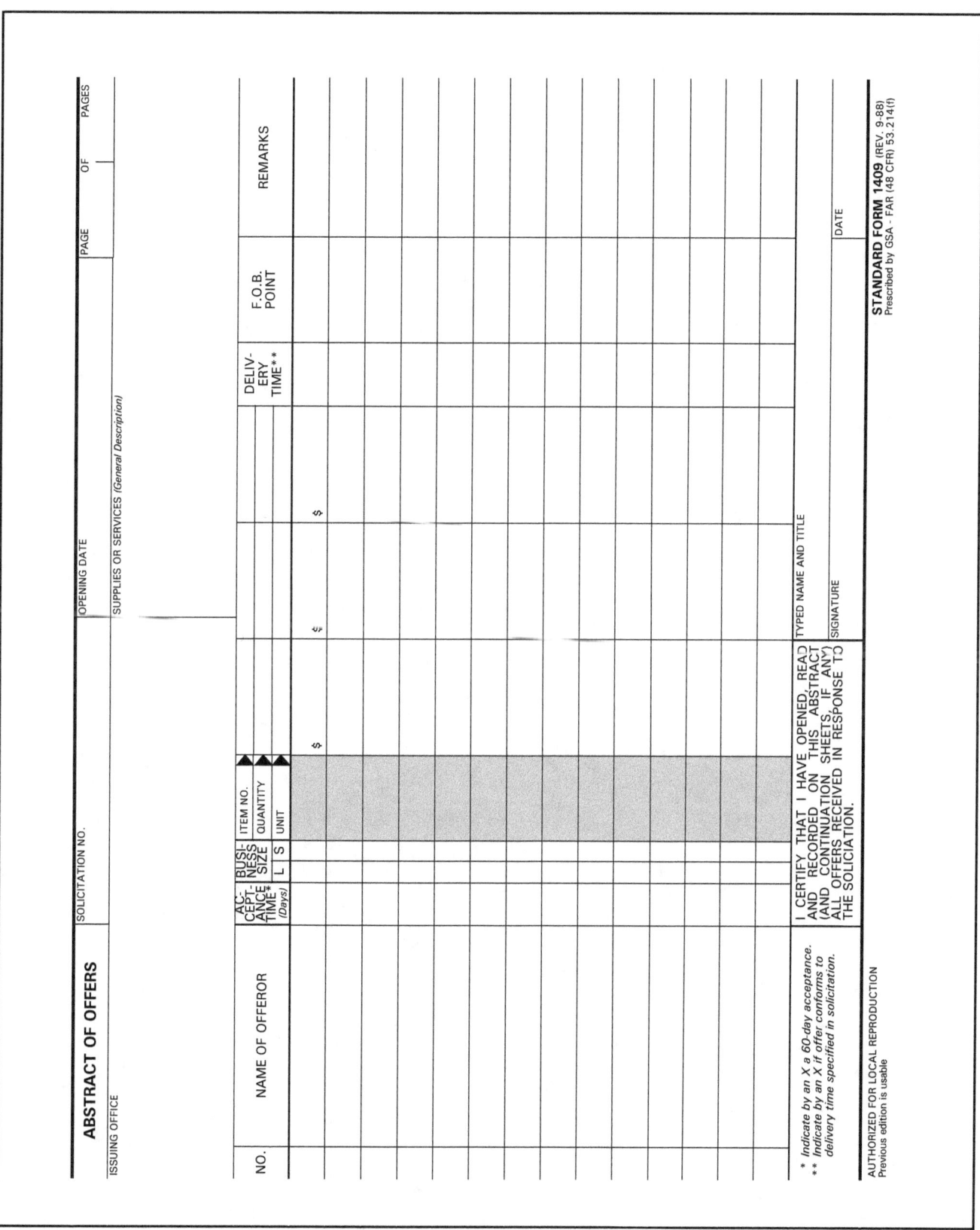

Standard Form 1410

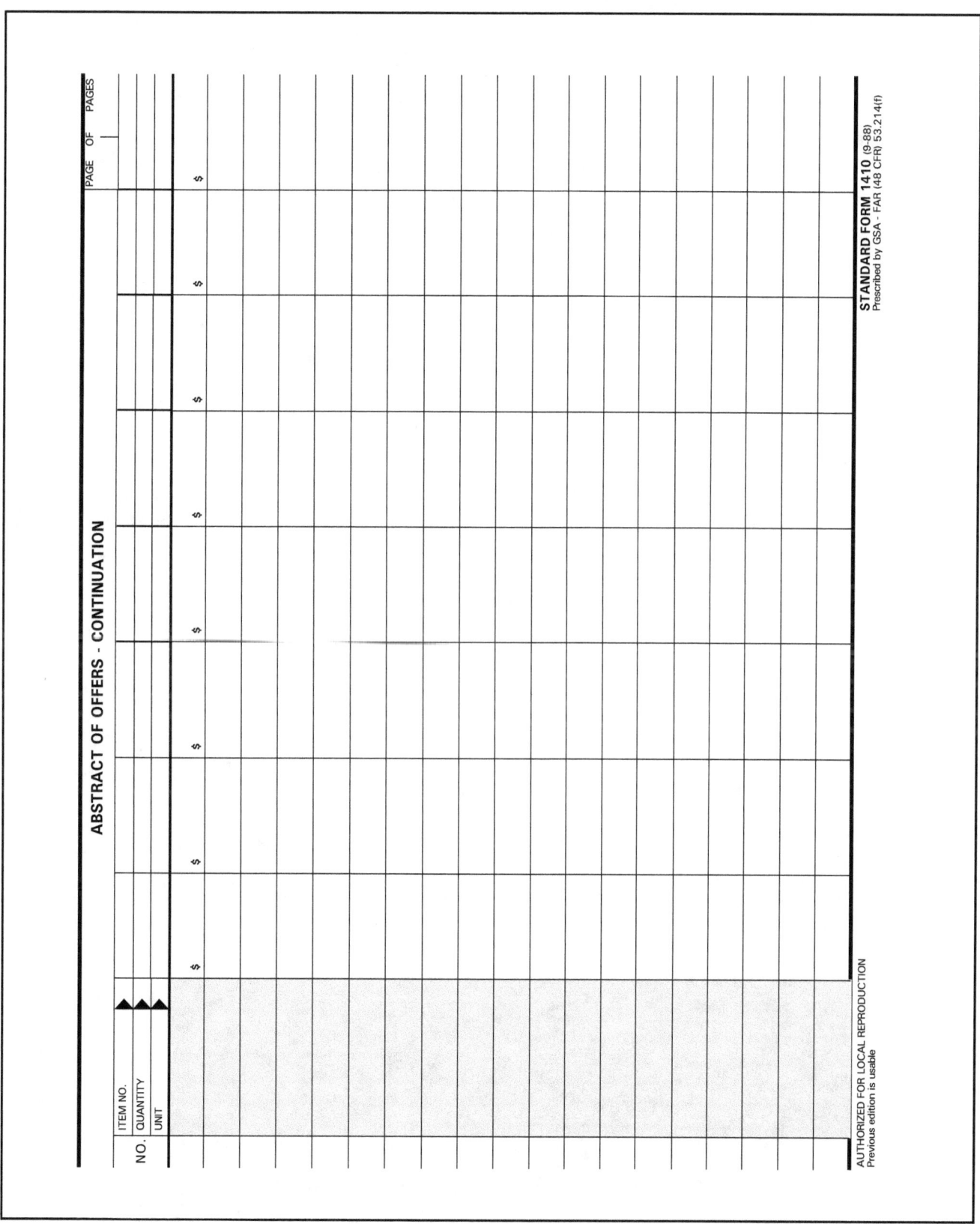

Standard Form 1413

STATEMENT AND ACKNOWLEDGMENT

OMB No.: 9000-0014
Expires: 6/30/2014

PAPERWORK REDUCTION ACT STATEMENT: Public reporting burden for this collection of information is estimated to average .05 hours per response, including the time for reviewing instructions, searching existing data sources, gathering and maintaining the data needed, and completing and reviewing the collection of information. Send comments regarding this burden estimate or any other aspects of this collection of information, including suggestions for reducing this burden, to U.S. General Services Administration, Regulatory Secretariat (MVCB)/IC 9000-0014, Office of Governmentwide Acquisition Policy, 1800 F Street, NW, Washington, DC 20405.

PART I - STATEMENT OF PRIME CONTRACTOR

1. PRIME CONTRACT NO.
2. DATE SUBCONTRACT AWARDED
3. SUBCONTRACT NUMBER

4. PRIME CONTRACTOR
a. NAME
b. STREET ADDRESS
c. CITY
d. STATE
e. ZIP CODE

5. SUBCONTRACTOR
a. NAME
b. STREET ADDRESS
c. CITY
d. STATE
e. ZIP CODE

6. The prime contract ☐ does, ☐ does not contain the clause entitled "Contract Work Hours and Safety Standards Act -- Overtime Compensation."

7. The prime contractor states that under the contract shown in Item 1, a subcontract was awarded on the date shown in Item 2 to the subcontractor identified in item 5 by the following firm:

a. NAME OF AWARDING FIRM

b. DESCRIPTION OF WORK BY SUBCONTRACTOR

8. PROJECT
9. LOCATION
10a. NAME OF PERSON SIGNING
10b. TITLE OF PERSON SIGNING
11. BY (Signature)
12. DATE SIGNED

PART II - ACKNOWLEDGMENT OF SUBCONTRACTOR

13. The subcontractor acknowledges that the following clauses of the contract shown in Item 1 are included in this subcontract:

- Contract Work Hours and Safety Standards Act - Overtime Compensation (If included in prime contract see Block 6)
- Payrolls and Basic Records
- Withholding of Funds
- Disputes Concerning Labor Standards
- Compliance with Construction Wage Rate Requirements and Related Regulations
- Construction Wage Rate Requirements
- Apprentices and Trainees
- Compliance with Copeland Act Requirements
- Subcontracts (Labor Standards)
- Contract Termination - Debarment
- Certification of Eligibility

14. NAME(S) OF ANY INTERMEDIATE SUBCONTRACTORS, IF ANY

A
B
C
D

15a. NAME OF PERSON SIGNING
15b. TITLE OF PERSON SIGNING
16. BY (Signature)
17. DATE SIGNED

AUTHORIZED FOR LOCAL REPRODUCTION
PREVIOUS EDITION IS NOT USABLE

STANDARD FORM 1413 (REV. 4/2013)
Prescribed by GSA/FAR (48 CFR) 53.222(e)

PART 53.3—ILLUSTRATION OF FORMS 53.301-1414

Standard Form 1414

CONSENT OF SURETY	1. CONTRACT NUMBER	2. MODIFICATION NUMBER	3. DATED

The Surety (Co-Sureties) consents (consent) to the foregoing contract modification and agrees (agree) that its (their) bond or bonds shall apply and extend to the contract as modified or amended.

4. INDIVIDUAL PRINCIPAL	a. NAME OF PRINCIPAL			c. SIGNATURE	*(Affix Seal)*
	b. BUSINESS ADDRESS			d. TYPED NAME	
	STREET ADDRESS			e. TYPED TITLE	
	CITY	STATE	ZIP CODE	f. DATE THIS CONSENT EXECUTED	

5. CORPORATE PRINCIPAL	a. CORPORATE NAME			c. PERSON EXECUTING CONSENT *(Signature)*	*(Affix Seal)*
	b. BUSINESS ADDRESS			d. TYPED NAME	
	STREET ADDRESS			e. TYPED TITLE	
	CITY	STATE	ZIP CODE	f. DATE THIS CONSENT EXECUTED	

6. CORPORATE/INDIVIDUAL SURETY (CO-SURETIES)

The Principal or authorized representative shall execute this consent of surety with the modification to which it pertains. If the rpresentative (e.g., attorney-in-fact) that signs the consent is not a member of the partnership, or joint venture, or an officer of the corporation involved, a Power-of-Attorney or a Certificate of Corporate Principal must accompany the consent.

A	a. CORPORATE/INDIVIDUAL SURETY'S NAME			c. PERSON EXECUTING CONSENT *(Signature)*	*(Affix Seal)*
	b. BUSINESS ADDRESS			d. TYPED NAME	
	STREET ADDRESS			e. TYPED TITLE	
	CITY	STATE	ZIP CODE	f. DATE THIS CONSENT EXECUTED	

B	a. CORPORATE/INDIVIDUAL SURETY'S NAME			c. PERSON EXECUTING CONSENT *(Signature)*	*(Affix Seal)*
	b. BUSINESS ADDRESS			d. TYPED NAME	
	STREET ADDRESS			e. TYPED TITLE	
	CITY	STATE	ZIP CODE	f. DATE THIS CONSENT EXECUTED	

C	a. CORPORATE/INDIVIDUAL SURETY'S NAME			c. PERSON EXECUTING CONSENT *(Signature)*	*(Affix Seal)*
	b. BUSINESS ADDRESS			d. TYPED NAME	
	STREET ADDRESS			e. TYPED TITLE	
	CITY	STATE	ZIP CODE	f. DATE THIS CONSENT EXECUTED	

(Add similar signature blocks on the back of this form if necessary for additional co-Sureties)

AUTHORIZED FOR LOCAL REPRODUCTION
Previous edition is usable

STANDARD FORM 1414 (REV. 5-97)
Prescribed by GSA - FAR (48 CFR) 53.228(k)

Standard Form 1415

CONSENT OF SURETY AND INCREASE OF PENALTY

	1. CONTRACT NUMBER	2. MODIFICATION NUMBER	3. DATED

4. The surety (co-sureties) consents (consent) to the foregoing contract modification and agrees (agree) that its (their) bond or bonds shall apply and extend to the contract as modified or amended. The principal and surety (co-sureties) further agree that on or after the execution of this consent, the penalty of the performance bond or bonds increased by _____ dollars ($_____) and the penalty of the payment bond or bonds is increased by _____ dollars ($_____). However, the increase of the liability of each co-surety resulting from this consent shall not exceed the sums shown below.

5. NAME OF SURETY(IES)	6. INCREASE IN LIABILITY LIMIT UNDER	7. INCREASE IN LIABILITY LIMIT UNDER
A.	$	$
B.	$	$
C.	$	$

8. INDIVIDUAL PRINCIPAL
- A. BUSINESS ADDRESS
- B. SIGNATURE
- C. TYPED NAME AND TITLE
- D. DATE THIS CONSENT EXECUTED
- *(Affix Seal)*

9. CORPORATE PRINCIPAL
- A. CORPORATE NAME AND BUSINESS ADDRESS
- B. PERSON EXECUTING CONSENT *(Signature)* BY
- C. TYPED NAME AND TITLE
- D. DATE THIS CONSENT EXECUTED
- *(Affix Corporate Seal)*

The Principal or authorized representative shall execute this Consent of Surety with the modification to which it pertains. If the representative (e.g., attorney-in-fact) that signs the consent is not a member of the partnership, or joint venture, or an officer of the corporation involved, a Power-of-Attorney or a Certificate of Corporate Principal must accompany the consent.

10. CORPORATE/INDIVIDUAL SURETY (CO-SURETIES)

A
- A. CORPORATE/INDIVIDUAL SURETY'S NAME AND ADDRESS
- B. PERSON EXECUTING CONSENT *(Signature)* BY
- C. TYPED NAME AND TITLE
- F. DATE THIS CONSENT EXECUTED
- *(Affix Corporate Seal)*

B
- A. CORPORATE/INDIVIDUAL SURETY'S NAME
- B. PERSON EXECUTING CONSENT *(Signature)* BY
- C. TYPED NAME AND TITLE
- D. DATE THIS CONSENT EXECUTED
- *(Affix Corporate Seal)*

C
- A. CORPORATE/INDIVIDUAL SURETY'S NAME
- B. PERSON EXECUTING CONSENT *(Signature)* BY
- C. TYPED NAME AND TITLE
- D. DATE THIS CONSENT EXECUTED
- *(Affix Corporate Seal)*

Add similar signature blocks on the back of this form if necessary for additional co-sureties.

AUTHORIZED FOR LOCAL REPRODUCTION
Previous edition is usable

STANDARD FORM 1415 (REV. 7-1993)
Prescribed by GSA-FAR (48 CFR) 53.228(l)

Standard Form 1416

PAYMENT BOND FOR OTHER THAN CONSTRUCTION CONTRACTS
(See instructions on reverse)

DATE BOND EXECUTED (Must not be later than bid opening date)

OMB NO.: 9000-0045

Public reporting burden for this collection of information is estimated to average 25 minutes per response, including the time for reviewing instructions, searching existing data sources, gathering and maintaining the data needed, and completing and reviewing the collection of information. Send comments regarding this burden estimate or any other aspect of this collection of information, including suggestions for reducing this burden, to the FAR Secretariat (MVR), Federal Acquisition Policy Division, GSA, Washington, DC 20405.

PRINCIPAL (Legal name and business address)

TYPE OF ORGANIZATION ("X" one)
☐ INDIVIDUAL   ☐ PARTNERSHIP
☐ JOINT VENTURE   ☐ CORPORATION

STATE OF INCORPORATION

SURETY(IES) (Name(s) and business address(es)) (Include ZIP code)

PENAL SUM OF BOND
MILLION(S)	THOUSAND(S)	HUNDRED(S)	CENTS

CONTRACT DATE   CONTRACT NO.

We, the Principal and Surety(ies) are firmly bound to the United States of America (hereinafter called the Government) in the above penal sum. For payment of the penal sum, we bind ourselves, our heirs, executors, administrators, and successors, jointly and severally. However, where the Sureties are corporations acting as co-sureties, we, the Sureties, bind ourselves in such sum "jointly and severally" as well as "severally" only for the purpose of allowing a joint action or actions against any or all of us. For all other purposes, each Surety binds itself, jointly and severally with the Principal, for the payment of the sum shown opposite the name of the Surety. If no limit of liability is indicated, the limit of liability is the full amount of the penal sum.

CONDITIONS:

The Principal has entered into the contract identified above.

THEREFORE:

(a) The above obligation is void if the Principal promptly makes payment to all persons (claimants) having a contract relationship with the Principal or a subcontractor of the Principal for furnishing labor, material or both in the prosecution of the work provided for in the contract identified above and any duly authorized modifications thereof. Notice of those modifications to the Surety(ies) are waived.

(b) The above obligation shall remain in full force if the Principal does not promptly make payments to all persons (claimants) having a contract relationship with the principal or a subcontractor of the Principal for furnishing labor, material or both in the prosecution of the contract identified above. In these cases, persons not paid in full before the expiration of ninety (90) days after the date of which the last labor was performed or material furnishing, have a direct right of action against the principal and Surety(ies) on this bond for the sum or sums justly due. The claimant, however, may not bring a suit or any action -

(1) Unless claimant, other than one having a direct contract with the Principal, had given written notice to the Principal within ninety (90) days after the claimant did or performed the last of the work or labor, or furnished or supplied the last of the materials for which the claim is made. The notice is to state with substantial accuracy the amount claimed and the name of the party to whom the materials were furnished or supplied, or for whom the work or labor was done or performed. Such notice shall be served by mailing the same by registered or certified mail, postage prepaid, in an envelope addressed to the Principal at any place where an office is regularly maintained for the transaction of business, or served in any manner in which legal process is served in the state in which the contract is being performed, save that such service need not be made by a public officer.

(2) After the expiration one (1) year following the date on which claimant did or performed the last of the work or labor, or furnished or suppled the last of the materials for which the suit is brought.

(3) Other than in the United States District court for the district in which the the contract, or any part thereof, was performed and executed, and not elsewhere.

WITNESS:

The Principal and Surety(ies) executed this bid bond and affixed their seals on the above date.

AUTHORIZED FOR LOCAL REPRODUCTION
Previous edition is usable

STANDARD FORM 1416 (REV. 10-98)
Prescribed by GSA - FAR (48 CFR) 53.228(m)

Standard Form 1416 (Back)

	PRINCIPAL			
SIGNATURE(S)	1. (Seal)	2. (Seal)	3. (Seal)	Corporate Seal
NAME(S) & TITLE(S) (Typed)	1.	2.	3.	

	INDIVIDUAL SURETY(IES)	
SIGNATURE(S)	1. (Seal)	2. (Seal)
NAME(S) & TITLE(S) (Typed)	1.	2.

	CORPORATE SURETY(IES)			
SURETY A NAME & ADDRESS		STATE OF INC.	LIABILITY LIMIT $	Corporate Seal
SIGNATURE(S)	1.	2.		
NAME(S) & TITLE(S) (Typed)	1.	2.		
SURETY B NAME & ADDRESS		STATE OF INC.	LIABILITY LIMIT $	Corporate Seal
SIGNATURE(S)	1.	2.		
NAME(S) & TITLE(S) (Typed)	1.	2.		

INSTRUCTIONS

1. This form is authorized for use when payment bonds are required under FAR (48 CFR) 28.103-3, i.e., payment bonds for other than construction contracts. Any deviation from this form will require the written approval of the Administrator of General Services.

2. Insert the full legal name and business address of the Principal in the space designated "Principal" on the face of the form. An authorized person shall sign the bond. Any person signing in a representative capacity (e.g., an attorney-in-fact) must furnish evidence of authority if that representative is not a member of the firm, partnership, or joint venture, or an officer of the corporation involved.

3. (a) Corporations executing the bond as sureties must appear on the Department of the Treasury's list of approved sureties and must act within the limitation listed therein. Where more than one corporate surety is involved, their names and addresses shall appear in the spaces (Surety A, Surety B, etc.) headed "CORPORATE SURETY(IES)." In the space designed "SURETY(IES)" on the face of the form, insert only the letter identification of the sureties.

(b) Where individual Sureties are involved, a completed Affidavit of Individual Surety (Standard Form 28), for each individual surety, shall accompany the bond. The Government may require the surety to furnish additional substantiating information concerning its financial capability.

4. Corporations executing the bond shall affix their corporate seals. Individuals shall execute the bond opposite the word "Corporate Seal"; and shall affix an adhesive seal if executed in Maine, New Hampshire, or any other jurisdiction requiring adhesive seals.

5. Type the name and title of each person signing this bond in the space provided.

STANDARD FORM 1416 (REV. 10-98) BACK

PART 53.3—ILLUSTRATION OF FORMS

53.301-1418

Standard Form 1418

PERFORMANCE BOND FOR OTHER THAN CONSTRUCTION CONTRACTS (See instructions on reverse)	DATE BOND EXECUTED *(Must be same or later than date of contract)*	OMB No.: **9000-0045**

Public reporting burden for this collection of information is estimated to average 25 minutes per response, including the time for reviewing instructions, searching existing data sources, gathering and maintaining the data needed, and completing and reviewing the collection of information. Send comments regarding this burden estimate or any other aspect of this collection of information, including suggestions for reducing this burden, to the FAR Secretariat (MVR), Federal Acquisition Policy Division, GSA, Washington, DC 20405

PRINCIPAL *(Legal name and business address)*	TYPE OF ORGANIZATION *("X" one)*
	☐ INDIVIDUAL ☐ PARTNERSHIP
	☐ JOINT VENTURE ☐ CORPORATION
	STATE OF INCORPORATION

SURETY(IES) *(Name(s) and business address(es)*	PENAL SUM OF BOND			
	MILLION(S)	THOUSAND(S)	HUNDRED(S)	CENTS
	CONTRACT DATE		CONTRACT NO.	
	OPTION DATE		OPTION NO.	

OBLIGATION:

We, the Principal and Surety(ies), are firmly bound to the United States of America (hereinafter called the Government) in the above penal sum. For payment of the penal sum, we bind ourselves, our heirs, executors, administrators, and successors, jointly and severally. However, where the Sureties are corporations acting as co-sureties, we, the Sureties, bind ourselves in such sum "jointly and severally" as well as "severally" only for the purpose of allowing a joint action or actions against any or all of us. For all other purposes, each Surety binds itself, jointly and severally with the Principal, for the payment of the sum shown opposite the name of the Surety. If no limit of liability is indicated, the limit of liability is the full amount of the penal sum.

CONDITIONS:

The Principal has entered into the contract identified above.

THEREFORE:

The above obligation is void if the Principal: (1) Performs and fulfills all the undertakings, covenants, terms, conditions, and agreements of the contract during either the base term or an optional term of the contract and any extensions thereof that are granted by the Government, with or without notice to the Surety(ies), and during the life of any guaranty required under the contract, and (2) performs and fulfills all the undertakings, covenants, terms, conditions, and agreements of any and all duly authorized modifications of the contract that hereafter are made. Notice of those modifications to the Surety(ies) is waived.

The guaranty for a base term covers the initial period of performance of the contract and any extensions thereof excluding any options. The guaranty for an option term covers the period of performance for the option being exercised and any extensions thereof.

The failure of a surety to renew a bond for any option term shall not result in a default of any bond previously furnished covering any base or option term.

WITNESS:

The Principal and Surety(ies) executed this performance bond and affixed their seals on the above date.

PRINCIPAL		
SIGNATURE(S)	1. (Seal)	2. (Seal)
NAME(S) & TITLE(S) *(Typed)*	1.	2.
		Corporate Seal

INDIVIDUAL SURETY(IES)		
SIGNATURE(S)	1. (Seal)	2. (Seal)
NAME(S) *(Typed)*	1.	2.

CORPORATE SURETY(IES)				
SURETY A	NAME & ADDRESS		STATE OF INC.	LIABILITY LIMIT $
	SIGNATURE(S)	1.	2.	Corporate Seal
	NAME(S) & TITLE(S) *(Typed)*	1.	2.	

AUTHORIZED FOR LOCAL REPRODUCTION
Previous edition not usable

STANDARD FORM 1418 (REV. 2-99)
Prescribed by GSA-FAR (48 CFR) 53.228(b)

Standard Form 1418 (Back)

			STATE OF INC.	LIABILITY LIMIT $	
SURETY B	NAME & ADDRESS				Corporate Seal
	SIGNATURE(S)	1.	2.		
	NAME(S) & TITLE(S) (Typed)	1.	2.		
SURETY C	NAME & ADDRESS		STATE OF INC.	LIABILITY LIMIT $	Corporate Seal
	SIGNATURE(S)	1.	2.		
	NAME(S) & TITLE(S) (Typed)	1.	2.		
SURETY D	NAME & ADDRESS		STATE OF INC.	LIABILITY LIMIT $	Corporate Seal
	SIGNATURE(S)	1.	2.		
	NAME(S) & TITLE(S) (Typed)	1.	2.		
SURETY E	NAME & ADDRESS		STATE OF INC.	LIABILITY LIMIT $	Corporate Seal
	SIGNATURE(S)	1.	2.		
	NAME(S) & TITLE(S) (Typed)	1.	2.		
SURETY F	NAME & ADDRESS		STATE OF INC.	LIABILITY LIMIT $	Corporate Seal
	SIGNATURE(S)	1.	2.		
	NAME(S) & TITLE(S) (Typed)	1.	2.		
SURETY G	NAME & ADDRESS		STATE OF INC.	LIABILITY LIMIT $	Corporate Seal
	SIGNATURE(S)	1.	2.		
	NAME(S) & TITLE(S) (Typed)	1.	2.		

BOND PREMIUM ▶	RATE PER THOUSAND ($)	TOTAL ($)

INSTRUCTIONS

1. This form is authorized for use in connection with Government contracts. Any deviation from this form will require the written approval of the Administrator of General Services.

2. Insert the full legal name and business address of the Principal in the space designated "Principal" on the face of the form. An authorized person shall sign the bond. Any person signing in a representative capacity (e.g., an attorney-in-fact) must furnish evidence of authority if that representative is not a member of the firm, partnership, or joint venture, or an officer of the coporation involved.

3. (a) Corporations executing the bond as sureties must appear on the Department of the Treasury's list of approved sureties and must act within the limitation listed therein. Where more than one corporate surety is involved, their names and addresses shall appear in the spaces (Surety A, Surety B, etc.) headed "CORPORATE SURETY(IES)." In the space designated "SURETY(IES)" on the face of the form, insert only the letter identification of the sureties.

(b) Where individual sureties are involved, a completed Affidavit of Individual Surety (Standard Form 28) for each individual surety, shall accompany the bond. The Government may require the surety to furnish additional substantiating information concerning their financial capability.

4. Corporations executing the bond shall affix their corporate seals. Individuals shall execute the bond opposite the word "Corporate Seal", and shall affix an adhesive seal if executed in Maine, New Hampshire, or any other jurisdiction requiring adhesive seals.

5. Type the name and title of each person signing this bond in the space provided.

6. Unless otherwise specified, the bond shall be submitted to the contracting office that awarded the contract.

Standard Form 1420

[Standard Form 1420 has been removed.]

Standard Form 1421

[Standard Form 1421 has been removed.]

PART 53.3—ILLUSTRATION OF FORMS　　　　　　　　　　　　　　　　　　　　　　　　　　53.301-1423

Standard Form 1423

INVENTORY VERIFICATION SURVEY (See FAR 45.602-1(b)(1))			DATE	
SECTION I - GENERAL				
1. FROM: *(Include ZIP Code)*		2. TO: *(Include ZIP Code)*		
3. CONTRACT NUMBER AND TYPE		4. CONTRACTOR/SUBCONTRACTOR		
5A. SCHEDULES OF INVENTORY TO BE INSPECTED AND VERIFIED			5B. PLANT CLEARANCE CASE NUMBER/DOCUMENT NUMBER	
REFERENCE NUMBER	PAGES START NO. / END NO.	AMOUNT ($)		

SECTION II - TECHNICAL VERIFICATION

	YES	NO		YES	NO
6. IS PROPERTY LISTED ON THE INVENTORY DISPOSAL SCHEDULES ON HAND AND IN THE QUANTITIES INDICATED?		*	12. ARE THE WEIGHTS OF THE ITEMS APPROXIMATELY CORRECT? IF WEIGHTS ARE NOT SHOWN, GIVE ESTIMATE OF WEIGHT BY BASIC MATERIAL CONTENT:		*
7. IS THE PROPERTY CORRECTLY DESCRIBED ON THE INVENTORY DISPOSAL SCHEDULES?		*			
8. IS THE PROPERTY SEGREGATED OR ADEQUATELY PROTECTED?		*	13. DO THE ITEMS APPEAR TO HAVE COMMERCIAL VALUE OTHER THAN SCRAP?	*	*
9. IS THE PROPERTY PROPERLY TAGGED?		*	14. DID CONTRACTOR MAKE REASONABLE EFFORTS TO RETURN THE PROPERTY?		*
10. ARE THE CONDITION CODES ACCURATE?		*	15. DO ANY ITEMS REQUIRE DEMILITARIZATION OR SPECIAL PROCESSING *(sensitive items)*?	*	
11. IS THE PROPERTY CLASSIFICATION CORRECTLY IDENTIFIED?		*	16. ARE COMMON ITEMS INCLUDED ON THE INVENTORY DISPOSAL SCHEDULE?	*	

SECTION III - TERMINATION INVENTORY

COMPLETION OF THIS SECTION ☐ IS ☐ IS NOT REQUIRED *(Requester, check one)*

	YES	NO		YES	NO
17. DID WORK STOP PROMPTLY UPON RECEIPT OF THE TERMINATION NOTICE? DATE OF NOTICE:		*	20. DOES THE INVENTORY INCLUDE REJECTS? IF YES, EXPLAIN SPECIFIC LINE ITEM ENTRIES. OBTAIN FROM CONTRACTOR ESTIMATED COST OF REWORKING REJECTS ON SPECIFIC LINE ITEM BASIS.	*	*
18a. DO THE QUANTITIES OF MATERIAL EXCEED THE AMOUNTS THAT WOULD HAVE BEEN REQUIRED TO COMPLETE THE TERMINATED PORTION OF THE CONTRACT?	*		21a. HAVE COMPLETED ARTICLES BEEN INSPECTED AS TO QUALITY AND CONFORMANCE TO SPECIFICATIONS?		
			b. DO THE COMPLETED ITEMS INSPECTED CONFORM TO CONTRACT SPECIFICATIONS?		*
b. CAN THE ITEMS OF TERMINATION INVENTORY BE USED ON THE CONTINUING PORTION OF THE CONTRACT?		*	c. DO OTHER THAN COMPLETED ITEMS CONFORM WITH TECHNICAL REQUIREMENTS OF THE CONTRACT OR ORDER?		*
19. ARE ALL ITEMS AND QUANTITIES ALLOCABLE TO THE TERMINATION PORTION OF THIS CONTRACT OR ORDER?		*	22. FOR WORK-IN-PROCESS, IS THE PERCENTAGE OF COMPLETION ACCURATE?		*

23. REQUESTING OFFICE REMARKS *(Where the answer to any question is placed in a block containing an asterisk (*) detailed comments of the verifier shall be included on the reverse of this form and identified by section and item number.)*

24. SIGNATURE OF REQUESTER

INVENTORY VERIFICATION
The above information is based on a physical verification of inventory listed under Item 5.

25. NAME AND TITLE	26. SIGNATURE OF VERIFIER	27. DATE

AUTHORIZED FOR LOCAL REPRODUCTION
Previous edition not usable

STANDARD FORM 1423 (REV. 5/2004)
Prescribed by GSA-FAR (48 CFR) 53.245(c)

Standard Form 1424

INVENTORY DISPOSAL REPORT
(See FAR 45.605)

PLANT CLEARANCE CASE NUMBER

TO: *(Include ZIP Code)*

FROM: *(Include ZIP Code)*

1. DATE PLANT CLEARANCE CASE OPENED
2. DATE PLANT CLEARANCE CASE CLOSED
3. NUMBER OF DAYS BETWEEN OPENING AND CLOSING
4. NAME AND ADDRESS OF CONTRACTOR/SUBCONTRACTOR *(Include ZIP Code)*
5. IF SUBCONTRACTOR, STATE NAME AND ADDRESS OF PRIME CONTRACTOR *(Include ZIP Code)*
6. LOCATION OF PROPERTY *(City and State)*
7. CONTRACT NUMBER
8. DOCKET NUMBER *(Termination only)*
9. SUBCONTRACT NUMBER
10. CONTRACTOR REFERENCE NUMBER

DISPOSITION OF PROPERTY

ITEM DESCRIPTION	LINE ITEMS	ACQUISITION COST	PROCEEDS
11. TOTAL INVENTORY AS SUBMITTED			
12. ADJUSTMENTS *(Pricing errors, shortages, etc.)*			
13. ADJUSTED INVENTORY *(Line 11 + or - Line 12)*			
14. PURCHASE OR RETENTION AT COST			
15. RETURN TO SUPPLIERS *(Net Proceeds)*			
16. REDISTRIBUTIONS			
A. WITHIN OWNING AGENCY			
B. OTHER AGENCIES			
TOTAL			
17. DONATIONS			
18. SALES			
19. SALES - SCRAP PROCEEDS TO OVERHEAD			
20.			
21.			
22. TOTAL PROCEEDS CREDIT *(Total Lines 14, 15, and 18)*			
23. ABANDONED			
24. DESTROYED/ABANDONED			
25. DESTROYED/SCRAPPED			
26. OTHER *(Explain in Item 28, Remarks)*			
27. TOTAL DISPOSITIONS			

28. REMARKS *(Identify contract number in which proceeds were applied, or disbursing office where proceeds were deposited)*

To the best of my knowledge, disposition of all property on this case has been effected in accordance with existing regulations, all property has been accounted for and all disposal credits properly applied.

CONTRACT ADMINISTRATION OFFICE *(Authorized signature and title)*

DATE

AUTHORIZED FOR LOCAL REPRODUCTION
Previous edition is not usable

STANDARD FORM 1424 (REV. 5/2004)
Prescribed by GSA - FAR (48 CFR) 53.245(d)

PART 53.3—ILLUSTRATION OF FORMS 53.301-1427

Standard Form 1427

INVENTORY SCHEDULE A - CONTINUATION SHEET (METALS IN MILL PRODUCT FORM)

TYPE: ☐ TERMINATION ☐ NONTERMINATION

DATE

OMB No.: 9000-0015
Expires: 04/30/92

Public reporting burden for this collection of information is estimated to average 1 hour per response, including the time for reviewing instructions, searching existing data sources, gathering and maintaining the data needed, and completing and reviewing the collection of information. Send comments regarding this burden estimate or any other aspect of this collection of information, including suggestions for reducing this burden, to the FAR Secretariat (VRS), Office of Federal Acquisition and Regulatory Policy, GSA, Washington, DC 20405; and to the Office of Management and Budget, Paperwork Reduction Project (9000-0015), Washington, DC 20503.

GOVERNMENT PRIME CONTRACT NO.   SUBCONTRACT OR P.O. NO.   REFERENCE NO.   PROPERTY CLASSIFICATION   PAGE NO.   NO. OF PAGES

FOR USE OF CONTRACTING AGENCY ONLY	ITEM NO. (a)	DESCRIPTION			DIMENSIONS				CONDITION (Use code) (c)	QUANTITY (d)	UNIT OF MEASURE (d1)	COST		CONTRACTOR'S OFFER (g)	FOR USE OF CONTRACTING AGENCY ONLY
		FORM, SHAPE, ROLLING TREATMENT (b)	HEAT TREATMENT, TEMPER, HARDNESS, FINISH, ETC. (b1)	SPECIFICATIONS, AND ALLOY OR OTHER VARIABLE DESIGNATION IN THE SPECIFICATION (b2)	THICKNESS (b3)	WIDTH (b4)	LENGTH (b5)					UNIT (e)	TOTAL (f)		
							FEET/METER	INCHES/CM							

AUTHORIZED FOR LOCAL REPRODUCTION
Previous edition is usable

STANDARD FORM 1427 (REV. 7-89)
Prescribed by GSA-FAR (48 CFR) 53.245(f)

53.3-125

Standard Form 1428

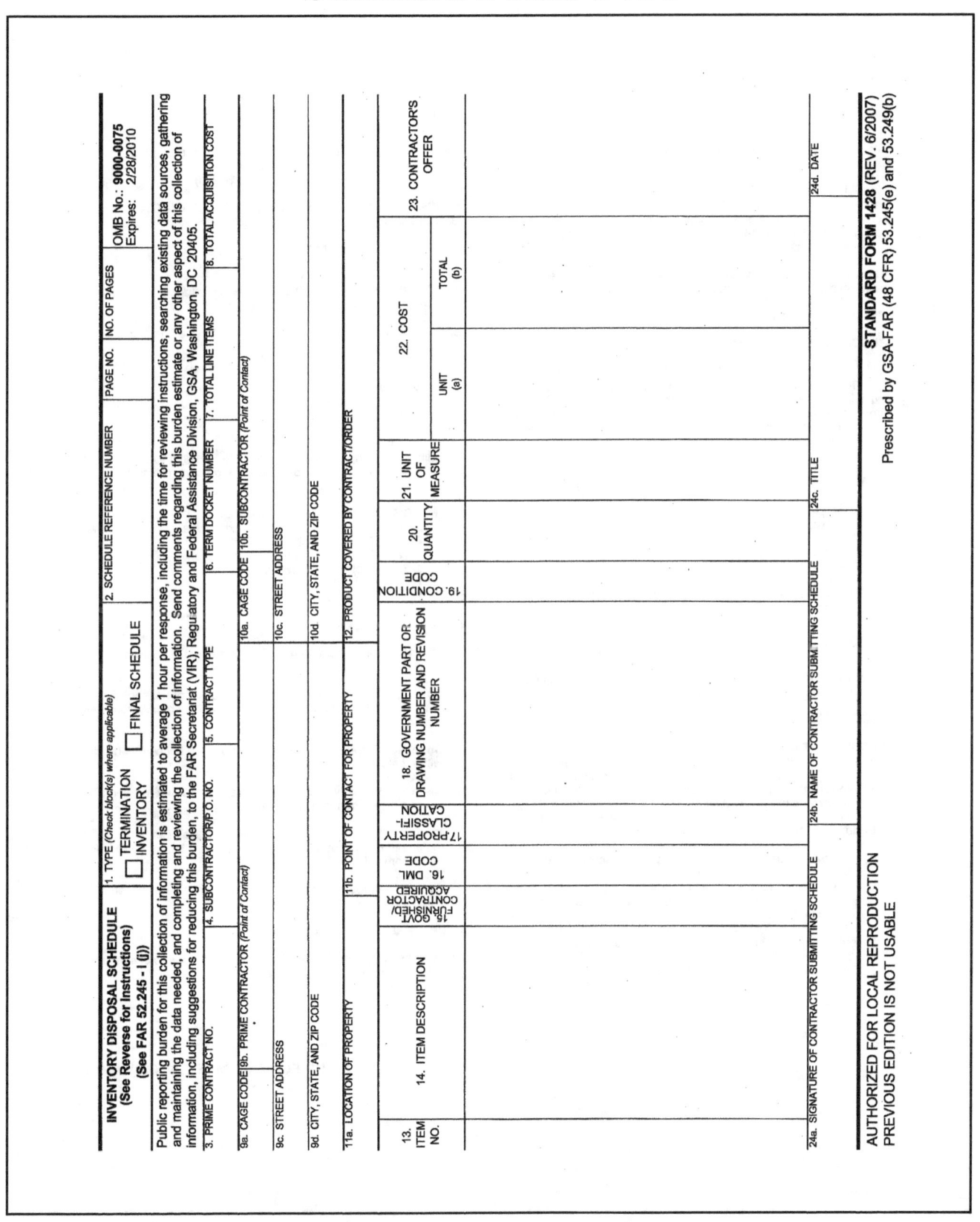

Standard Form 1428 (Back)

INSTRUCTIONS

The Contractor shall submit all schedules to the Plant Clearance Officer.

Manual submissions. Prepare a separate schedule for items in each property classification (block 17) and a separate schedule for scrap. Submit an original and 2 copies of each scrap schedule and continuation sheet (SF 1429). For other schedules, an original and 7 copies are required.

Electronic submissions. Group all items of the same property classification. Submit separate schedules for scrap.

General instructions.

BLOCKS 1, 2 & 4 - Self-explanatory.

BLOCK 3 - PRIME CONTRACT NO. *(For contract modifications and BOAs).* If the property applies solely to one contract modification indicate the modification number after the contract number. For task orders and orders under basic ordering agreements, enter the contract number or BOA number followed by the order number under which the property is accountable.

BLOCK 5 - CONTRACT TYPE. Use one of the following codes:

- J - Fixed-Price
- O - Other
- S - Cost-Reimbursement
- Y - Time-and-Material
- Z - Labor-Hour
- 9 - Task Order Contracts and Orders under Basic Ordering Agreements (BOAs)

BLOCKS 6 - 8 - Self-explanatory.

BLOCKS 9a and 10a - CAGE CODE. Enter the Commercial and Government Entity code when applicable.

BLOCKS 9b-d, 10b-d, and 11a-13 - Self-explanatory.

BLOCK 14 - ITEM DESCRIPTION. Describe each item in sufficient detail to permit the Government to determine its appropriate disposition. Scrap may be described as a lot including metal content, estimated weight and estimated acquisition cost. For all other property, provide the information required by FAR 52.245 - 1 (f)(1)(iii). List the national stock number (NSN) first. For the following, also provide:

Special tooling and special test equipment. Identify each part number with which the item is used.
Computers, components thereof, peripheral and related equipment. The manufacturer's name, model and serial number, and date manufactured.
Work in process. The estimated percentage of completion.
Precious metals. The metal type and estimated weight.
Hazardous material or property contaminated with hazardous material. The type of hazardous material.

Metals in mill product form. The form, shape, treatments, hardness, temper, specification (commercial or Government), and dimensions (thickness, width, and length).

BLOCK 15 - GOVERNMENT FURNISHED/CONTRACTOR ACQUIRED. Per line item, enter one of the following:

- GF - Government furnished
- CA - Contractor acquired

BLOCK 16 - DML CODE. *(Demilitarization code).* If applicable, enter the code specified in DoD 4160.21-M-1.

BLOCK 17 - PROPERTY CLASSIFICATION. Use one of the following classifications for each line item:

- EQ - Equipment
- M - Material
- STE - Special test equipment
- ST - Special tooling

In addition, when applicable, list one of the following sub classifications for each line item below the property classification:

- COM - Computers, peripherals, etc.
- AAE - Arms, ammunition and explosives
- PM - Precious metals
- HAZ - Hazardous materials
- ME - Metals in mill product form
- WIP - Work in process
- CL - Classified

BLOCK 18 - Self-Explanatory.

BLOCK 19 - CONDITION CODE. Assign one of the following codes to each item:

Code 1. Property which is in new condition or unused condition and can be used immediately without modifications or repairs.

Code 4. Property which shows some wear, but can be used without significant repair.

Code 7. Property which is unusable in its current condition but can be economically repaired.

Code X. Property which has value in excess of its basic material content, but repair or rehabilitation is impractical and/or uneconomical.

Code S. Property has no value except for its basic material content.

BLOCKS 20 - 22 - Self-explanatory.

BLOCK 23 - CONTRACTOR'S OFFER. The Contractor's offer to purchase the item if it survives screening.

STANDARD FORM 1428 (REV. 6/2007) BACK

Standard Form 1429

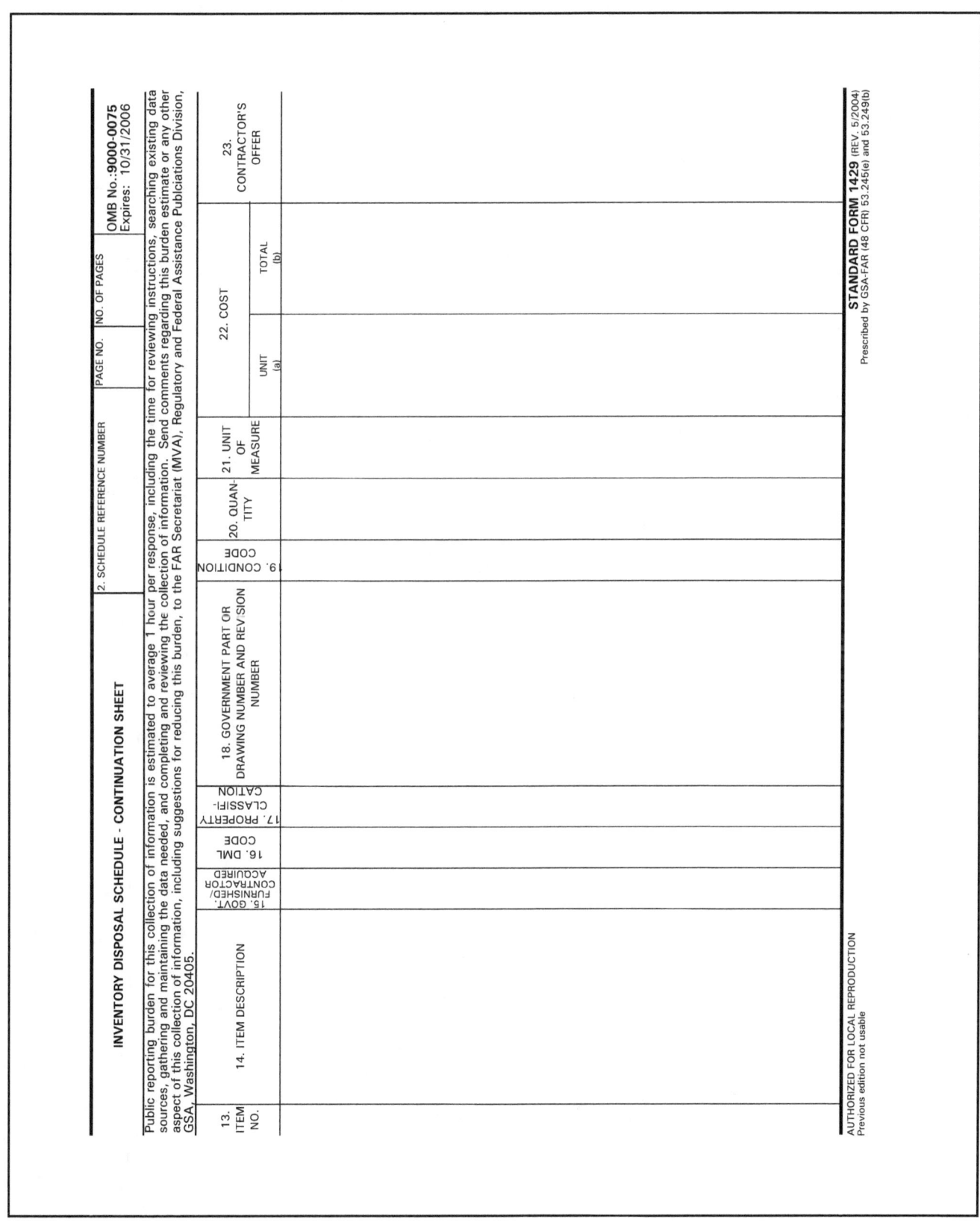

Standard Form 1435

SETTLEMENT PROPOSAL (INVENTORY BASIS)

OMB No.: 9000-0012
Expires: 05/31/98

Public reporting burden for this collection of information is estimated to average 2.5 hours per response, including the time for reviewing instructions, searching existing data sources, gathering and maintaining the data needed, and completing and reviewing the collection of information. Send comments regarding this burden estimate or any other aspect of this collection of information, including suggestions for reducing this burden, to the FAR Secretariat (MVR), Federal Acquisition Policy Division, GSA, Washington, DC 20405.

FOR USE BY A FIXED-PRICE PRIME CONTRACTOR OR FIXED-PRICE SUBCONTRACTOR

THIS PROPOSAL APPLIES TO (Check one)
☐ A PRIME CONTRACT WITH THE GOVERNMENT
☐ SUBCONTRACT OR PURCHASE ORDER

SUBCONTRACT OR PURCHASE ORDER NO(S).

COMPANY

STREET ADDRESS

CONTRACTOR WHO SENT NOTICE OF TERMINATION

NAME

ADDRESS (Include ZIP Code)

CITY AND STATE (Include ZIP Code)

NAME OF GOVERNMENT AGENCY

GOVERNMENT PRIME CONTRACT NO. | CONTRACTOR'S REFERENCE NO.

If moneys payable under the contract have been assigned, give the following:
NAME OF ASSIGNEE

EFFECTIVE DATE OF TERMINATION

ADDRESS (Include ZIP Code)

PROPOSAL NO.

CHECK ONE
☐ INTERIM ☐ FINAL

SF 1439, SCHEDULE OF ACCOUNTING INFORMATION ☐ IS ☐ IS NOT ATTACHED (If not, explain below)

SECTION I - STATUS OF CONTRACT OR ORDER AT EFFECTIVE DATE OF TERMINATION

PRODUCTS COVERED BY TERMINATED CONTRACT OR PURCHASE ORDER (a)		FINISHED			UNFINISHED OR NOT COMMENCED		TOTAL COVERED BY CONTRACT OR ORDER (g)
		PREVIOUSLY SHIPPED AND INVOICED (b)	ON HAND		TO BE COMPLETED (Partial termination only) (e)	NOT TO BE COMPLETED (f)	
			PAYMENT TO BE RECEIVED THROUGH INVOICING (c)	INCLUDED IN THIS PROPOSAL (d)			
	QUANTITY						
	$						
	QUANTITY						
	$						
	QUANTITY						
	$						

SECTION II - PROPOSED SETTLEMENT

NO.	ITEM (a)	(Use Columns (b) and (c) only where previous proposal has been filed)		TOTAL PROPOSED TO DATE (d)	FOR USE OF CONTRACTING AGENCY ONLY (e)
		TOTAL PREVIOUSLY PROPOSED (b)	INCREASE OR DECREASE BY THIS PROPOSAL (c)		
1	METALS				
2	RAW MATERIALS (other than metals)				
3	PURCHASED PARTS				
4	FINISHED COMPONENTS				
5	MISCELLANEOUS INVENTORY				
6	WORK-IN-PROCESS				
7	SPECIAL TOOLING AND SPECIAL TEST EQUIPMENT				
8	OTHER COSTS (from Schedule B)				
9	GENERAL AND ADMINISTRATIVE EXPENSES (from Schedule C)				
10	TOTAL (Items 1 to 9 inclusive)				
11	PROFIT (explain in Schedule D)				
12	SETTLEMENT EXPENSES (from Schedule E)				
13	TOTAL (Items 10 to 12 inclusive)				
14	SETTLEMENTS WITH SUBCONTRACTORS (from Schedule F)				
15	ACCEPTABLE FINISHED PRODUCT				
16	GROSS PROPOSED SETTLEMENT (Items 13 thru 15)				
17	DISPOSAL AND OTHER CREDITS (from Schedule G)				
18	NET PROPOSED SETTLEMENT (Item 16 less 17)				
19	ADVANCE, PROGRESS & PARTIAL PAYMENTS (from Schedule H)				
20	NET PAYMENT REQUESTED (Item 18 less 19)				

(When the space provided for any information is insufficient, continue on a separate sheet.)

AUTHORIZED FOR LOCAL REPRODUCTION
Previous edition is unusable

STANDARD FORM 1435 (REV. 9-97)
Prescribed by GSA - FAR (48 CFR) 53.249(a)(2)

Standard Form 1435 (Page 2)

SCHEDULE A - ANALYSIS OF INVENTORY COST *(Items 4 and 6)*

Furnish the following information (unless not reasonably available) for inventories of finished components and work-in-progress included in this proposal:

	TOTAL DIRECT LABOR	TOTAL DIRECT MATERIALS	TOTAL INDIRECT EXPENSES	TOTAL
FINISHED COMPONENTS				
WORK-IN-PROGRESS				

NOTE: Individual items of small amounts may be grouped into a single entry in Schedules B, C, D, and G.

SCHEDULE B - OTHER COSTS *(Item 8)*

ITEM	EXPLANATION	AMOUNT	FOR USE OF CONTRACTING AGENCY ONLY

SCHEDULE C - GENERAL AND ADMINISTRATIVE EXPENSES *(Item 9)*

DETAIL OF EXPENSES	AMOUNT	FOR USE OF CONTRACTING AGENCY ONLY

SCHEDULE D - PROFIT *(Item 11)*

EXPLANATION	AMOUNT	FOR USE OF CONTRACTING AGENCY ONLY

(Where the space provided for any information is insufficient, continue on a separate sheet.)

STANDARD FORM 1435 (REV. 9-97) **PAGE 2**

Standard Form 1435 (Page 3)

SCHEDULE E - SETTLEMENT EXPENSES (Item 12)

ITEM	EXPLANATION	AMOUNT	FOR USE OF CONTRACTING AGENCY ONLY

SCHEDULE F - SETTLEMENTS WITH IMMEDIATE SUBCONTRACTORS AND SUPPLIERS (Item 14)

NAME AND ADDRESS OF SUBCONTRACTOR	BRIEF DESCRIPTION OF PRODUCT CANCELED	AMOUNT OF SETTLEMENT	FOR USE OF CONTRACTING AGENCY ONLY

SCHEDULE G - DISPOSAL AND OTHER CREDITS (Item 17)

DESCRIPTION	AMOUNT	FOR USE OF CONTRACTING AGENCY ONLY

(If practicable, show separately amount of disposal credits applicable to acceptable finished product included in Item 15.)
(Where the space provided for any information is insufficient, continue on a separate sheet.)

STANDARD FORM 1435 (REV. 9-97) PAGE 3

Standard Form 1435 (Page 4)

SCHEDULE H - ADVANCE, PROGRESS AND PARTIAL PAYMENTS *(Item 19)*			
DATE	TYPE OF PAYMENT	AMOUNT	FOR USE OF CONTRACTING AGENCY ONLY

(Where the space provided for any information is insufficient, continue on a separate sheet.)

CERTIFICATE

This is to certify that the undersigned, individually, and as an authorized representative of the Contractor, has examined this termination settlement proposal and that, to the best knowledge and belief of the undersigned:

(a) AS TO THE CONTRACTOR'S OWN CHARGES. The proposed settlement (exclusive of charges set forth in Item 14) and supporting schedules and explanations have been prepared from the books of account and records of the Contractor in accordance with recognized commercial accounting practices; they include only those charges allocable to the terminated portion of this contract; they have been prepared with knowledge that they will, or may, be used directly or indirectly as the basis of settlement of a termination settlement proposal or claim against an agency of the United States; and the charges as stated are fair and reasonable.

(b) AS TO THE SUBCONTRACTORS' CHARGES. (1) The Contractor has examined, or caused to be examined, to an extent it considered adequate in the circumstances, the termination settlement proposals of its immediate subcontractors (exclusive of proposals filed against these immediate subcontractors by their subcontractors); (2) The settlements on account of immediate subcontractors own charges are fair and reasonable, the charges are allocable to the terminated portion of this contract, and the settlements were negotiated in good faith and are not more favorable to its immediate subcontractors than those that the Contractor would make if reimbursement by the Government were not involved; (3) The Contractor has received from all its immediate subcontractors appropriate certificates with respect to their termination settlement proposals, which certificates are substantially in the form of this certificate; and (4) The Contractor has no information leading it to doubt (i) the reasonableness of the settlements with more remote subcontractors or (ii) that the charges for them are allocable to this contract. Upon receipt by the Contractor of amounts covering settlements with its immediate subcontractors, the Contractor will pay or credit them promptly with the amounts so received, to the extent that it has not previously done so. The term "subcontractors," as used above, includes suppliers.

NOTE: The Contractor shall, under conditions stated in FAR 15.403, be required to submit a Certificate of Current Cost or Pricing Data (see FAR 15.406-2 and 15.408 Table 15-2).

NAME OF CONTRACTOR	BY *(Signature of authorized official)*	
	TITLE	DATE
NAME OF SUPERVISORY ACCOUNTING OFFICIAL	TITLE	

STANDARD FORM 1435 (REV. 9-97) PAGE 4

Standard Form 1436

SETTLEMENT PROPOSAL (TOTAL COST BASIS)

OMB No.: 9000-0012
Expires: 06/30/2004

Public reporting burden for this collection of information is estimated to average 2.5 hours per response, including the time for reviewing instructions, searching existing data sources, gathering and maintaining the data needed, and completing and reviewing the collection of information. Send comments regarding this burden estimate or any other aspect of this collection of information, including suggestions for reducing this burden, to the FAR Secretariat (MVA), Regulatory and Federal Assistance Publications Division, GSA, Washington, DC 20405.

FOR USE BY A FIXED-PRICE PRIME CONTRACTOR OR FIXED-PRICE SUBCONTRACTOR

THIS PROPOSAL APPLIES TO (Check one)
☐ A PRIME CONTRACT WITH THE GOVERNMENT
☐ SUBCONTRACT OR PURCHASE ORDER

COMPANY

SUBCONTRACT OR PURCHASE ORDER NO(S).

STREET ADDRESS

CONTRACTOR WHO SENT NOTICE OF TERMINATION
NAME

CITY AND STATE (Include ZIP Code)

ADDRESS (Include ZIP Code)

NAME OF GOVERNMENT AGENCY

GOVERNMENT PRIME CONTRACT NO.   CONTRACTOR'S REFERENCE NO.

If moneys payable under the contract have been assigned, give the following:
NAME OF ASSIGNEE

EFFECTIVE DATE OF TERMINATION

ADDRESS (Include ZIP Code)

PROPOSAL NO.

CHECK ONE
☐ INTERIM   ☐ FINAL

SF 1439, SCHEDULE OF ACCOUNTING INFORMATION   ☐ IS   ☐ IS NOT ATTACHED (If not, explain below)

SECTION I - STATUS OF CONTRACT OR ORDER AT EFFECTIVE DATE OF TERMINATION

PRODUCTS COVERED BY TERMINATED CONTRACT OR PURCHASE ORDER (a)		PREVIOUSLY SHIPPED AND INVOICED (b)	FINISHED ON HAND		UNFINISHED OR NOT COMMENCED		TOTAL COVERED BY CONTRACT OR ORDER (g)
			PAYMENT TO BE RECEIVED THROUGH INVOICING (c)	PAYMENT NOT TO BE RECEIVED THROUGH INVOICING (d)	SUBSEQUENTLY COMPLETED AND INVOICED* (e)	NOT TO BE COMPLETED (f)	
	QUANTITY						
	$						
	QUANTITY						
	$						
	QUANTITY						
	$						

SECTION II - PROPOSED SETTLEMENT

NO.	ITEM (a)	TOTAL PREVIOUSLY PROPOSED (b)	INCREASE OR DECREASE BY THIS PROPOSAL (c)	TOTAL PROPOSED TO DATE (d)	FOR USE OF CONTRACTING AGENCY ONLY (e)
1	DIRECT MATERIAL				
2	DIRECT LABOR				
3	INDIRECT FACTORY EXPENSE (from Schedule A)				
4	SPECIAL TOOLING AND SPECIAL TEST EQUIPMENT (SF 1428)				
5	OTHER COSTS (from Schedule B)				
6	GENERAL AND ADMINISTRATIVE EXPENSES (from Schedule C)				
7	TOTAL COSTS (Items 1 thru 6)				
8	PROFIT (Explain in Schedule D)				
9	TOTAL (Items 7 and 8)				
10	DEDUCT FINISHED PRODUCT INVOICED OR TO BE INVOICED*				
11	TOTAL (Item 9 less Item 10)				
12	SETTLEMENT EXPENSES (from Schedule E)				
13	TOTAL (Items 11 and 12)				
14	SETTLEMENTS WITH SUBCONTRACTORS (from Schedule F)				
15	GROSS PROPOSED SETTLEMENT (Items 13 thru 14)				
16	DISPOSAL AND OTHER CREDITS (from Schedule G)				
17	NET PROPOSED SETTLEMENT (Item 15 less 16)				
18	ADVANCE, PROGRESS & PARTIAL PAYMENTS (from Schedule H)				
19	NET PAYMENT REQUESTED (Item 17 less 18)				

*Column (e), Section I, should only be used in the event of a partial termination, in which the total cost reported in Section II should be accumulated to date of completion of the continued portion of the contract and the deduction for finished product (Item 10, Section II) should be the contract price of finished product in Column (b), (c), and (e), Section I.

NOTE: File inventory schedule (SF 1428) for allocable inventories on hand at date of termination (See 49.206).

(When the space provided for any information is insufficient, continue on a separate sheet.)

AUTHORIZED FOR LOCAL REPRODUCTION
Previous edition is unusable

STANDARD FORM 1436 (REV. 5/2004)
Prescribed by GSA FAR (48 CFR) 53.249(a)(3)

Standard Form 1436 (Page 2)

SCHEDULE A - INDIRECT FACTORY EXPENSE *(Item 3)*

DETAIL OF EXPENSES	METHOD OF ALLOCATION	AMOUNT	FOR USE OF CONTRACTING AGENCY ONLY

NOTE: Individual items of small amounts may be grouped into a single entry in Schedules B, C, D, E, and G.

SCHEDULE B - OTHER COSTS *(Item 5)*

ITEM	EXPLANATION	AMOUNT	FOR USE OF CONTRACTING AGENCY ONLY

SCHEDULE C - GENERAL AND ADMINISTRATIVE EXPENSES *(Item 6)*

DETAIL OF EXPENSES	METHOD OF ALLOCATION	AMOUNT	FOR USE OF CONTRACTING AGENCY ONLY

SCHEDULE D - PROFIT *(Item 8)*

EXPLANATION	AMOUNT	FOR USE OF CONTRACTING AGENCY ONLY

Standard Form 1436 (Page 3)

SCHEDULE E - SETTLEMENT EXPENSES (Item 12)

ITEM	EXPLANATION	AMOUNT	FOR USE OF CONTRACTING AGENCY ONLY

SCHEDULE F - SETTLEMENTS WITH IMMEDIATE SUBCONTRACTORS AND SUPPLIERS (Item 14)

NAME AND ADDRESS OF SUBCONTRACTOR	BRIEF DESCRIPTION OF PRODUCT CANCELED	AMOUNT OF SETTLEMENT	FOR USE OF CONTRACTING AGENCY ONLY

SCHEDULE G - DISPOSAL AND OTHER CREDITS (Item 16)

DESCRIPTION	AMOUNT	FOR USE OF CONTRACTING AGENCY ONLY

(If practicable, show separately amount of disposal credits applicable to acceptable finished product included on SF 1428.)

(Where the space provided for any information is insufficient, continue on a separate sheet.)

STANDARD FORM 1436 (REV. 5/2004) PAGE 3

Standard Form 1436 (Page 4)

	SCHEDULE H - ADVANCE, PROGRESS AND PARTIAL PAYMENTS *(Item 19)*		FOR USE OF CONTRACTING AGENCY ONLY
DATE	TYPE OF PAYMENT	AMOUNT	

(Where the space provided for any information is insufficient, continue on a separate sheet.)

CERTIFICATE

This is to certify that the undersigned, individually, and as an authorized representative of the Contractor, has examined this termination settlement proposal and that, to the best knowledge and belief of the undersigned:

(a) AS TO THE CONTRACTOR'S OWN CHARGES. The proposed settlement (exclusive of charges set forth in Item 14) and supporting schedules and explanations have been prepared from the books of account and records of the Contractor in accordance with recognized commercial accounting practices; they include only those charges allocable to the terminated portion of this contract; they have been prepared with knowledge that they will, or may, be used directly or indirectly as the basis of settlement of a termination settlement proposal or claim against an agency of the United States; and the charges as stated are fair and reasonable.

(b) AS TO THE SUBCONTRACTORS' CHARGES. (1) The Contractor has examined, or caused to be examined, to an extent it considered adequate in the circumstances, the termination settlement proposals of its immediate subcontractors (exclusive of proposals filed against these immediate subcontractors by their subcontractors); (2) The settlements on account of immediate subcontractors own charges are fair and reasonable, the charges are allocable to the terminated portion of this contract, and the settlements were negotiated in good faith and are not more favorable to its immediate subcontractors than those that the Contractor would make if reimbursement by the Government were not involved; (3) The Contractor has received from all its immediate subcontractors appropriate certificates with respect to their termination settlement proposals, which certificates are substantially in the form of this certificate; and (4) The Contractor has no information leading it to doubt (i) the reasonableness of the settlements with more remote subcontractors or (ii) that the charges for them are allocable to this contract. Upon receipt by the Contractor of amounts covering settlements with its immediate subcontractors, the Contractor will pay or credit them promptly with the amounts so received, to the extent that it has not previously done so. The term "subcontractors," as used above, includes suppliers.

NOTE: The Contractor shall, under conditions stated in FAR 15.403, be required to submit a Certificate of Current Cost or Pricing Data (see FAR 15.406-2 and 15.408 Table 15-2).

NAME OF CONTRACTOR	BY *(Signature of authorized official)*		
	TITLE		DATE
NAME OF SUPERVISORY ACCOUNTING OFFICIAL	TITLE		

STANDARD FORM 1436 (REV. 5/2004) PAGE 4

Standard Form 1437

SETTLEMENT PROPOSAL FOR COST-REIMBURSEMENT TYPE CONTRACTS

OMB No.: 9000-0012
Expires: 05/31/98

Public reporting burden for this collection of information is estimated to average 2.5 hours per response, including the time for reviewing instructions, searching existing data sources, gathering and maintaining the data needed, and completing and reviewing the collection of information. Send comments regarding this burden estimate or any other aspect of this collection of information, including suggestions for reducing this burden, to the FAR Secretariat (MVR), Federal Acquisition Policy Division, GSA, Washington, DC 20405.

To be used by prime contractors submitting settlement proposals on cost-reimbursement type contracts under Part 49 of the Federal Acquisition Regulation. Also suitable for use in connection with terminated cost-reimbursement type subcontracts.

COMPANY	PROPOSAL NUMBER	CHECK ONE ☐ PARTIAL ☐ FINAL
STREET ADDRESS	GOVERNMENT PRIME CONTRACT NO.	REFERENCE NO.
CITY AND STATE (Include ZIP Code)	EFFECTIVE DATE OF TERMINATION	

ITEM (a)	TOTAL PREVIOUSLY SUBMITTED (b)	INCREASE OR DECREASE BY THIS PROPOSAL (c)	TOTAL SUBMITTED TO DATE (d)
1. DIRECT MATERIAL	$	$	$
2. DIRECT LABOR			
3. INDIRECT FACTORY EXPENSE			
4. SPECIAL TOOLING AND SPECIAL TEST EQUIPMENT			
5. OTHER COSTS			
6. GENERAL AND ADMINISTRATIVE EXPENSE			
7. TOTAL COST (Items 1 thru 6)	$	$	$
8. FEE			
9. SETTLEMENT EXPENSES			
10. SETTLEMENTS WITH SUBCONTRACTORS			
11. GROSS PROPOSED SETTLEMENT (Items 7 thru 10)			
12. DISPOSAL AND OTHER CREDITS			
13. NET PROPOSED SETTLEMENT (Item 11 less 12)	$	$	$
14. PRIOR PAYMENTS TO CONTRACTOR	¢	$	$
15. NET PAYMENT REQUESTED (Item 13 less 14)	$	$	$

CERTIFICATE

This is to certify that the undersigned, individually, and as an authorized representative of the Contractor, has examined this termination settlement proposal and that, to the best knowledge and belief of the undersigned:

(a) AS TO THE CONTRACTOR'S OWN CHARGES. The proposed settlement (exclusive of charges set forth in Item 10) and supporting schedules and explanations have been prepared from the books of account and records of the Contractor in accordance with recognized commercial accounting practices; they include only those charges allocable to the terminated portion of this contract; they have been prepared with knowledge that they will, or may, be used directly or indirectly as the basis of settlement of a termination settlement proposal or claim against an agency of the United States; and the charges as stated are fair and reasonable.

(b) AS TO THE SUBCONTRACTORS' CHARGES. (1) The Contractor has examined, or caused to be examined, to an extent it considered adequate in the circumstances, the termination settlement proposals of its immediate subcontractors (exclusive of proposals filed against these immediate subcontractors by their subcontractors); (2) The settlements on account of immediate subcontractors' own charges are fair and reasonable, the charges are allocable to the terminated portion of this contract, and the settlements were negotiated in good faith and are not more favorable to its immediate subcontractors than those that the Contractor would make if reimbursement by the Government were not involved; (3) The Contractor has received from all its immediate subcontractors appropriate certificates with respect to their termination settlement proposals, which certificates are substantially in the form of this certificate; and (4) The Contractor has no information leading it to doubt (i) the reasonableness of the settlements with more remote subcontractors or (ii) that the charges for them are allocable to this contract. Upon receipt by the Contractor of amounts covering settlements with its immediate subcontractors, the Contractor will pay or credit them promptly with the amounts so received, to the extent that it has not previously done so. The term "subcontractors," as used above, includes suppliers.

NOTE: The Contractor shall, under conditions stated in FAR 15.403, be required to submit a Certificate of Current Cost or Pricing Data (see FAR 15.406-2 and 15.408 Table 15-2).

NAME OF CONTRACTOR	BY (Signature of authorized official)	
	TITLE	DATE
NAME OF SUPERVISORY ACCOUNTING OFFICIAL	TITLE	

AUTHORIZED FOR LOCAL REPRODUCTION
Previous edition is unusable

STANDARD FORM 1437 (REV. 9-97)
Prescribed by GSA - FAR (48 CFR) 53.249(a)(4)

PART 53.3—ILLUSTRATION OF FORMS   53.301-1438

Standard Form 1438

SETTLEMENT PROPOSAL (SHORT FORM)

OMB No.: 9000-0012
Expires: 06/30/2004

Public reporting burden for this collection of information is estimated to average 2.5 hours per response, including the time for reviewing instructions, searching existing data sources, gathering and maintaining the data needed, and completing and reviewing the collection of information. Send comments regarding this burden estimate or any other aspect of this collection of information, including suggestions for reducing this burden, to the FAR Secretariat (MVA), Regulatory and Federal Assistance Publications Division, GSA, Washington, DC 20405.

For Use by a Prime Contractor or Subcontractor in Settlement of a Fixed Price Terminated Contract When Total Charges Claimed Are Less Than $10,000.

THIS PROPOSAL APPLIES TO (Check one)
☐ A PRIME CONTRACT WITH THE GOVERNMENT
☐ SUBCONTRACT OR PURCHASE ORDER

SUBCONTRACT OR PURCHASE ORDER NO.(S)

COMPANY (Prime or Subcontractor)

STREET ADDRESS

CONTRACTOR WHO SENT NOTICE OF TERMINATION
NAME

ADDRESS (Include ZIP Code)

CITY AND STATE (Include ZIP code)

NAME OF GOVERNMENT AGENCY | GOVERNMENT PRIME CONTRACT NO.

If moneys payable under the contract have been assigned, give the following:
NAME OF ASSIGNEE

CONTRACTOR'S REFERENCE NO. | EFFECTIVE DATE OF TERMINATION

ADDRESS (Include ZIP Code)

SECTION I - STATUS OF CONTRACT OR ORDER AT EFFECTIVE DATE OF TERMINATION

PRODUCTS COVERED BY TERMINATED CONTRACT OR PURCHASE ORDER (a)		PREVIOUSLY SHIPPED AND INVOICED (b)	FINISHED ON HAND		UNFINISHED OR NOT COMMENCED		TOTAL COVERED BY CONTRACT OR ORDER (g)
			PAYMENT TO BE RECEIVED THROUGH INVOICING (c)	INCLUDED IN THIS PROPOSAL (d)	TO BE COMPLETED (Partial termination only) (e)	NOT TO BE COMPLETED (f)	
	QUANTITY						
	$						
	QUANTITY						
	$						
	QUANTITY						
	$						

SECTION II - PROPOSED SETTLEMENT

NO.	ITEM (Include only items allocable to the terminated portion of contract)	AMOUNT OF CHARGE ($)
1	CHARGE FOR ACCEPTABLE FINISHED PRODUCT NOT COVERED BY INVOICING (from SF 1428)	
2	CHARGE FOR WORK-IN-PROGRESS, RAW MATERIAL, ETC. ON HAND (from SF 1428)	
3	OTHER CHARGES INCLUDING PROFIT AND SETTLEMENT EXPENSES	
4	CHARGES FOR SETTLEMENT(S) WITH SUBCONTRACTORS	
5	GROSS PROPOSED SETTLEMENT (Sum of Items 1 thru 4)	
6	DISPOSAL AND OTHER CREDITS (from SF 1424, Item 27, Col. 3)	
7	NET PROPOSED SETTLEMENT (Item 5 less 6)	
8	ADVANCE, PROGRESS, AND PARTIAL PAYMENTS	
9	NET PAYMENT REQUESTED (Item 7 less 8)	

List your inventory on SF 1428 and attach a copy thereto. Retain for the applicable period specified in the prime contract all papers and records relating to this proposal for future examination.

GIVE A BRIEF EXPLANATION OF HOW YOU ARRIVED AT THE AMOUNTS SHOWN IN ITEMS 3, 4, 6, AND 7

I CERTIFY that the above proposed settlement includes only charges allocable to the terminated portion of the contract or purchase order, that the total charges (Item 5) and the disposal credits (Item 6) are fair and reasonable, and that this proposal has been prepared with knowledge that it will, or may, be used directly or indirectly as a basis for reimbursement under a settlement proposal(s) against agencies of the United States.

NAME OF YOUR COMPANY

BY (Signature of authorized official)

TITLE | DATE

(Where the space provided for any information is insufficient, continue on a separate sheet.)

AUTHORIZED FOR LOCAL REPRODUCTION
Previous edition is not usable

STANDARD FORM 1438 (REV. 5/2004)
Prescribed by GSA-FAR (48 CFR) 53.249(a)(5)

53.3-141

Standard Form 1438 (Back)

INSTRUCTIONS

1. This settlement proposal should be submitted to the contracting officer, if you are a prime contractor, or to your customer, if you are a subcontractor. The term contract as used hereinafter includes a subcontract or a purchase order.

2. Proposals that would normally be included in a single settlement proposal, such as those based on a series of separate orders for the same item under one contract should be consolidated wherever possible, and must not be divided in such a way as to bring them below $10,000.

3. You should review any aspects of your contract relating to termination and consult your customer or contracting officer for further information. Government regulations pertaining to the basis for determining a fair and reasonable termination settlement are contained in Part 49 of the Federal Acquisition Regulation. Your proposal for fair compensation should be prepared on the basis of the costs shown by your accounting records. Where your costs are not so shown, you may use any reasonable basis for estimating your costs which will provide for fair compensation for the preparations made and work done for the terminated portion of the contract, including a reasonable profit on such preparation and work.

4. Generally your settlement proposal may include under Items 2, 3, and 4, the following:

    a. COSTS - Costs incurred which are reasonably necessary and are properly allocable to the terminated portion of your contract under recognized commerical accounting practices, including direct and indirect manufacturing, selling and distribution, administrative, and other costs and expenses incurred.

    b. SETTLEMENT WITH SUBCONTRACTORS - Reasonable settlements of proposals of subcontractors allocable to the terminated portion of the subcontract. Copies of such settlements will be attached hereto.

    c. SETTLEMENT EXPENSES - Reasonable costs of protecting and preserving termination inventory in your possession and preparing your proposal.

    d. PROFIT - A reasonable profit with respect to the preparations you have made and work you have actually done for the terminated portion of your contract. No profit should be included for work which has not been done, nor shall profit be included for settlement expenses, or for settlement with subcontractors.

5. If you use this form, your total charges being proposed (line 5), must be less than $10,000. The Government has the right to examine your books and records relative to this proposal, and if you are a subcontractor, your customer must be satisfied with your proposal.

STANDARD FORM 1438 (REV. 5/2004) BACK

PART 53.3—ILLUSTRATION OF FORMS   53.301-1439

Standard Form 1439

SCHEDULE OF ACCOUNTING INFORMATION	OMB No.: **9000-0012** Expires: 05/31/98

Public reporting burden for this collection of information is estimated to average 2.5 hours per response, including the time for reviewing instructions, searching existing data sources, gathering and maintaining the data needed, and completing and reviewing the collection of information. Send comments regarding this burden estimate or any other aspect of this collection of information, including suggestions for reducing this burden, to the FAR Secretariat (VRS), Office of Acquisition and Regulatory Policy, GSA, Washington, DC 20405; and to the Office of Management and Budget, Paperwork Reduction Project (9000-0012), Washington, DC 20503.

To be used by prime contractors submitting termination proposals under part 49 of the Federal Acquisition Regulation. Also suitable for use by subcontractor in effecting subcontract settlements with prime contractor or immediate subcontractor.

THIS PROPOSAL APPLIES TO *(Check one)* ☐ A PRIME CONTRACT WITH THE GOVERNMENT ☐ SUBCONTRACT OR PURCHASE ORDER	COMPANY *(Prime or Subcontractor)*
SUBCONTRACT OR PURCHASE ORDER NO.(S)	STREET ADDRESS
CONTRACTOR WHO SENT NOTICE OF TERMINATION NAME AND ADDRESS *(Include ZIP Code)*	CITY AND STATE *(Include ZIP Code)*
	NAME OF GOVERNMENT AGENCY
	GOVERNMENT PRIME CONTRACT NO.	CONTRACTOR'S REFERENCE NO.	EFFECTIVE DATE OF TERMINATION

1. INDIVIDUAL IN YOUR ORGANIZATION FROM WHOM ADDITIONAL INFORMATION MAY BE REQUESTED ON QUESTIONS RELATING TO:

ACCOUNTING MATTERS		PROPERTY DISPOSAL	
NAME		NAME	
TITLE	TELEPHONE NUMBER	TITLE	TELEPHONE NUMBER
ADDRESS *(Include ZIP Code)*		ADDRESS *(Include ZIP Code)*	

2. ARE THE ACCOUNTS OF THE CONTRACTOR SUBJECT TO REGULAR PERIODIC EXAMINATION BY INDEPENDENT PUBLIC ACCOUNTANTS?
☐ YES ☐ NO *(Name and address of accountants)*

3. INDEPENDENT ACCOUNTANTS, IF ANY, WHO HAVE REVIEWED OR ASSISTED IN THE PREPARATION OF THE ATTACHED PROPOSAL

NAME	ADDRESS *(Include ZIP Code)*

4. GOVERNMENTAL AGENCY(IES) WHICH HAVE REVIEWED YOUR ACCOUNTS IN CONNECTION WITH PRIOR SETTLEMENT PROPOSALS DURING THE CURRENT AND PRECEDING FISCAL YEAR

NAME	ADDRESS *(Include ZIP Code)*

5. HAVE THERE BEEN ANY SIGNIFICANT DEVIATIONS FROM YOUR REGULAR ACCOUNTING PROCEDURES AND POLICIES IN ARRIVING AT THE COSTS SET FORTH IN THE ATTACHED PROPOSAL? *(If "yes," explain briefly)*
☐ YES ☐ NO

6. WERE THE DETAILED COST RECORDS USED IN PREPARING THE PROPOSAL CONTROLLED BY AND IN AGREEMENT WITH YOUR GENERAL BOOKS OF ACCOUNT?
☐ YES ☐ NO

7. STATE METHOD OF ACCOUNTING FOR TRADE AND CASH DISCOUNTS EARNED, REBATES, ALLOWANCES, AND VOLUME PRICE ADJUSTMENTS. ARE SUCH ITEMS EXCLUDED FROM COSTS PROPOSED?
☐ YES ☐ NO

(Where the space provided for any information is insufficient, continue on a separate sheet.)

AUTHORIZED FOR LOCAL REPRODUCTION
Previous edition is usable

STANDARD FORM 1439 (REV. 7-89)
Prescribed by GSA-FAR (48 CFR) 53.249(a)(6)

Standard Form 1439 (Page 2)

8. STATE METHOD OF RECORDING AND ABSORBING (1) GENERAL ENGINEERING AND GENERAL DEVELOPMENT EXPENSE AND (2) ENGINEERING AND DEVELOPMENT EXPENSE DIRECTLY APPLICABLE TO THE TERMINATED CONTRACT.

9. STATE TYPES AND SOURCE OF MISCELLANEOUS INCOME AND CREDITS AND MANNER OF RECORDING IN THE INCOME OR THE COST ACCOUNTS SUCH AS RENTAL OF YOUR FACILITIES TO OUTSIDE PARTIES, ETC.

10. METHOD OF ALLOCATING GENERAL AND ADMINISTRATIVE EXPENSE.

11. ARE COSTS AND INCOME FROM CHANGE ORDERS SEGREGATED FROM OTHER CONTRACT COSTS AND INCOME? *(If "Yes," by what methods?)*
☐ YES ☐ NO

12. METHOD OF COMPUTING PROFIT SHOWN IN THE ATTACHED PROPOSAL AND REASON FOR SELECTING THE METHOD USED. FURNISH ESTIMATE OF AMOUNT OR RATE OF PROFIT IN DOLLARS OR PERCENT ANTICIPATED HAD THE CONTRACT BEEN COMPLETED.

13. ARE SETTLEMENT EXPENSES APPLICABLE TO PREVIOUSLY TERMINATED CONTRACTS EXCLUDED FROM THE ATTACHED PROPOSALS? *(If "NO," explain.)*
☐ YES ☐ NO

14. DOES THIS PROPOSAL INCLUDE CHARGES FOR MAJOR INVENTORY ITEMS AND PROPOSALS OF SUBCONTRACTORS COMMON TO THIS TERMINATED CONTRACT AND OTHER WORK OF THE CONTRACTOR? *(If "Yes," explain the method used in allocating amounts to the terminated portion of this contract.)*
☐ YES ☐ NO

15. EXPLAIN BRIEFLY YOUR METHOD OF PRICING INVENTORIES, INDICATING WHETHER MATERIAL HANDLING COST HAS BEEN INCLUDED IN CHARGES FOR MATERIALS.

16. ARE ANY PARTS, MATERIALS, OR FINISHED PRODUCT, KNOWN TO BE DEFECTIVE, INCLUDED IN THE INVENTORIES? *(If "Yes," explain.)*
☐ YES ☐ NO

(Where the space provided for any information is insufficient, continue on a separate sheet.)

STANDARD FORM 1439 (REV. 7-83) **PAGE 2**

Standard Form 1439 (Page 3)

17. WERE INVENTORY QUANTITIES BASED ON A PHYSICAL COUNT AS OF THE DATE OF TERMINATION? *(If "No," explain exceptions.)*
☐ YES ☐ NO

18. DESCRIBE BRIEFLY THE NATURE OF INDIRECT EXPENSE ITEMS INCLUDED IN INVENTORY COSTS *(See Schedule A, SF 1435)* AND EXPLAIN YOUR METHOD OF ALLOCATION USED IN PREPARING THIS PROPOSAL, INCLUDING IF PRACTICABLE, THE RATES USED AND THE PERIOD OF TIME UPON WHICH THEY ARE BASED.

19. STATE GENERAL POLICIES RELATING TO DEPRECIATION AND AMORTIZATION OF FIXED BASES, UNDERLYING POLICIES.

20. DO THE COSTS SET FORTH IN THE ATTACHED PROPOSAL INCLUDE PROVISIONS FOR ANY RESERVES OTHER THAN DEPRECIATION RESERVES? *(If "Yes," list such reserves.)*
☐ YES ☐ NO

21. STATE POLICY OR PROCEDURE FOR RECORDING AND WRITING OFF STARTING LOAD.

22. STATE POLICIES FOR DISTINGUISHING BETWEEN CHARGES TO CAPITAL (FIXED) ASSET ACCOUNTS AND TO REPAIR AND MAINTENANCE ACCOUNTS.

23. ARE PERISHABLE TOOLS AND MANUFACTURING SUPPLIES CHARGED DIRECTLY TO CONTRACT COSTS OR INCLUDED IN INDIRECT EXPENSES?

(Where the space provided for any information is insufficient, continue on a separate sheet.)

STANDARD FORM 1439 (REV. 7-83) **PAGE 3**

Standard Form 1439 (Page 4)

24. HAVE ANY CHARGES FOR SERVANCE, DISMISSAL, OR SEPARATION PAY BEEN INCLUDED IN THIS PROPOSAL? *(If "Yes," furnish brief explanation and estimates of amounts included.)*

☐ YES   ☐ NO

25. STATE POLICIES RELATING TO RECORDING OF OVERTIME SHIFT PREMIUMS AND PRODUCTION BONUSES.

26. DOES CONTRACTOR HAVE A PENSION PLAN? *(If "YES," state method of funding and absorption of past and current pension service costs.)*

☐ YES   ☐ NO

27. IS THIS SETTLEMENT PROPOSAL BASED ON STANDARD COSTS?

☐ YES *(If "Yes," has adjustment to actual cost or adjustment for any significant variaions been made?)*   ☐ YES   ☐ NO *(If "No," explain)*
☐ NO

28. DOES THIS PROPOSAL INCLUDE ANY ELEMENT OF PROFIT TO THE CONTRACTOR OR RELATED ORGANIZATION, OTHER THAN (a) PROFIT SET FORTH SEPARATELY IN THE PROPOSAL OR (b) PROFIT INCLUDED IN THE CONTRACT PRICE AT WHICH ACCEPTABLE FINISHED PRODUCT, IF ANY, IS INCLUDED IN THE PROPOSAL? *(If "Yes," explain briefly.)*

☐ YES   ☐ NO

29. WHAT IS LENGTH OF TIME (PRODUCTION CYCLE) REQUIRED TO PRODUCE ONE OF THE END ITEMS FROM THE TIME THE MATERIAL ENTERS THE PRODUCTION LINE TO THE COMPLETION AS THE FINISHED PRODUCT?

30. STATE POLICY AND PROCEDURE FOR VERIFICATION AND NEGOTIATION OF SETTLEMENTS WITH SUBCONTRACTORS AND VENDORS.

CERTIFICATE

THIS CERTIFIES THAT, TO THE BEST KNOWLEDGE AND BELIEF OF THE UNDERSIGNED, THE ABOVE STATMENTS ARE TRUE AND CORRECT

NAME OF CONTRACTOR	BY *(Signature of supervisory accounting official)*	
	TITLE	DATE

(Where the space provided for any information is insufficient, continue on a separate sheet.)

STANDARD FORM 1439 (REV. 7-83) PAGE 4

PART 53.3—ILLUSTRATION OF FORMS

Standard Form 1440

APPLICATION FOR PARTIAL PAYMENT

OMB No.: 9000-0012
Expires: 05/31/98

Public reporting burden for this collection of information is estimated to average 2.5 hours per response, including the time for reviewing instructions, searching existing data sources, gathering and maintaining the data needed, and completing and reviewing the collection of information. Send comments regarding this burden estimate or any other aspect of this collection of information, including suggestions for reducing this burden, to the FAR Secretariat (VRS), Office of Federal Acquisiton Policy ,GSA, Washington, DC 20405; and to the Office of Management and Budget, Paperwork Reduction Project (9000-0012), Washington, DC 20503.

For use by Prime Contractor or Subcontractor under contracts terminated for the convenience of the Government

THIS APPLICATION APPLIES TO *(Check one)*
☐ A PRIME CONTRACT WITH THE GOVERNMENT
☐ SUBCONTRACT OR PURCHASE ORDER

SUBCONTRACT OR PURCHASE ORDER NUMBER(S)

APPLICANT

STREET ADDRESS

CONTRACTOR WHO SENT NOTICE OF TERMINATION

NAME

CITY AND STATE *(Include ZIP Code)*

ADDRESS *(Include ZIP Code)*

NAME OF GOVERNMENT AGENCY

IF CONTRACTOR HAS GUARANTEED LOANS OR HAS ASSIGNED MONEYS DUE UNDER THE CONTRACT, GIVE THE FOLLOWING:

GOVERNMENT PRIME CONTRACT NUMBER

NAME AND ADDRESS OF FINANCING INSTITUTION *(Include ZIP Code)*

CONTRACTOR'S REFERENCE NUMBER

NAME AND ADDRESS OF GUARANTOR *(Include ZIP Code)*

EFFECTIVE DATE OF TERMINATION | DATE OF THIS APPLICATION

NAME AND ADDRESS OF ASSIGNEE *(Include ZIP Code)*

AMOUNT REQUESTED
$

APPLICATION NUMBER UNDER THIS TERMINATION

SECTION I - STATUS OF CONTRACT OR ORDER AT EFFECTIE DATE OF TERMINATION

PRODUCTS COVERED BY TERMINATED CONTRACT OR PURCHASE ORDER (a)		FINISHED			UNFINISHED OR NOT COMMENCED		TOTAL COVERED BY CONTRACT OR ORDER (g)
		PREVIOUSLY SHIPPED AND INVOICED (b)	ON HAND		TO BE COMPLETED (e)	NOT TO BE COMPLETED (f)	
			PAYMENT TO BE RECEIVED THROUGH INVOICING (c)	INCLUDED IN THIS APPLICATION (d)			
	QUANTITY						
	$						
	QUANTITY						
	$						
	QUANTITY						
	$						

SECTION II - APPLICANT'S OWN TERMINATION CHARGES
(Exclusive of its Subcontractors' Charges)

SETTLEMENT PROPOSAL
☐ ATTACHED
☐ PREVIOUSLY SUBMITTED

NO.	ITEM	CHARGES AS LISTED IN SETTLEMENT PROPOSAL
1.	ACCEPTABLE FURNISHED PRODUCT *(at contract price)*	$
2.	WORK-IN-PROCESS	
3.	RAW MATERIALS, PURCHASED PARTS, AND SUPPLIES	
4.	GENERAL AND ADMINISTRATIVE EXPENSES	
5.	**TOTAL** *(Sum of lines 1, 2, 3, and 4)*	$
6.	SPECIAL TOOLING AND SPECIAL TEST EQUIPMENT	
7.	OTHER COSTS	
8.	SETTLEMENT EXPENSES	
9.	**TOTAL** *(Sum of lines 5, 6, 7, and 8)*	$
10.	SUBCONTRACTOR SETTLEMENTS APPROVED BY CONTRACTING OFFICER OR SETTLED UNDER A DELEGATION OF AUTHORITY AND PAID BY APPLICANT	$
11.	AMOUNT RECEIVED	
(a)	UNLIQUIDATED PARTIAL, PROGRESS, AND ADVANCE PAYMENTS RECEIVED	$
(b)	DISPOSAL AND OTHER CREDITS	
(c)	**TOTAL** *(Sum of lines a and b)*	
(d)	AMOUNT OF PARTIAL PAYMENT REQUESTED	
(e)	**TOTAL** *(Sum of lines c and d)*	$

AUTHORIZED FOR LOCAL REPRODUCTION
Previous edition is usable

STANDARD FORM 1440 (REV. 1-95)
Prescribed by GSA-FAR (48 CFR) 53.249(a)(7)

Standard Form 1440 (Back)

SECTION III - AGREEMENT OF APPLICANT

IN CONSIDERATION OF PARTIAL PAYMENT THAT MAY BE MADE, THE APPLICANT AGREES AS FOLLOWS:

(a) Repayment of Excess. If any partial payment made to the Contractor is in excess of the amount finally determined to be due on its termination settlement proposal or claim, the Contractor shall repay the excess to the Government upon demand together with interest at the rate established by the Secretary of the Treasury under 50 U.S.C. (app.) 1215(b)(2). Interest shall be computed for the period from the date of the excess payment to the date the excess is repaid. Interest shall not be charged however, for any (1) excess payment due to a reduction in the Contractor's proposal or claim because of retention or other disposition of termination inventory, until 10 days after the date of the retention or disposition, or any later date determined by the Contracting Officer because of the circumstances, or for (2) overpayment under cost-reimbursement research and development contracts (without profit or fee to the Contractor) if the overpayments are repaid to the Government within 30 days after demand.

(b) Prompt Settlement of Proposal. The applicant will make every effort to expedite final settlement of the termination settlement proposal and any proposals of its subcontractors.

(c) Disposal and Retention of Inventory. The applicant shall, within 10 days, notify the Contracting Officer whenever the proceeds received from the disposal of termination inventory, when added to the cost or agreed value of inventory retained by the applicant, exceeds the amount of its charges (Section II, Line 9) and the amount of such credits has not been included on Section II, Line b (Disposal and Other Credits).

SECTION IV - CERTIFICATE OF APPLICANT

I certify that the amount of charges **(exclusive of subcontractors' charges)** due as of the date of this application and allocable to the terminated portion of contract number _____ dated _____ with _____, is not less than $ _____ (From Section II, Line 9) ; that, to the best of my knowledge, the amounts received are set forth above; and that I have not assigned any moneys payable under this contract, except as set forth above.

NAME OF APPLICANT	BY (Signature of authorized official)	
	TITLE	DATE

SECTION V - RECOMMENDATION OF FIRST REVIEWING CONTRACTOR

The undersigned states that it has examined this application and has considered the applicant's general reputation. It has no reason to doubt the accuracy of the information contained in this application or that amount certified by the applicant as due will constitute a proper charge to be included in the undersigned's termination settlement proposal against _____

It recommends that the requested partial payment be made.

The undersigned agrees that it will promptly pay over to the applicant or credit against amounts owing from the applicant any amount received for the benefit of the applicant under this application, and that it will repay to the Government on demand any amount not so paid or credited.

NAME OF CONTRACTOR	BY (Signature of authorized official)	
	TITLE	DATE

SECTION VI - RECOMMENDATION OF OTHER REVIEWING CONTRACTORS

Each of the undersigned states that it has no reason to doubt that the amount of the partial payment requested, and recommended above is due the applicant will constitute a proper charge in the termination settlement proposal of the undersigned.

Each of the undersigned agrees that it will promptly pay over to its immediate subcontractor or credit against amounts owing from such subcontractor any amount received for the benefit of the applicant under this application, and that it will repay to the Government on demand any amount not so paid or credited.

	CONTRACTOR	DATE	IDENTIFICATION OF YOUR CONTRACT	SIGNATURE OF OFFICER, PARTNER, OR OWNER
1				
2				
3				

(Where the space provided for any information is insufficient, continue on a separate sheet.)

STANDARD FORM 1440 (REV. 1-95) BACK

Standard Form 1442

| SOLICITATION, OFFER, AND AWARD *(Construction, Alteration, or Repair)* | 1. SOLICITATION NO. | 2. TYPE OF SOLICITATION ☐ SEALED BID *(IFB)* ☐ NEGOTIATED *(RFP)* | 3. DATE ISSUED | PAGE | OF | PAGES |

IMPORTANT - The "offer" section on the reverse must be fully completed by offeror.

| 4. CONTRACT NO. | 5. REQUISITION/PURCHASE REQUEST NO. | 6. PROJECT NO. |

| 7. ISSUED BY | CODE | 8. ADDRESS OFFER TO |

| 9. FOR INFORMATION CALL: | a. NAME | b. TELEPHONE NO. *(Include area code) (NO COLLECT CALLS)* |

SOLICITATION

NOTE: In sealed bid solicitations "offer" and "offeror" mean "bid and "bidder".

10. THE GOVERNMENT REQUIRES PERFORMANCE OF THE WORK DESCRIBED IN THESE DOCUMENTS *(Title, identifying no., date)*

11. The Contractor shall begin performance _____ calendar days and complete it within _____ calendar days after receiving ☐ award, ☐ notice to proceed. This performance period is ☐ mandatory ☐ negotiable. *(See _____ .)*

| 12a. THE CONTRACTOR MUST FURNISH ANY REQUIRED PERFORMANCE AND PAYMENT BONDS? *(If "YES," indicate within how many calendar days after award in Item 12b).* ☐ YES ☐ NO | 12b. CALENDAR DAYS |

13. ADDITIONAL SOLICITATION REQUIREMENTS:

a. Sealed offers in original and _____ copies to perform the work required are due at the place specified in Item 8 by _____ *(hour)* local time _____ *(date)*. If this is a sealed bid solicitation, offers will be publicly opened at that time. Sealed envelopes containing offers shall be marked to show the offeror's name and address, the solicitation number, and the date and time offers are due.

b. An offer guarantee ☐ is, ☐ is not required.

c. All offers are subject to the (1) work requirements, and (2) other provisions and clauses incorporated in the solicitation in full text or by

d. Offers providing less than _____ calendar days for Government acceptance after the date offers are due will not be considered and will be rejected.

NSN 7540-01-155-3212

STANDARD FORM 1442 (REV. 4-85)
Prescribed by GSA - FAR (48 CFR) 53.236-1(d)

Standard Form 1442 (Back)

OFFER (Must be fully completed by offeror)

14. NAME AND ADDRESS OF OFFEROR (Include ZIP Code)

15. TELEPHONE NO. (Include area code)

16. REMITTANCE ADDRESS (Include only if different than Item 14.)

CODE   FACILITY CODE

17. The offeror agrees to perform the work required at the prices specified below in strict accordance with the terms of this solicitation, if this offer is accepted by the Government in writing within _____ calendar days after the date offers are due. (Insert any number equal to or greater than the minimum requirement stated in Item 13d. Failure to insert any number means the offeror accepts the minimum in Item 13d.)

AMOUNTS ▶

18. The offeror agrees to furnish any required performance and payment bonds.

19. ACKNOWLEDGMENT OF AMENDMENTS
(The offeror acknowledges receipt of amendments to the solicitation -- give number and date of each)

AMENDMENT NO.									
DATE.									

20a. NAME AND TITLE OF PERSON AUTHORIZED TO SIGN OFFER (Type or print)

20. SIGNATURE

20c. OFFER DATE

AWARD (To be completed by Government)

21. ITEMS ACCEPTED:

22. AMOUNT

23. ACCOUNTING AND APPROPRIATION DATA

24. SUBMIT INVOICES TO ADDRESS SHOWN IN ▶ ITEM
(4 copies unless otherwise specified)

25. OTHER THAN FULL AND OPEN COMPETITION PURSUANT TO
☐ 10 U.S.C. 2304(c) (   )   ☐ 41 U.S.C. 253(c) (   )

26. ADMINISTERED BY

27. PAYMENT WILL BE MADE BY

CONTRACTING OFFICER WILL COMPLETE ITEM 28 OR 29 AS APPLICABLE

☐ **28. NEGOTIATED AGREEMENT** (Contractor is required to sign this document and return _____ copies to issuing office.) Contractor agrees to furnish and deliver all items or perform all work requirements identified on this form and any continuation sheets for the consideration stated in this contract. The rights and obligations of the parties to this contract shall be governed by (a) this contract award, (b) the solicitation, and (c) the clauses, representations, certifications, and specifications incorporated by reference in or attached to this contract.

☐ **29. AWARD** (Contractor is not required to sign this document.) Your offer on this solicitation is hereby accepted as to the items listed. This award consummates the contract, which consists of (a) the Government solicitation and your offer, and (b) this contract award. No further contractual document is necessary.

30a. NAME AND TITLE OF CONTRACTOR OR PERSON AUTHORIZED TO SIGN (Type or print)

31a. NAME OF CONTRACTING OFFICER (Type or print)

30b. SIGNATURE

30c. DATE

31b. UNITED STATES OF AMERICA
BY

30c. DATE

STANDARD FORM 1442 (REV. 4-85) BACK

Standard Form 1443

CONTRACTOR'S REQUEST FOR PROGRESS PAYMENT

Form Approved
OMB Number 9000-0010

IMPORTANT: This form is to be completed in accordance with instructions on the reverse.

SECTION I - IDENTIFICATION INFORMATION

1. TO: NAME AND ADDRESS OF CONTRACTING OFFICE ADMINISTERING THE CONTRACT *(Include ZIP Code)*

PAYING OFFICE

2. FROM: NAME AND ADDRESS OF CONTRACTOR *(Include ZIP Code)*

3. SMALL BUSINESS ☐ YES ☐ NO

4. CONTRACT NUMBER
   A. BASIC CONTRACT NUMBER   B. TASK OR DELIVERY ORDER NUMBER

5. CONTRACT PRICE $

6. RATES
   A. PROGRESS PAYMENTS %   B. LIQUIDATION %

7. DATE OF INITIAL AWARD
   A. YEAR   B. MONTH

8A. PROGRESS PAYMENT REQUEST NUMBER

8B. DATE OF THIS REQUEST

SECTION II - STATEMENT OF COSTS UNDER THIS CONTRACT THROUGH _____ *(Date)*

9. RESERVED	
10. RESERVED	
11. COSTS ELIGIBLE FOR PROGRESS PAYMENTS UNDER THE PROGRESS PAYMENTS CLAUSE	
12a. TOTAL CONTRACT COST(S) INCURRED TO DATE	
b. ESTIMATED COST TO COMPLETE c. TOTAL ESTIMATED COST OF PERFORMANCE	
13. ITEM 11 MULTIPLIED BY ITEM 6a	
14a. FINANCING PAYMENTS PAID TO SUBCONTRACTORS	
b. LIQUIDATED FINANCING PAYMENTS TO SUBCONTRACTORS	
c. UNLIQUIDATED FINANCING PAYMENTS PAID TO SUBCONTRACTORS *(Item 14a less 14b)*	
d. SUBCONTRACT FINANCING PAYMENTS APPROVED FOR CURRENT PAYMENT	
e. ELIGIBLE SUBCONTRACTOR FINANCING PAYMENTS *(Item 14c plus 14d)*	
15. TOTAL DOLLAR AMOUNT *(Item 13 plus 14e)*	
16. ITEM 5 MULTIPLIED BY ITEM 6b	
17. LESSER OF ITEM 15 OR ITEM 16	
18. TOTAL AMOUNT OF PREVIOUS PROGRESS PAYMENTS REQUESTED	
19. MAXIMUM BALANCE ELIGIBLE FOR PROGRESS PAYMENTS *(Item 17 less 18)*	

SECTION III - COMPUTATION OF LIMITS FOR OUTSTANDING PROGRESS PAYMENTS

20. COMPUTATION OF PROGRESS PAYMENT CLAUSE LIMITATION	
a. COSTS INCLUDED IN ITEM 11, APPLICABLE TO ITEMS DELIVERED, INVOICED, AND ACCEPTED TO THE DATE IN HEADING OF SECTION II	
b. COSTS ELIGIBLE FOR PROGRESS PAYMENTS, APPLICABLE TO UNDELIVERED ITEMS AND TO DELIVERED ITEMS NOT INVOICED AND ACCEPTED *(Item 11 less 20a)*	
c. ITEM 20b MULTIPLIED BY ITEM 6a	
d. ELIGIBLE SUBCONTRACTOR FINANCING PAYMENTS *(Same as Item 14e)*	
e. LIMITATION *(Item 20c plus 20d)*	
21. COMPUTATION OF PROGRESS PAYMENT CLAUSE LIMITATION	
a. CONTRACT PRICE OF ITEMS DELIVERED, ACCEPTED AND INVOICED AS OF THE DATE SHOWN IN THE HEADING OF SECTION II	
b. CONTRACT PRICE OF ITEMS NOT DELIVERED, ACCEPTED AND INVOICED *(Item 5 less 21a)*	
c. ITEM 21b MULTIPLIED BY ITEM 6b	
d. UNLIQUIDATED ADVANCE PAYMENTS PLUS ACCRUED INTEREST	
e. LIMITATION *(Item 21c less 21d)*	
22. MAXIMUM UNLIQUIDATED PROGRESS PAYMENTS *(Lesser of Item 20e or 21e)*	
23. TOTAL AMOUNT LIQUIDATED AND TO BE LIQUIDATED	
24. UNLIQUIDATED PROGRESS PAYMENTS *(Item 18 less 23)*	
25. MAXIMUM PERMISSIBLE PROGRESS PAYMENTS *(Item 22 less 24)*	
26. AMOUNT OF CURRENT INVOICE FOR PROGRESS PAYMENT *(Lesser of item 25 or 19)*	
27. AMOUNT APPROVED BY CONTRACTING OFFICER	

CERTIFICATION

DATE _____

I Certify that:

(a) The above statement (with attachments) has been prepared from the books and records of the above-named contractor in accordance with the contract and the instructions hereon, and to the best of my knowledge and belief, that it is correct;
(b) All the costs of contract performance (except as herewith reported in writing) have been paid to the extent shown herein, or where not shown as paid have been paid or will be paid currently, by the contractor, when due, in the ordinary course of business;
(c) The work reflected above has been performed;
(d) The quantities and amounts involved are consistent with the requirements of the contract;
(e) There are no encumbrances (except as reported in writing herewith, or on previous progress payment request number _____) against the property acquired or produced for, and allocated or properly chargeable to the contract which would affect or impair the Government's title;
(f) There has been no materially adverse change in the financial condition of the contractor since the contractor's (insert 'as of' date of financial information) _____ submission of its last financial information dated (insert date of prior submission/certification) _____ to the Government in connection with the contract;
(g) To the extent of any contract provision limiting progress payments pending first article approval, such provision has been complied with, and
(h) After the making of the requested progress payment the unliquidated progress payments will not exceed the maximum unliquidated progress payments permitted by the contract.

NAME AND TITLE OF CONTRACTOR REPRESENTATIVE SIGNING THIS FORM	SIGNATURE
NAME AND TITLE OF CONTRACTING OFFICER	SIGNATURE

NSN 7540-01-140-5523

STANDARD FORM 1443 (REV. 7/2009)
Prescribed by GSA FAR (48 CFR 53.232)

Standard Form 1443 (Back)

INSTRUCTIONS

GENERAL - All dollar amounts must be shown in whole dollars, rounded using a consistent methodology (e.g., always round up, always round down, always round to the nearest dollar). All line item numbers not included in the instructions below are self-explanatory.

SECTION I - IDENTIFICATION INFORMATION. Complete items 1 through 8b in accordance with the following instructions.

Item 1. TO - Enter the name and address of the cognizant Contract Administration Office (the office administering the contract).
PAYING OFFICE - Enter the designation of the paying office, as indicated on the contract.

Item 2. FROM - CONTRACTOR'S NAME AND ADDRESS/ZIP CODE - Enter the name and mailing address of the contractor. If applicable, the division of the company performing the contract should be entered immediately following the contractor's name.

Item 3. Enter an "X" in the appropriate block to indicate whether or not the contractor is a small business concern.

Item 4. Enter the contract number, including the task or delivery order number if applicable. Progress payment requests under individual orders shall be submitted as if the order constituted a separate contract, unless otherwise specified in this contract (FAR 52.232-16(m)).

Item 5. Enter the total contract price in accordance with the following (See FAR 32.501-3):
(1) Under firm-fixed-price contracts, the contract price is the current amount fixed by the contract plus the not-to-exceed amount for any unpriced modifications.
(2) If the contract is redeterminable or subject to economic price adjustment, the contract price is the initial price until modified.
(3) Under a fixed-price incentive contract, the contract price is the target price plus the not-to-exceed amount for any unpriced modifications. However, if the contractor's properly incurred costs exceed the target price, the contracting officer may provisionally increase the price up to the ceiling or maximum price.
(4) Under a letter contract, the contract price is the maximum amount obligated by the contract as modified.
(5) Under an unpriced order issued against a basic ordering agreement, the contract price is the maximum amount obligated by the order, as modified.
(6) Any portion of the contract specifically providing for reimbursement of costs only shall be excluded from the contract price.

Item 6A. PROGRESS PAYMENT RATES - Enter the 2-digit progress payment percentage rate shown in paragraph (a) (1) of the progress payment clause.

Item 6B. LIQUIDATED RATE - Enter the current progress payment liquidation rate prescribed in the contract (FAR 52.232-16(b)) using three digits - Example: show 80% as 800 - show 72.3% as 723. Decimals between tenths must be rounded up to the next highest tenth (not necessarily the nearest tenth), since rounding down would produce a rate below the minimum rate calculated (FAR 32.503-10(b) (4)).

Item 7. DATE OF INITIAL AWARD - Enter the four digit calendar year. Use two digits to indicate the month. Example: Show January 2005 as 2005/01.

Item 8A. PROGRESS PAYMENT REQUEST NUMBER - Enter the number assigned to this request. All requests under a single contract must be numbered consecutively, beginning with 1. Each subsequent request under the same contract must continue in sequence, using the same series of numbers without omission.

Item 8B. Enter the date of the request.

SECTION II - STATEMENT OF COSTS UNDER THIS CONTRACT.
Date. In the space provided in the heading enter the date through which costs have been accumulated from inception for inclusion in this request. This date is applicable to item entries in Sections II and III.

Cost Basis. In accordance with FAR 52.232-16 (a) (1), the basis for progress payments is the contractor's total costs incurred under this contract, whether or not actually paid, plus financing payments to subcontractors (computed in accordance with FAR 52.232-16(j)), less the sum of all previous progress payments made by the Government under this contract.

Item 11. Costs eligible for progress payments under the progress payments clause. Compute the eligible costs in accordance with the requirements at FAR 52.232-16(a)(1) through (4). First articles: Before first article approval, the acquisition of materials or components for, or the commencement of production of, the balance of the contract quantity is at the sole risk of the contractor. Before the first article approval, the costs thereof shall not be allowable for purposes of progress payments. (See FAR 52.209-3(g) and FAR 52.209-4(h)).

Item 12a. Enter the total contract costs incurred to date; if the actual amount is not known, enter the best possible estimate. If an estimate is used, enter (E) after the amount.

Item 12b. Enter the estimated cost to complete the contract. The contractor shall furnish estimates to complete that have been developed or updated within six months of the date of the progress payment request. The estimates to complete shall represent the contractor's best estimate of total costs to complete all remaining contract work required under the contract. The estimates shall include sufficient detail to permit Government verification.

Items 14a through 14e. Include only financing payments (progress payments, performance-based payments, and commercial item financing) on subcontracts which are in accordance with the requirements of FAR 52.232-16(j). Do not include interim payments under a cost reimbursement contract.

Item 14a. Enter only financing payments actually paid.
Item 14b. Enter total financing payments recouped from subcontractors.

Item 14d. Include the amount of unpaid subcontract progress payment billings which have been approved by the contractor for the current payment in the ordinary course of business.

SECTION III - ADVANCE PAYMENTS/ACCEPTED ITEMS. This Section must be completed only if the contractor has received advance payments against this contract, or if the items have been delivered, invoiced and accepted as of the date indicated in the heading of Section II above. EXCEPTION: Item 27 must be completed for all progress payment requests where the line 12c amount exceeds the amount on Line 5.

Item 20a. Of the costs reported in Item 11, compute and enter only costs which are properly allocable to items delivered, invoiced and accepted to the applicable date. In order of preference, these costs are to be computed on the basis of one of the following: (a) The actual unit cost of items delivered, giving proper consideration to the deferment of the starting load costs or (b) projected unit costs (based on experienced costs plus the estimated cost to complete the contract), where the contractor maintains cost data which will clearly establish the reliability of such estimates.

Item 23. Enter total progress payments liquidated (monies recouped from the contractor on prior billings) and those to be liquidated from billings submitted but not yet paid (monies to be recouped from the contractor on submitted but unpaid billings).

CERTIFICATION
Paragraph (f). If no financial information has been provided previously in connection with this contract, insert "N/A" in the submission date block and the financial information date block. Otherwise, insert respectively, the "as of" date of the financial information submitted last and the date of the last submission.

STANDARD FORM 1443 (REV. 7/2009) BACK

FAC 2005–73 MAY 29, 2014

PART 53.3—ILLUSTRATION OF FORMS 53.301-1444

Standard Form 1444

AUTHORIZED FOR LOCAL REPRODUCTION

REQUEST FOR AUTHORIZATION OF ADDITIONAL CLASSIFICATION AND RATE

CHECK APPROPRIATE BOX
☐ SERVICE CONTRACT
☐ CONSTRUCTION CONTRACT

OMB Number: 9000-0089
Expiration Date: 7/31/2014

PAPERWORK REDUCTION ACT STATEMENT: Public reporting burden for this collection of information is estimated to average .5 hours per response, including the time for reviewing instructions, searching existing data sources, gathering and maintaining the data needed, and completing and reviewing the collection of information. Send comments regarding this burden estimate or any other aspects of this collection of information, including suggestions for reducing this burden, to U.S. General Services Administration, Regulatory Secretariat (MVCB)/IC 9000-0089, Office of Governmentwide Acquisition Policy, 1800 F Street, NW, Washington, DC 20405.

INSTRUCTIONS: THE CONTRACTOR SHALL COMPLETE ITEMS 3 THROUGH 16, KEEP A PENDING COPY, AND SUBMIT THE REQUEST, IN QUADRUPLICATE, TO THE CONTRACTING OFFICER.

1. TO:
ADMINISTRATOR,
WAGE AND HOUR DIVISION
U.S. DEPARTMENT OF LABOR
WASHINGTON, D.C. 20210

2. FROM: *(REPORTING OFFICE)*

3. CONTRACTOR

4. DATE OF REQUEST

5. CONTRACT NUMBER | 6. DATE BID OPENED *(SEALED BIDDING)* | 7. DATE OF AWARD | 8. DATE CONTRACT WORK STARTED | 9. DATE OPTION EXERCISED *(IF APPLICABLE) (SERVICE CONTRACT ONLY)*

10. SUBCONTRACTOR *(IF ANY)*

11. PROJECT AND DESCRIPTION OF WORK *(ATTACH ADDITIONAL SHEET IF NEEDED)*

12. LOCATION *(CITY, COUNTY AND STATE)*

13. IN ORDER TO COMPLETE THE WORK PROVIDED FOR UNDER THE ABOVE CONTRACT, IT IS NECESSARY TO ESTABLISH THE FOLLOWING RATE(S) FOR THE INDICATED CLASSIFICATION(S) NOT INCLUDED IN THE DEPARTMENT OF LABOR DETERMINATION
NUMBER: DATED:

a. LIST IN ORDER: PROPOSED CLASSIFICATION TITLE(S); JOB DESCRIPTION(S); DUTIES; AND RATIONALE FOR PROPOSED CLASSIFICATIONS *(Service contracts only)*
(Use reverse or attach additional sheets, if necessary)

b. WAGE RATE(S)

c. FRINGE BENEFITS PAYMENTS

14. SIGNATURE AND TITLE OF SUBCONTRACTOR REPRESENTATIVE *(IF ANY)*

15. SIGNATURE AND TITLE OF PRIME CONTRACTOR REPRESENTATIVE

16. SIGNATURE OF EMPLOYEE OR REPRESENTATIVE | TITLE | CHECK APPROPRIATE BOX-REFERENCING BLOCK 13.
☐ AGREE ☐ DISAGREE

TO BE COMPLETED BY CONTRACTING OFFICER *(CHECK AS APPROPRIATE - SEE FAR 22.1019 (SERVICE CONTRACT LABOR STANDARDS) OR FAR 22.406-3 (CONSTRUCTION WAGE RATE REQUIREMENTS))*

☐ THE INTERESTED PARTIES AGREE AND THE CONTRACTING OFFICER RECOMMENDS APPROVAL BY THE WAGE AND HOUR DIVISION. AVAILABLE INFORMATION AND RECOMMENDATIONS ARE ATTACHED.

☐ THE INTERESTED PARTIES CANNOT AGREE ON THE PROPOSED CLASSIFICATION AND WAGE RATE. A DETERMINATION OF THE QUESTION BY THE WAGE AND HOUR DIVISION IS THEREFORE REQUESTED. AVAILABLE INFORMATION AND RECOMMENDATIONS ARE ATTACHED.
(Send 3 copies to the Department of Labor)

SIGNATURE OF CONTRACTING OFFICER OR REPRESENTATIVE | TITLE AND COMMERCIAL TELEPHONE NUMBER | DATE SUBMITTED

PREVIOUS EDITION IS USABLE

STANDARD FORM 1444 (REV. 4/2013)
Prescribed by GSA-FAR (48 CFR) 53.222(f)

PART 53.3—ILLUSTRATION OF FORMS   53.301-1445

Standard Form 1445

LABOR STANDARDS INTERVIEW

CONTRACT NUMBER	EMPLOYEE INFORMATION		
	LAST NAME	FIRST NAME	MI
NAME OF PRIME CONTRACTOR	STREET ADDRESS		
NAME OF EMPLOYER			
	CITY	STATE	ZIP CODE
SUPERVISOR'S NAME			
LAST NAME / FIRST NAME / MI	WORK CLASSIFICATION	WAGE RATE	

ACTION	CHECK BELOW	
	YES	NO
Do you work over 8 hours per day?		
Do you work over 40 hours per week?		
Are you paid at least time and a half for overtime hours?		
Are you receiving any cash payments for fringe benefits required by the posted wage determination decision?		

WHAT DEDUCTIONS OTHER THAN TAXES AND SOCIAL SECURITY ARE MADE FROM YOUR PAY?

HOW MANY HOURS DID YOU WORK ON YOUR LAST WORK DAY BEFORE THIS INTERVIEW?	TOOLS YOU USE
DATE OF LAST WORK DAY BEFORE INTERVIEW *(YYMMDD)*	
DATE YOU BEGAN WORK ON THIS PROJECT *(YYMMDD)*	

THE ABOVE IS CORRECT TO THE BEST OF MY KNOWLEDGE

EMPLOYEE'S SIGNATURE	DATE *(YYMMDD)*
INTERVIEWER SIGNATURE TYPED OR PRINTED NAME	DATE *(YYMMDD)*

INTERVIEWER'S COMMENTS

WORK EMPLOYEE WAS DOING WHEN INTERVIEWED	ACTION *(If explanation is needed, use comments section)*	YES	NO
	IS EMPLOYEE PROPERLY CLASSIFIED AND PAID?		
	ARE WAGE RATES AND POSTERS DISPLAYED?		

FOR USE BY PAYROLL CHECKER

IS ABOVE INFORMATION IN AGREEMENT WITH PAYROLL DATA?
☐ YES ☐ NO
COMMENTS

CHECKER

LAST NAME	FIRST NAME	MI	JOB TITLE
SIGNATURE			DATE *(YYMMDD)*

AUTHORIZED FOR LOCAL REPRODUCTION
Previous edition not usable

STANDARD FORM 1445 (REV. 12-96)
Prescribed by GSA - FAR (48 CFR) 53.222(g)

53.3-155

Standard Form 1446

LABOR STANDARDS INVESTIGATION SUMMARY SHEET

REPORTING OFFICE	CONTRACT NUMBER	CONTRACT AMOUNT	DATE OF CONTRACT

TYPE OF CONTRACT
☐ FIXED PRICE ☐ CPFF ☐ OTHER *(Specify)*

CONTRACTOR'S NAME AND ADDRESS *(Include ZIP Code)*	EMPLOYER'S NAME AND ADDRESS *(Include ZIP Code)* *(If other than prime contractor)*

PROJECT AND LOCATION

DESCRIPTION OF WORK

BASIS FOR INVESTIGATION

WAGE DETERMINATION NUMBER	WAGE DETERMINATION DATE

NATURE AND EXTENT OF VIOLATION

NO. EMPLOYEES INVOLVED	ARE VIOLATIONS CONSIDERED WILLFUL? ☐ Yes ☐ No	COPELAND ACT VIOLATIONS ☐ Yes ☐ No
CONSTRUCTION WAGE RATE REQUIREMENTS STATUTE UNDERPAYMENTS $	CWHSS* UNDERPAYMENTS $	CWHSS* LAW VIOLATIONS $

CORRECTIVE ACTIONS TAKEN

RESTITUTION MADE ☐ Yes ☐ No	AMOUNT OF RESTITUTION $	CONTRACTORS PAYMENT WITHHELD ☐ Yes ☐ No
WITHHELD FOR CONSTRUCTION WAGE RATE REQUIREMENTS STATUTE VIOLATIONS $	WITHHELD FOR CWHSS* UNDERPAYMENTS $	WITHHELD FOR CWHSS* VIOLATIONS $

REMARKS

PREPARED BY

DATE	TITLE	SIGNATURE

*Contract Work Hours and Safety Standards Statute

AUTHORIZED FOR LOCAL REPRODUCTION
Previous edition is usable

STANDARD FORM 1446 (REV. 4-2013)
Prescribed by GSA-FAR (48 CFR) 53.222(h)

Standard Form 1447

[Go to *http://www.gsa.gov/forms* to access form.]

Standard Form 1449

[Go to *http://www.gsa.gov/forms* to access form.]

Optional Form 17

OF-17 (12/93)
Offer Label
FAR (48) CFR 53.214(g))
FAR (48) CFR 53.215-1(h))

NOTICE TO OFFEROR

1. THIS LABEL MAY ONLY BE USED ON ENVELOPES LARGER THAN 156 mm (6 1/8 INCHES) IN HEIGHT AND 292 mm (11 1/2 INCHES) IN LENGTH.

2. Print or type your name and address in the UPPER left corner of the envelope containing your offer.

3. Complete the bottom portion of this form and paste it on the LOWER left corner of the envelope, unless the envelope is 156 mm by 292 mm (6 1/8 inches by 11 1/2 inches) or smaller.

OFFER

| SOLICITATION NO. |
| DATE FOR RECEIPT OF OFFERS |
| TIME FOR RECEIPT OF OFFERS   AM   PM |
| OFFICE DESIGNATED TO RECEIVE OFFERS |

SAMPLE ONLY

Optional Form 90

RELEASE OF LIEN ON REAL PROPERTY

Whereas _____, of _____, by a bond
         (Name)   (Place of Residence)
for the performance of U.S. Government Contract Number _____ ,
became a surety for the complete and successful performance of said contract, which bond inlcudes a lien upon certain real property further described hereafter, and

Whereas said surety established the said lien upon the following property

and recorded this pledge on _____
                              (Name of Land Records)
in the _____ of _____ ,
        (Locality)   (State)
and

Whereas, I, _____ , being a duly authorized representative of the United States Government as a warranted contracting officer, have determined that the lien is no longer required to ensure further performance of the said Government contract or satisfaction of claims arising therefrom,
and

Whereas the surety remains liable to the United States Government for continued performance of the said Government contract and satisfaction of claims pertaining thereto.

Now, therefore, this agreement witnesseth that the Government hereby releases the aforementioned lien.

[Date]   [Signature]
                                Seal

AUTHORIZED FOR LOCAL REPRODUCTION

OPTIONAL FORM 90 (REV. 1-90)
Prescribed by GSA-FAR (48 CFR) 53.228(n)

Optional Form 91

RELEASE OF PERSONAL PROPERTY FROM ESCROW

Whereas _____, of _____, by a bond
(Name) (Place of Residence)
for the performance of U.S. Government Contract Number _____,
became a surety for the complete and successful performance of said contract, and Whereas said surety has placed certain personal property in escrow

in Account Number _____ on deposit

at _____
(Name of Financial Institution)

located at _____ , and
(Address of Financial Institution)

Whereas I, _____ , being a duly authorized representative of the United States government as a warranted contracting officer, have determined that retention in escrow of the following property is no longer required to ensure further performance of the said Government contract or satisfaction of claims arising therefrom:

and
Whereas the surety remains liable to the United States Government for the continued performance of the said Government contract and satisfaction of claims pertaining thereto.

Now, therefore, this agreement witnesseth that the Government hereby releases from escrow the property listed above, and directs the custodian of the aforementioned escrow account to deliver the listed property to the surety. If the listed property comprises the whole of the property placed in escrow in the aforementioned escrow account, the Government further directs the custodian to close the account and to return all property therein to the surety, along with any interest accruing which remains after the deduction of any fees lawfully owed to

_____ .
(Name of Financial Institution)

[Date]   [Signature]

                                    Seal

AUTHORIZED FOR LOCAL REPRODUCTION

OPTIONAL FORM 91 (1-90)
Prescribed by GSA-FAR (48 CFR) 53.228(o)

Optional Form 307

CONTRACT AWARD

PAGE	OF	PAGES

1. CONTRACT NUMBER
2. EFFECTIVE DATE
3. SOLICITATION NUMBER
4. REQUISITION/PROJECT NUMBER
5. ISSUED BY   CODE
6. ADMINISTERED BY *(If other than Item 5)*   CODE
7. NAME AND ADDRESS OF CONTRACTOR   CODE
8. PAYMENT WILL BE MADE BY
9A. DUNS NUMBER
9B. TAXPAYER'S IDENTIFICATION NO.
10. SUBMIT INVOICES *(4 copies unless otherwise specified)* TO
    ☐ ITEM 5   ☐ ITEM 6   ☐ ITEM 8   ☐ OTHER *(Specify)*

11. TABLE OF CONTENTS

(X)	SEC.	DESCRIPTION	PAGE(S)	(X)	SEC.	DESCRIPTION	PAGE(S)
		PART I - THE SCHEDULE				PART II - CONTRACT CLAUSES	
	A	SOLICITATION/CONTRACT FORM			I	CONTRACT CLAUSES	
	B	SUPPLIES OR SERVICES AND PRICES/COSTS				PART III - LIST OF DOCUMENTS, EXHIBITS AND OTHER ATTACH.	
	C	DESCRIPTION/SPECS./WORK STATEMENT			J	LIST OF ATTACHMENTS	
	D	PACKAGING AND MARKING				PART IV - REPRESENTATIONS AND INSTRUCTIONS	
	E	INSPECTION AND ACCEPTANCE			K	REPRESENTATIONS, CERTIFICATIONS AND OTHER STATEMENTS OF OFFERORS	
	F	DELIVERIES OR PERFORMANCE					
	G	CONTRACT ADMINISTRATION DATA			L	INSTRS., CONDS., AND NOTICES TO OFFERORS	
	H	SPECIAL CONTRACT REQUIREMENTS			M	EVALUATION FACTORS FOR AWARD	

12. BRIEF DESCRIPTION

13. TOTAL AMOUNT OF CONTRACT ▶

14. CONTRACTOR'S AGREEMENT. Contractor agrees to furnish and deliver the items or perform services to the extent stated in this document for the consideration stated. The rights and obligations of the parties to this contract shall be subject to and governed by this document and any documents attached or incorporated by reference.

15. AWARD. The Government hereby accepts your offer on the solicitation identified in item 3 above as reflected in this award document. The rights and obligations of the parties to this contract shall be subject to and governed by this document and any documents attached or incorporated by reference.

☐ A. CONTRACTOR IS REQUIRED TO SIGN THIS DOCUMENT AND RETURN FOUR COPIES TO THE ISSUING OFFICE. *(Check if applicable)*

B. SIGNATURE OF PERSON AUTHORIZED TO SIGN

A. UNITED STATES OF AMERICA *(Signature of Contracting Officer)*

C. NAME OF SIGNER

D. TITLE OF SIGNER

B. NAME OF CONTRACTING OFFICER

E. DATE

C. DATE

AUTHORIZED FOR LOCAL REPRODUCTION

OPTIONAL FORM 307 (9-97)
Prescribed by GSA - FAR (48 CFR) 53.215-1(e)

Optional Form 308

SOLICITATION AND OFFER - NEGOTIATED ACQUISITION

PAGE   OF   PAGES

I. SOLICITATION

1. SOLICITATION NUMBER	2. DATE ISSUED	3. OFFERS DUE BY	4. OFFERS VALID FOR 60 DAYS UNLESS A DIFFERENT PERIOD IS ENTERED HERE

5. ISSUED BY

6. ADDRESS OFFER TO *(If other than Item 5)*

7. FOR INFORMATION CALL *(No collect calls)*

A. NAME	B. TELEPHONE		C. E-MAIL ADDRESS
	AREA CODE	PHONE NUMBER	

8. BRIEF DESCRIPTION

9. TABLE OF CONTENTS

(X)	SEC.	DESCRIPTION	PAGE(S)	(X)	SEC.	DESCRIPTION	PAGE(S)
		PART I - THE SCHEDULE				PART II - CONTRACT CLAUSES	
	A	SOLICITATION/CONTRACT FORM			I	CONTRACT CLAUSES	
	B	SUPPLIES OR SERVICES AND PRICES/COSTS				PART III - LIST OF DOCUMENTS, EXHIBITS AND OTHER ATTACH.	
	C	DESCRIPTION/SPECS./WORK STATEMENT			J	LIST OF ATTACHMENTS	
	D	PACKAGING AND MARKING				PART IV - REPRESENTATIONS AND INSTRUCTIONS	
	E	INSPECTION AND ACCEPTANCE			K	REPRESENTATIONS, CERTIFICATIONS AND OTHER STATEMENTS OF OFFERORS	
	F	DELIVERIES OR PERFORMANCE					
	G	CONTRACT ADMINISTRATION DATA			L	INSTRS., CONDS., AND NOTICES TO OFFERORS	
	H	SPECIAL CONTRACT REQUIREMENTS			M	EVALUATION FACTORS FOR AWARD	

II. OFFER

The undersigned agrees to furnish and deliver the items or perform services to the extent stated in this document for the consideration stated. The rights and obligations of the parties to the resultant contract shall be subject to and governed by this document and any documents attached or incorporated by reference.

10A. PERSONS AUTHORIZED TO NEGOTIATE	10B. TITLE	10C. TELEPHONE	
		AREA CODE	NUMBER

11. NAME AND ADDRESS OF OFFEROR

12A. SIGNATURE OF PERSON AUTHORIZED TO SIGN

12B. NAME OF SIGNER

12C. TITLE OF SIGNER

12D. DATE	12E. TELEPHONE	
	AREA CODE	NUMBER

AUTHORIZED FOR LOCAL REPRODUCTION

OPTIONAL FORM 308 (9-97)
Prescribed by GSA - FAR (48 CFR) 53.215-1(f)

Optional Form 309

AMENDMENT OF SOLICITATION
(Negotiated Procurements)

PAGE   OF   PAGES

NOTICE: Offerors must acknowledge receipt of this amendment in writing, by the date and time specified for proposal submissions or the date and time specified in Block 6, whichever is later. IF YOUR ACKNOWLEDGMENT IS NOT RECEIVED AT THE DESIGNATED LOCATION BY THE SPECIFIED DATE AND TIME, YOUR OFFER MAY BE REJECTED. If, by virtue of this amendment, you wish to change your offer, such change must make reference to the solicitation and this amendment and be received prior to the date and time specified in Block 6.

I. AMENDMENT

1. SOLICITATION NUMBER	2. SOLICITATION DATE	3. AMENDMENT NUMBER	4. AMENDMENT DATE

5. ISSUED BY

6. DUE DATE
THIS AMENDMENT DOES NOT CHANGE THE DATE BY WHICH OFFERS ARE DUE UNLESS A DATE AND TIME IS INSERTED BELOW.

A. DATE	B. TIME

7. FOR INFORMATION CALL *(No collect calls)*

A. NAME	B. TELEPHONE		C. E-MAIL ADDRESS
	AREA CODE	PHONE NUMBER	

8. DESCRIPTION OF AMENDMENT

Except as provided herein, all terms and conditions of the solicitation remain unchanged and in full force and effect.

II. ACKNOWLEDGMENT OF AMENDMENT

In lieu of other written methods of acknowledgment, the offeror may complete Blocks 9 and 10 and return this amendment to the address in Block 5.

9. NAME AND ADDRESS OF OFFEROR	10A. OFFEROR *(Signature of person authorized to sign)*
	10B. NAME OF SIGNER
	10C. TITLE OF SIGNER
	10D. DATE

AUTHORIZED FOR LOCAL REPRODUCTION

OPTIONAL FORM 309 (9-97)
Prescribed by GSA - FAR (48 CFR) 53.215-1(g)

Optional Form 312

[Standard Form 98 has been removed.]

Optional Form 312 (Back)

[Standard Form 98 has been removed.]

Optional Form 336

CONTINUATION SHEET	REFERENCE NO. OF DOCUMENT BEING CONTINUED	PAGES
NAME OF OFFEROR OR CONTRACTOR		

ITEM NO.	SUPPLIES/SERVICES	QUANTITY	UNIT	UNIT PRICE	AMOUNT

NSN 7540-01-152-8067

OPTIONAL FORM 336 (4-86)
Sponsored by GSA FAR (48 CFR) 53.110

Optional Form 347

[Go to *http://www.gsa.gov/forms* to access form.]

Optional Form 348

**ORDER FOR SUPPLIES OR SERVICES
SCHEDULE - CONTINUATION**

PAGE NO.

IMPORTANT: Mark all packages and papers with contract and/or order numbers.

DATE OF ORDER | CONTRACT NO. | ORDER NO.

ITEM NO. (a)	SUPPLIES OR SERVICES (b)	QUANTITY ORDERED (c)	UNIT (d)	UNIT PRICE (e)	AMOUNT (f)	QUANTITY ACCEPTED (g)

TOTAL CARRIED FORWARD TO 1ST PAGE (ITEM 17h)

AUTHORIZED FOR LOCAL REPRODUCTION
PREVIOUS EDITION NOT USABLE

OPTIONAL FORM 348 REV. (4/2006)
Prescribed by GSA - FAR (48 CFR) 53.213(f)

PART 53.3—ILLUSTRATION OF FORMS

Optional Form 1419

Optional Form 1419A

ABSTRACT OF OFFERS - CONSTRUCTION CONTINUATION SHEET

1. SOLICITATION NUMBER

PAGE OF PAGES

INSTRUCTIONS Attach this form to OF 1419, Abstract of Offers - Construction, when more than 2 offers are received on a construction project. Each Continuation Sheet will accommodate 13 contract items to conform to the number of items which can be entered on the OF 1419. Use additional OF 1419's for contract items in excess of 13 and attach additional Continuation Sheets (OF 1419A) as needed.

2. PROJECT TITLE

4. OFFERS *(Continued)*

- A. OFFEROR NO.:
- B. BID SECURITY *(Type and amount)*
- C. AMENDMENTS ACKNOWLEDGED
- D. UNIT PRICE
- E. ESTIMATED AMOUNT

3. CONTRACT ITEMS
- A. ITEM NO.
- B. ESTIMATED QUANTITY
- C. UNIT

AUTHORIZED FOR LOCAL REPRODUCTION
Previous edition is usable

OPTIONAL FORM 1419A (11-88)

PART 53.3—ILLUSTRATION OF FORMS

Form DD 254

DEPARTMENT OF DEFENSE CONTRACT SECURITY CLASSIFICATION SPECIFICATION *(The requirements of the DoD Industrial Security Manual apply to all security aspects of this effort.)*	1. CLEARANCE AND SAFEGUARDING
	a. FACILITY CLEARANCE REQUIRED
	b. LEVEL OF SAFEGUARDING REQUIRED

2. THIS SPECIFICATION IS FOR: *(X and complete as applicable)*	3. THIS SPECIFICATION IS: *(X and complete as applicable)*		
a. PRIME CONTRACT NUMBER	a. ORIGINAL *(Complete date in all cases)*		DATE *(YYYYMMDD)*
b. SUBCONTRACT NUMBER	b. REVISED *(Supersedes all previous specs)*	REVISION NO.	DATE *(YYYYMMDD)*
c. SOLICITATION OR OTHER NUMBER — DUE DATE *(YYYYMMDD)*	c. FINAL *(Complete Item 5 in all cases)*		DATE *(YYYYMMDD)*

4. IS THIS A FOLLOW-ON CONTRACT? ☐ YES ☐ NO. If Yes, complete the following:
Classified material received or generated under _____ *(Preceding Contract Number)* is transferred to this follow-on contract.

5. IS THIS A FINAL DD FORM 254? ☐ YES ☐ NO. If Yes, complete the following:
In response to the contractor's request dated _____, retention of the classified material is authorized for the period of _____

6. CONTRACTOR *(Include Commercial and Government Entity (CAGE) Code)*

a. NAME, ADDRESS, AND ZIP CODE	b. CAGE CODE	c. COGNIZANT SECURITY OFFICE *(Name, Address, and Zip Code)*

7. SUBCONTRACTOR

a. NAME, ADDRESS, AND ZIP CODE	b. CAGE CODE	c. COGNIZANT SECURITY OFFICE *(Name, Address, and Zip Code)*

8. ACTUAL PERFORMANCE

a. LOCATION	b. CAGE CODE	c. COGNIZANT SECURITY OFFICE *(Name, Address, and Zip Code)*

9. GENERAL IDENTIFICATION OF THIS PROCUREMENT

10. CONTRACTOR WILL REQUIRE ACCESS TO:	YES	NO	11. IN PERFORMING THIS CONTRACT, THE CONTRACTOR WILL:	YES	NO
a. COMMUNICATIONS SECURITY (COMSEC) INFORMATION			a. HAVE ACCESS TO CLASSIFIED INFORMATION ONLY AT ANOTHER CONTRACTOR'S FACILITY OR A GOVERNMENT ACTIVITY		
b. RESTRICTED DATA			b. RECEIVE CLASSIFIED DOCUMENTS ONLY		
c. CRITICAL NUCLEAR WEAPON DESIGN INFORMATION			c. RECEIVE AND GENERATE CLASSIFIED MATERIAL		
d. FORMERLY RESTRICTED DATA			d. FABRICATE, MODIFY, OR STORE CLASSIFIED HARDWARE		
e. INTELLIGENCE INFORMATION			e. PERFORM SERVICES ONLY		
(1) Sensitive Compartmented Information (SCI)			f. HAVE ACCESS TO U.S. CLASSIFIED INFORMATION OUTSIDE THE U.S., PUERTO RICO, U.S. POSSESSIONS AND TRUST TERRITORIES		
(2) Non-SCI			g. BE AUTHORIZED TO USE THE SERVICES OF DEFENSE TECHNICAL INFORMATION CENTER (DTIC) OR OTHER SECONDARY DISTRIBUTION CENTER		
f. SPECIAL ACCESS INFORMATION			h. REQUIRE A COMSEC ACCOUNT		
g. NATO INFORMATION			i. HAVE TEMPEST REQUIREMENTS		
h. FOREIGN GOVERNMENT INFORMATION			j. HAVE OPERATIONS SECURITY (OPSEC) REQUIREMENTS		
i. LIMITED DISSEMINATION INFORMATION			k. BE AUTHORIZED TO USE THE DEFENSE COURIER SERVICE		
j. FOR OFFICIAL USE ONLY INFORMATION			l. OTHER *(Specify)*		
k. OTHER *(Specify)*					

DD FORM 254, DEC 1999   PREVIOUS EDITION IS OBSOLETE.   [Reset]

Form DD 254 (Reverse)

12. PUBLIC RELEASE. Any information *(classified or unclassified)* pertaining to this contract shall not be released for public dissemination except as provided by the Industrial Security Manual or unless it has been approved for public release by appropriate U.S. Government authority. Proposed public releases shall be submitted for approval prior to release ☐ Direct ☐ Through *(Specify)*

to the Directorate for Freedom of Information and Security Review, Office of the Assistant Secretary of Defense (Public Affairs)* for review.
*In the case of non-DoD User Agencies, requests for disclosure shall be submitted to that agency.

13. SECURITY GUIDANCE. The security classification guidance needed for this classified effort is identified below. If any difficulty is encountered in applying this guidance or if any other contributing factor indicates a need for changes in this guidance, the contractor is authorized and encouraged to provide recommended changes; to challenge the guidance or the classification assigned to any information or material furnished or generated under this contract; and to submit any questions for interpretation of this guidance to the official identified below. Pending final decision, the information involved shall be handled and protected at the highest level of classification assigned or recommended. *(Fill in as appropriate for the classified effort. Attach, or forward under separate correspondence, any documents/guides/extracts referenced herein. Add additional pages as needed to provide complete guidance.)*

14. ADDITIONAL SECURITY REQUIREMENTS. Requirements, in addition to ISM requirements, are established for this contract. ☐ Yes ☐ No
(If Yes, identify the pertinent contractual clauses in the contract document itself, or provide an appropriate statement which identifies the additional requirements. Provide a copy of the requirements to the cognizant security office. Use Item 13 if additional space is needed.)

15. INSPECTIONS. Elements of this contract are outside the inspection responsibility of the cognizant security office. ☐ Yes ☐ No
(If Yes, explain and identify specific areas or elements carved out and the activity responsible for inspections. Use Item 13 if additional space is needed.)

16. CERTIFICATION AND SIGNATURE. Security requirements stated herein are complete and adequate for safeguarding the classified information to be released or generated under this classified effort. All questions shall be referred to the official named below.

a. TYPED NAME OF CERTIFYING OFFICIAL	b. TITLE	c. TELEPHONE *(Include Area Code)*
d. ADDRESS *(Include Zip Code)*	17. REQUIRED DISTRIBUTION	
	☐ a. CONTRACTOR	
	☐ b. SUBCONTRACTOR	
	☐ c. COGNIZANT SECURITY OFFICE FOR PRIME AND SUBCONTRACTOR	
e. SIGNATURE	☐ d. U.S. ACTIVITY RESPONSIBLE FOR OVERSEAS SECURITY ADMINISTRATION	
	☐ e. ADMINISTRATIVE CONTRACTING OFFICER	
	☐ f. OTHERS AS NECESSARY	

DD FORM 254 (BACK), DEC 1999

Reset

Form DD 441

**DEPARTMENT OF DEFENSE
SECURITY AGREEMENT**

Form Approved
OMB No. 0704-0194
Expires Sep 30, 2007

The public reporting burden for this collection of information is estimated to average 14 minutes per response, including the time for reviewing instructions, searching existing data sources, gathering and maintaining the data needed, and completing and reviewing the collection of information. Send comments regarding this burden estimate or any other aspect of this collection of information, including suggestions for reducing the burden, to the Department of Defense, Executive Services and Communications Directorate (0704-0194). Respondents should be aware that notwithstanding any other provision of law, no person shall be subject to any penalty for failing to comply with a collection of information if it does not display a currently valid OMB control number.

PLEASE DO NOT RETURN YOUR FORM TO THE ABOVE ORGANIZATION. RETURN COMPLETED FORM TO YOUR RESPECTIVE COGNIZANT SECURITY OFFICE.

This DEPARTMENT OF DEFENSE SECURITY AGREEMENT *(hereinafter called the Agreement)*, entered into this _____ day of

_____ , _____ by and between THE UNITED STATES OF AMERICA through the Defense Security Service

acting for the Department of Defense and other governmental User Agencies *(hereinafter called the Government)*, and

_____ *(hereinafter called the Contractor)*, which is:

(1) a corporation organized and existing under the laws of the state of _____

(2) a partnership consisting of _____

(3) an individual trading as _____

with its principal office and place of business at *(Street, City, State and ZIP Code)*

_____

WITNESSETH THAT:

WHEREAS, the Government has in the past purchased or may in the future purchase from the Contractor supplies or services, which are required and necessary to the national security of the United States; or may invite bids or request quotations on proposed contracts for the purchase of supplies or services, which are required and necessary to the national security of the United States; and

WHEREAS, it is essential that certain security measures be taken by the Contractor prior to and after being accorded access to classified information; and

WHEREAS, the parties desire to define and set forth the precautions and specific safeguards to be taken by the Contractor and the Government in order to preserve and maintain the security of the United States through the prevention of improper disclosure of classified information, sabotage, or any other acts detrimental to the security of the United States;

NOW, THEREFORE, in consideration of the foregoing and of the mutual promises herein contained, the parties hereto agree as follows.

Section I - SECURITY CONTROLS

(A) The Contractor agrees to provide and maintain a system of security controls within the organization in accordance with the requirements of the "National Industrial Security Program Operating Manual," DoD 5220.22-M (hereinafter called the Manual) attached hereto and made a part of this agreement, subject, however, (i) to any revisions of the Manual required by the demands of national security as determined by the Government, notice of which shall be furnished to the Contractor, and (ii) to mutual agreements entered into by the parties in order to adapt the Manual to the Contractor's business and necessary procedures thereunder. In order to place in effect such security controls, the Contractor further agrees to prepare Standard Practice Procedures for internal use, such procedures to be consistent with the Manual. In the event of any inconsistency between the Manual, as revised, and the Contractor's Standard Practice Procedures, the Manual shall control.

(B) The Government agrees that it shall indicate when necessary, by security classification (TOP SECRET, SECRET, or CONFIDENTIAL), the degree of importance to the national security of information pertaining to supplies, services, and other matters to be furnished by the Contractor to the Government or by the Government to the Contractor, and the Government shall give written notice of such security classification to the Contractor and of any subsequent changes thereof, provided, however, that matters requiring security classification will be assigned the least restricted security classification consistent with proper safeguarding of the matter concerned, since overclassification causes unnecessary operational delays and depreciates the importance of correctly classified matter. Further, the Government agrees that when Atomic Energy information is involved it will, when necessary, indicate by a marking additional to the classification marking that the information is "RESTRICTED DATA." The "Department of Defense Contract Security Classification Specification" (DD Form 254) is the basic document by which classification, regrading, and declassification specifications are documented and conveyed to the Contractor.

(C) The Government agrees, on written application, to grant personnel security clearances to eligible employees of the Contractor who require access to information classified TOP SECRET, SECRET, or CONFIDENTIAL.

(D) The Contractor agrees to determine that any subcontractor, subbidder, individual, or organization proposed for the furnishing of supplies or services which will involve access to classified information, has been granted an appropriate facility security clearance, which is still in effect prior to according access to such classified information.

Section II - SECURITY REVIEWS

Designated representatives of the Government responsible for reviews pertaining to industrial plant security shall have the right to review, at reasonable intervals, the procedures, methods, and facilities utilized by the Contractor in complying with the requirements of the terms and conditions of the Manual. Should the Government, through its authorized representative, determine that the Contractor's security methods, procedures, or facilities do not comply with such requirements, it shall submit a written report to the Contractor advising of the deficiencies.

DD FORM 441, OCT 2004 PREVIOUS EDITION IS OBSOLETE.

Form DD 441 (Reverse)

Section III - MODIFICATION

Modification of this Agreement may be made only by written agreement of the parties hereto. The Manual may be modified in accordance with Section I of this Agreement.

Section IV - TERMINATION

This Agreement shall remain in effect until terminated through the giving of 30 days' written notice to the other party of intention to terminate; provided, however, notwithstanding any such termination, the terms and conditions of this Agreement shall continue in effect so long as the Contractor possesses classified information.

Section V - PRIOR SECURITY AGREEMENTS

As of the date hereof, this Agreement replaces and succeeds any and all prior security or secrecy agreements, understandings, and representations, with respect to the subject matter included herein, entered into between the Contractor and the Government; provided, that the term "security or secrecy agreements, understandings, and representations: shall not include agreements, understandings, and representations contained in contracts for the furnishing of supplies or services to the Government which were previously entered into between the Contractor and the Government.

Section VI - SECURITY COSTS

This Agreement does not obligate Government funds, and the Government shall not be liable for any costs or claims of the Contractor arising out of this Agreement or instructions issued hereunder. It is recognized, however, that the parties may provide in other written contracts for security costs, which may be properly chargeable thereto.

IN WITNESS WHEREOF, the parties hereto have executed this Agreement as of the day and year written above:

THE UNITED STATES OF AMERICA

By _____
(Signature of Authorized Government Representative)

_____
(Typed Name of Authorized Government Representative)

_____
(Typed Name of Authorized Government Agency)

WITNESS

_____
(Typed Name of Contractor Entering Agreement)

By _____
(Signature of Authorized Contractor Representative)

_____
(Typed Name of Authorized Contractor Representative)

_____
(Title of Authorized Contractor Representative)

_____
(Contractor Address)

_____
(Contractor Address)

NOTE: In case of a corporation, a witness is not required but the certificate must be completed. Type or print names under all signatures.

NOTE: Contractor, if a corporation, should cause the following certificate to be executed under its corporate seal, provided that the same officer shall not execute both the Agreement and the Certificate.

CERTIFICATE

I, _____, certify that I am the _____ of the corporation named as Contractor herein; that _____ who signed this Agreement on behalf of the Contractor, was then _____ of said corporation; that said Agreement was duly signed for and in behalf of said corporation by authority of its governing body, and is within the scope of its corporate powers.

(Corporate Seal)   (Signature and Date)

DD FORM 441 (BACK), OCT 2004

Form WH-347

[Go to *http://www.dol.gov/whd/forms/wh347.pdf* to access form.]

FEDERAL ACQUISITION REGULATION

APPENDIX

The official codified Cost Accounting Standards appear at 48 CFR Chapter 99.
This Chapter may be accessed via the website at *www.gpoaccess.gov/cfr/index.html*.

This page intentionally left blank.

Appendix—Cost Accounting Standards Preambles and Regulations*

Part III—Preambles Published Under the FAR System

* This Appendix is provided for the convenience of user of the looseleaf FAR. The official codified Cost Accounting Standards appear at 48 CFR 99.

This page intentionally left blank.

Part III—Preambles Published Under the FAR System

This page intentionally left blank.

PART III—PREAMBLES PUBLISHED UNDER THE FAR SYSTEM

PREAMBLE A TO 30.404, CAPITALIZATION OF TANGIBLE ASSETS

This final rule, in Federal Acquisition Circular (FAC) 84-38, revises 30.404-40(b)(1), 30.404-60(a)(1), and 30.404-60(a)(1)(i).

SUMMARY

Section 30.404 requires that contractors have written policies for capitalization which must include a minimum acquisition cost criterion of $1000. The standard is being amended to raise the threshold to $1500. The purpose of the change is to permit contractors to adopt practices appropriate in today's economy.

Effective Date: The effective date of this modification is September 19, 1988.

BACKGROUND

Supplementary Information. The CAS Board established the minimum acquisition cost criterion for capitalization at $500 when it originally promulgated CAS 404 in 1973. The Board's initial $500 limitation encompassed the practices of 97 percent of the companies whose Disclosure Statements were filed with the Board. In the promulgation comments to the Standard, the Board recommended that the special limits in the standard "…may need to be reviewed in the future…(and will be revised) promptly if developments warrant a change."

On March 3, 1980, the Board did revise the limitation upward to $1000 as it recognized that circumstances had changed significantly since the promulgation of Standard 404. The Board found that the performance of several official indices showed increases from 60 to 80 percent, and a survey of companies not influenced by the limitation of Standard 404 showed a significant number using $1000 as the minimum criterion for capitalization.

The impact of inflation has continued over the 7 years since 1980, although at a lower level. Indices from the Commerce Department for the implicit price deflators on nonresidential structures and machinery and equipment showed increases from 30 to 35 percent over the period 1979 through 1985. When applied to the current $1000 criterion, this yields values from $1300 to $1350. In addition, economic projections showed inflation levels rising slightly from 1986 through 1989. Consequently, this change increases the minimum acquisition cost criterion for capitalization of tangible capital assets to $1500 to cover both actual and projected price increases.

The amendment which is now being promulgated is derived directly from the proposed rule which was published in the *Federal Register* on July 9, 1986 (51 FR 24971), with an invitation for interested parties to submit comments.

Four letters of comment were received on the July 9, 1986, proposal. Only one letter directly addressed the appropriateness of the proposed revisions to 30.404. That comment stated that inflation should not be the motivating factor in determining significant costs for capitalization, but rather materiality of the cost should be the factor in determining significance.

The CAS Board's comments in the CAS 404 preamble and its action to increase the capitalization threshold based upon inflation, discussed above, indicate that the Board considered the materiality and significance of asset acquisition cost to be directly related to the level of prices in the economy. The Defense Acquisition Regulations Council and the Civilian Agency Acquisition Council agree with the CAS Board's outlook on this matter and expect the increase in capitalization threshold provided in this modification to 30.404 will be beneficial to Government contract costing by not requiring capitalization of assets that are of insignificant value.

PREAMBLE A TO 30.416, ACCOUNTING FOR INSURANCE COSTS

This final rule, in Federal Acquisition Circular (FAC) 84-38, revises 30.416-50(a)(3)(ii).

SUMMARY

FAR 30.416-50(a)(3)(ii) revisions delete the requirement to use state rates in discounting certain self-insured losses to present value.

Effective Date: The effective date of this modification is September 19, 1988.

This modification shall be followed by each contractor on or after the start of its next cost accounting period, beginning after receipt of a contract to which this modification is applicable.

BACKGROUND

Supplementary Information. Section 30.416 provides that the amount of insurance cost to be assigned to a cost accounting period is the projected average loss (PAL) for that period plus insurance administration expense in that period. The PAL is either the insurance premium, where the risk of loss is covered by the purchase of insurance, or a self-insurance charge, where the exposure to risk is not covered by the purchase of insurance. Where it is probable that the actual amount of losses will not differ significantly from the PAL, the actual amount of losses may be considered to represent the PAL for the period as the self-insurance charge.

In self-insurance, when the actual amount of losses is being used to represent the PAL, contractors are to discount those losses to present value, where payments to the claimant will not take place for over a year after the loss occurs. If a state provides a discount rate for computing lump-sum settlements, 30.416 requires that the state rate be used for computing present value. Otherwise, the Pub. L. 92-41 Treasury rate is to be used. The differing rates specified by the states, and the lack of specified rates in some states, result in inconsistent treatment of self-insurance charges on defense contracts.

The purpose of requiring a present value computation for contract cost accounting purposes is to recognize the time value of money for funds advanced to and used by the contractor for extended periods before being disbursed. The Pub. L. 92-41 Treasury rate is generally specified for this purpose. The majority of state laws covering worker's compensation insurance specify a rate in the range of 3-6 percent. The use of a low rate results in a larger settlement than would use of a current money market rate. The purpose of low state rates is to discourage lump-sum settlements. This purpose is unrelated to that of fair valuation for contract cost accounting purposes. The use of state rates may produce inaccurate measures of present values and will most certainly create inconsistencies in the pricing of contracts due to the lack of consistent determinations of present values. Consequently, the proposed rule, published in the *Federal Register* on July 8, 1986 (51 FR 24788), deleted the reference to state discount rates at 30.416-50(a)(3)(ii) and required use of the Pub. L. 92-41 Treasury rate in all cases.

Four comments were received in response to the proposed rule. None of the comments directly challenged the appropriateness of the proposed revision. Therefore, no changes were made to the proposed rule as a result of the public comments.

FAC 2005–65 JANUARY 29, 2013

FEDERAL ACQUISITION REGULATION

INDEX PAGES 1-144 [REMOVED]

FAR Correction(s)

Please complete this form to notify the Regulatory Secretariat of errors, omissions, or inconsistencies in the text of the FAR or FACs and submit via mail or facsimile to:

> General Services Administration
> Regulatory Secretariat Division (MVCB)
> 1800 F Street, NW
> Washington, DC 20405
>
> Telephone: (202) 501-4755
> Facsimile: (202) 501-4067

FAR Part, Subpart, or Section: _____

Page Number: _____

Nature of Error(s): _____

_____

_____

_____

Name: _____

Telephone: _____

E-mail Address: _____

Address: _____

_____